Henry Riddell Montgomery

Specimens of the Early Native Poetry of Ireland, in English Metrical Translations

Henry Riddell Montgomery

Specimens of the Early Native Poetry of Ireland, in English Metrical Translations

ISBN/EAN: 9783337323592

Printed in Europe, USA, Canada, Australia, Japan

Cover: Foto ©Thomas Meinert / pixelio.de

More available books at **www.hansebooks.com**

SPECIMENS

OF THE

EARLY NATIVE POETRY

OF

IRELAND,

In English Metrical Translations,

BY

MISS BROOKE, S. (SIR S.) FERGUSON, WM. LEAHY, J. C. MANGAN,
T. FURLONG, J. D'ALTON, H. G. CURRAN,
E. WALSH, AND J. ANSTER, LL.D.,
ETC.

WITH

INTRODUCTION AND RUNNING COMMENTARY,

Historic, Biographic, and Critical,

BY

HENRY R. MONTGOMERY,

Author of "Memoirs of Sir R. Steele and his Contemporaries," "Thomas Moore: his
Life and Writings," "Famous Literary Impostures," "Bickerstaff," &c., &c.

NEW AND ENLARGED EDITION.

DUBLIN:
HODGES, FIGGIS, AND CO., GRAFTON STREET.
LONDON:
SIMPKIN, MARSHALL, HAMILTON, KENT, AND CO.
1892.

TO HER EXCELLENCY

THE MARCHIONESS OF DUFFERIN AND AVA,

British Embassy, Paris,

IN THE BELIEF THAT ALL THE FULL SHARE WHICH, ON THE BEST
AUTHORITY, WE ARE ASSURED SHE CONTRIBUTED TO THE
SUCCESS OF HIGH OFFICIAL FUNCTIONS,

Vice-regal and Diplomatic,

IN ONE OF THE MOST CONTINUOUSLY SUCCESSFUL AND BRILLIANT
OFFICIAL CAREERS ON RECORD,
BOTH IN THE WEST AND THE EAST—
IN ADDITION TO SPECIAL PHILANTHROPIC EFFORTS, WHICH HAVE
ENSHRINED HER NAME IN THE HINDOO ZENANAS
HAVE NOT DIMINISHED (WITH ALL THEIR FAULTS) HER INTEREST
IN HER OWN LAND AND PEOPLE, TO WHICH ANOTHER
LADY DUFFERIN GAVE SUCH TOUCHING EXPRESSION
IN HER "EMIGRANT'S FAREWELL,"—

This Volume

IS WITH KIND PERMISSION INSCRIBED BY HER LADYSHIP'S OBLIGED,
OBEDIENT SERVANT,

H. R. MONTGOMERY.

PREFACE

TO REVISED AND ENLARGED EDITION.

THE large original edition of the present volume, published so far back as to exceed the average life of a book, has long been out of print, and is now re-issued in a revised form, with nearly half as much more matter incorporated. If the aim had been to make a great book, the bulk might easily have been increased by giving the pieces in full, instead of only, especially with the longer pieces, the spirit. In the original prefatory notice it is stated—"The object of the present volume is to bring together, in a small compass, some of the choicest gems of native poetry, scattered over the pages of periodicals, and of heavy quartos and expensive collections—unaccompanied by the originals, which, however valuable in themselves, would possess no interest to the mere English reader. It seems a prominent characteristic of the present day, both in these islands and on the continent, that the popular taste is recurring to the productions of early times, and reviving the spirit of primitive literary ages. Of this, the institution of national Archæological Societies, both in England

and Ireland, would of itself afford sufficient evidence. Nor is the increased attention which begins to be paid to the history and literature of Ireland, less obvious; and the idea occurred, that somewhat towards promoting both of these objects might be effected, by placing before the public, in a more accessible and popular form than they have hitherto appeared, a small collection of such fragments of Irish poetry as possessed historical interest, and which, with a running commentary, might serve to illustrate the ages to which they respectively belong."

In some cases pieces are inserted from the interest of the matter, historically or traditionally, where they may not have had the benefit of the highest poetical merit in their English dress, and others which have had, on similar grounds; but on the whole it is hoped the present will be found a great improvement on the former edition.

In addition to a remark on Scottish patriotism at the conclusion, it was intended to have alluded to the fact that in almost every considerable town throughout the world where English is spoken, the memory of Burns is annually celebrated; while Moore, who has left a body of national song which, in quality and quantity, is absolutely unparalleled, receives no such recognition, even in the land whose melodies he has immortalized.

January, 1892.

CHRONOLOGICAL TABLE OF CONTENTS.

		Translator's Name.	Page
CIRCA.	PREFACE	..	ix
B.C. 500.	Introduction—Poetry in general—Claims of Ancient Poetry of Ireland	..	1-10
	Historic Notices of the Origin and Progress of the Bards	..	11
	Notice of the royal law-giver Ollamh Fodhla (Ollav Foala), and the Palace of Tara	..	16
	Notice of the Red Branch Knights of Ulster	..	18
25.	Ancient Historic Tale of Deirdre and the Sons of Usna	..	19
	Deirdre's Farewell to Alba	W. LEAHY	20
	——	S. (SIR S.) FERGUSON	21
	—— Foreboding, Dream, and Warning	W. LEAHY	22-23
	—— Lavarcum's Forebodings	Do.	25
	—— Lament for the Sons of Usna	Do.	26
	——	S. (SIR S.) FERGUSON	30
	Conloch, a Heroic Poem of Cuchullin	MISS BROOKE	33
A.D.	Cuchullin's Lament for his Son	Do.	40
2.	—— Death	..	43
10.	Reformation of the Bardic Order	..	44
174. 177.	Testament of Cathaeir Mor, King of Ireland	J. C. MANGAN.	45
	Conn of the Hundred Battles—Leith Cuin and Leath Modha	..	52
190.	Battle of Cnucha. War Ode to Goll, the Son of Morna	O'HALLORAN	53
213.	Notice of the Monarch Cormac O'Con— Lament for his queen	J. C. MANGAN	55
	Notice of the Ossianic Heroes—Finn MacCumhal and his son Oisin		5

TABLE OF CONTENTS.

A.D.		Translator's Name.	Page
250.	Notice of the Dalraid Colony from Ireland to Argyleshire	..	60
	Scotia one of the ancient names of Ireland	..	61
	The Fenian Heroes—Fergus, not Oisin, their Bard	..	65
	Contest between Fion and Goll M'Morni	..	66
	Ode to Gaul (or Goll), the son of Morni	Miss Brooke	67
	Notice of the Celtic War Songs—The Battle of Gabhra (Gaura)	..	73
296.	War Ode of Fergus, to Osgur (or Oscar) son of Oisin	Miss Brooke	75
400.	Torna Egeas, the last of the Pagan Bards	..	81
	———— his Lament for his princely wards, Corc and Niall	S. (Sir S.) Ferguson	83
	———— his verses on the Ancient Royal Cemetery of Croghan	Keating	86
432.	Introduction of Christianity—Dubtach (Duvach) M'Lughair, chief bard of the kingdom, becomes a convert..	..	88
	Hymn on St. Patrick, attributed to Fiech, Bishop of Sletty	..	89
450.	Rhythmical structure of the Bards—Coelius Sedulius, or Shiel	..	90
560.	Poets of sixth century—Eochy Eigeas, Dallan Forgail, and Seanchan Torpest—Dallan's Odes to Prince of Orgiall	H. G. Curran	94-95
	Abuses of the Bardic influence Reformation of the Order	..	96
597.	Seanchan Torpest—his Lament for Dallan	{ H. G. Curran { J. C. Mangan	97 98
	Notice of Columba and his Latin poetry	Dr. Smith	100
543. 615. }	Notice of Columbanus and his Latin poetry	Do.	106
	Early fame of the Academies of Ireland	..	111
684.	Prince Aldfrid's (of Northumbria) Itinerary of Ireland	J. C. Mangan	112
795.	Notice of the first Incursions of the Norsemen, or Danes	..	115
840.	Donat, Bishop of Fesulæ—his Latin verses in eulogy of Ireland	Rev. Dr. Dunkin	ib.
940.	Cormacan Eigeas, chief bard of Ulster..	..	116
	Continuation of the Invasions of the Norsemen	..	117
	Checked by the reign of Brian Boroihme (Boru) note on Sir C. G. Duffy	..	118
1014.	Battle of Clontarf, and treacherous death of the aged king	..	ib.
	Lament of M'Liag, his Secretary and Biographer	J. C. Mangan	119

TABLE OF CONTENTS.   xiii

A.D.		Translator's Name.	Page
	M'Liag in Exile remembers Brian	W. H. Drummond, D.D.	121
	Note respecting usurpation of Brian	.. .. ..	122
1015.	MacGilly Caw or Kew mournfully remembers Brian	W. H. Drummond, D.D.	126
	Notice of the Fenian Poems, with specimens	.. .. ..	129
	Poem of the Chase	W. H. Drummond, D.D.	130
	Poem of Magnus the Great	Miss Brooke	140
	Macpherson's Ossian and Dr. Drake (note)	..	151
	Fenian Poems continued—Lay of Bhin Bolbin	Dr. Drummond	155
	Dr. Petrie's description of the valley of Glanasmole (note)	.. .. ..	ib.
	The Blackbird of the Grove of Carna	Wm. Leahy	158
	Ode to the Hill of Howth	Dr. Drummond	160
	Tale, the Son of Trone	Wm. Leahy	161
	Renewal of the Norse Incursions	.. ..	166
1169-70.	Anglo-Norman Invasion (and note)	..	169
1185.	Notice of Giraldus Cambrensis, and his eulogy of Irish music	.. .. ..	170
	Donogh More O'Daly and Carol O'Daly	.. ..	172
1200.	Eileen-a-Roon, by the latter	{T. Furlong / J. C. Mangan}	174-75
1265.	The Fortification of Ross—Ballad	Mrs. Maclean (L.E.L.)	177
1372.	Carroll O'Daly (the Second) and Echo	J. D'Alton, M.R.I.A.	187
1350.	John O'Dugan—his Kings of Cashell	M. Kearney	189
1380.	The Chiefs of O'Cahan or O'Kane—Battle of Roe	Anonymous	191-93
1400.	Darkness of the fifteenth century—Earl of Desmond's Song	Ed. Lawson	195-96
1468.	Donall O'Mulconry on the Inauguration of Turlogh O'Brien	J. C. Mangan	197-98
15—.	Cruel Persecution of the Bards—the poet Spenser's Notice of them—their influence still exemplified in the case of Lord Thomas Fitzgerald (Silken Thomas)	.. ..	204, 206
	Bards of sixteenth century	.. .. ..	207
1556.	O'Gnive's Downfall of the Gael	S. (Sir S.) Ferguson	207
	Other version of the same, reference to	J. J. Callinan	210
	Fitzgerald's Maritime Ode	Miss Brooke	211
1600.	Bards of early part of seventeenth century—their contention	..	215
	Notice of Hugh Roe O'Donnell	..	ib.
1601.	Elegy on the Ruins of Donegal Castle by Mulmurry Ward	J. C. Mangan	219
1610.	Owen Roe Ward's Lament for O'Neill of Tyrone, and O'Donnell of Tyrconnell	Do.	224

A.D.		Translator's Name.	Page
	Contrast between the policy of Elizabeth and James I. towards these princes ..	.. ..	.. 230
1630.	O'Hussey, last hereditary bard of the Maguire of Fermanagh—his Ode to the Maguire in a perilous expedition ..	J. C. Mangan	231
	Political tone of much of the poetry of this period	.. ..	.. 234
1650.	John O'Dugan—the Coolin	S. (Sir S.) Ferguson	235-36
	John O'Dwyer of the Glen (a Lament)..	T. Furlong ..	.. 237
	The Roman Vision, historical poem ..	H. G. Curran	.. 239
	Ode to Thomas O'Connellan, a famous minstrel	S. (Sir S.) Ferguson	248
1690.	Edmond O'Ryan, or Emon-a-Knock—his Love Elegy	Miss Brooke	.. 249
	Peculiar aptitude of the Irish language for lyric poetry	.. ..	.. 254
	Anonymous Verses	Miss Brooke	.. 254
	Fergus and M'Nally—Bridget Fergus ..	J. D'Alton, m.r.i.a.	.. 255
	Bacchanalian Poetry. Prevalence of Intemperance probably of recent origin..	.. ..	.. 257
	Ode to Drunkenness	T. Furlong ..	.. 258
	Bards of early part of the eighteenth century—O'Neachtan, M'Donnell, and O'Carolan—Lament for Mary D'Este	H. G. Curran	.. 261
	Maggy Lauder	T. Furlong	.. 261
	Jacobite Poetry—John Claragh M'Donnell		.. 264
	The Lady of Albany's Lament for Prince Charles	E. Walsh	.. 265
1670.	O'Carolan (Turlogh), Notice of ..	..	.. 267
	———— Bridget Cruise, his first love, lines to	T. Furlong ..	.. 268
	———— her reply to	Anonymous ..	.. 270
	———— Verses in his eulogy, by a brother Bard		.. 272
	———— Tradition of the poet Goldsmith being taken as a child to see him		ib.
	———— His (Goldsmith's) anecdote of the origin of his Concerto	.. ..	.. ib.
	———— Mild Mable, his song to ..	S. (Sir S. Ferguson..	273
	———— O'More's Fair Daughter, his Ode to	T. Furlong ..	.. 275
	———— Grace Nugent, his song to ..	S. Sir S.) Ferguson..	278
1733.	———— Monody on the Death of his Wife	Miss Brooke	.. 279
1738.	———— his last days—Plays his "Farewell to Music"	.. ..	.. 280
	———— M'Cabe's Elegy to his memory	Miss Brooke.	.. 281

TABLE OF CONTENTS.

A.D.		Translator's Name.	Page
	Decline of the Irish Language subsequently—Origin (probable) of Bulls ..	..	292
	O'Cullane, a Poet of County Cork after Carolan		ib.
	———— ——his Elegy on the Ruins of Timoleague Abbey	.. S. (Sir S.) Ferguson..	293
	Concluding Observations	..	288
	MISCELLANEOUS ADDENDA—		
	The Dirge of Dargo ..	.. J. Anster, ll.d.	.. 291
	The Woman of Three Cows	.. J. C. Mangan	.. 293
	O'Byrne's Bard to the Clans of Wicklow	.. S. (Sir S.) Ferguson..	295
	Molly Astore	Do.	.. 298
	The Fair-haired Girl	Do.	.. 299
	Casbel of Munster ..· ..	Do.	.. 300
	Nora of the Amber Hair	Do.	.. 300
	Boatman's Hymn	Do.	.. 301
	The Fair Hills of Ireland ..	Do.	.. 302
	INDEX	Do.	.. 305

SPECIMENS

OF THE

EARLY NATIVE POETRY OF IRELAND.

"Lov'd land of the bards and saints, to me
There's nought so dear as thy minstrelsy;
Bright is nature in every dress,
Rich in unborrow'd loveliness;
Winning in every shape she wears,
Winning she is in thine own sweet airs;
What to the spirit more cheering can be
 Than the lay, whose ling'ring notes recal
The thoughts of the holy, the fair, the free,
 Belov'd in life, or deplor'd in their fall?
Fling, fling the forms of art aside,—
 Dull is the ear that those forms enthral;
Let the simple songs of our sires be tried,
 They go to the heart, and the heart is all.
Give me the full responsive sigh,
The glowing cheek and the moisten'd eye;
Let these the minstrel's might attest,
And the vain and the idle may share the rest."

THOMAS FURLONG.

MUCH ingenuity has been needlessly expended in a vain attempt to account for the first rise of profane poetry. A somewhat fantastic hypothesis, adopted by several distinguished writers, assumes it to have had its origin in the principle of natural religion, or its perversion, and to have been addressed by the primeval inhabitants of the world in grateful adoration to the sun, the moon, the stars, and other great natural objects, whose mysterious movements impressed them with awe, and whose beneficence they continually experienced.* Others have attributed the earliest poetic inspiration to the heroic age and spirit, and partial evidence might easily be found for the most opposite views on the subject, in the actual themes of the early children of song. Thus in Orpheus and Corinus, if we may place any dependence in the existence of such shadowy and unsubstantial beings, we have some of the earliest examples (in their attributed remains) both of the heroic and devotional species. It is, however, very justly remarked by an elegant writer of the last century, to whose authority we shall have frequent occasion to refer, that "the early ages of every nation are enveloped in dark clouds, impervious to the rays of historic light. An attempt, therefore, to trace the arts of poetry and music to their source, in this or any other country, must be unsuccessful, for man is both a poet and musician by nature."†

---

* No such theories are necessary with regard to the noblest poetry in existence—that of the Scriptures—which, in the language of a late eloquent writer, "In lyric flow and fire, in crushing force, in majesty which seems still to echo the awful sounds once heard beneath the thunder-clouds of Sinai, is the most superb that ever burned within the breast of man."—Sir D. K. Sandford's *Dissertation on the Rise and Progress of Literature, Part I.*

† *Historical Memoirs of the Irish Bards,* by J. C. Walker, M.R.I.A.—A work in which, though the writer takes the liberty occasionally to dissent from his authority, every event connected with the bards will be found detailed with a degree of minuteness, elegance, and learning which will repay by its perusal those who may wish for more minute information than would suit the limits of the present volume.

But from whatever source the inspiration of the earliest poetry may have been derived, it is a powerful tribute to the influence of the gentle art over the springs of the human heart, that the sages of antiquity have made it a vehicle of the earliest historic records, philosophy, and laws. The Greeks, who so gracefully conveyed their moral lessons in the form of fable—the secret of much of their mythology—have even intimated its divine origin as well as its potency as a moral agent, in the otherwise extravagant story of Orpheus and the gift of Apollo.

Poetry thus appears, contrary to what we would naturally expect, to have been the elder sister of prose composition. Nor is it less remarkable to find it take precedence of those arts which, though less refined, would seem of a more imperative and pressing nature. Yet such appears to have been frequently, if not always, the case; nor will this inverse order appear, on a little reflection, altogether unnatural. Poetry and music, which have ever been closely united, are the gifts of nature; the useful arts, as they are termed, are the offspring of time and necessity, arising out of the increase of the species. But in the infancy of society the wants of men were few and easy of procurement. Many circumstances, besides, in the modes of life at such periods, have a tendency to call forth the romantic conceptions and wild images of poetry. A certain tincture of superstition, inherent in human nature at all times, was more strongly infused in

> "Those days of song and dreams,
> When the shepherds gather'd their flocks of old
> By the blue Arcadian streams."

The roving fancy of these children of nature conjured up imaginary spirits in every grove. Hence the Dryads,

Hama-dryads, Satyrs, Fauns, and all the host of pastoral and sylvan deities. "Thus the woods and wilds became peopled with shadowy beings, whose cries were fancied to be heard in the piping winds or in the roar of the foaming cataract."*

With this imaginative spirit the primitive tribes of this secluded island were peculiarly and deeply imbued. Poetry and its inseparable companion, music, they cultivated with the most enthusiastic ardour, and brought to singular perfection. Hence it is, as we are informed by a venerable authority, whose ancestors were the last native sovereigns who swayed the destinies of this island, that in early times "a knowledge of the arts of music and poetry was absolutely necessary. The manners of the nation were wholly engrafted on this stock. The arts in question were deemed of divine original, and made a principal part of their public policy."†

"Give me the making of a people's ballads, and I care not who makes their laws," was the well-known remark of Fletcher of Saltoun—a man who had mixed much and variously in the world, and who took an active and conspicuous part in the most stirring and eventful period of British history. It was an exaggerated form of expressing a substantial truth.

It was in this view, far more than with any merely literary

---

* *Historical Memoirs of the Irish Bards*, quarto edition, p. 18.— Walker gives the above remark in reference to the importance attached to the ancient *caoine*, or funeral song, the spirits of those whose requiem was not thus sung being deemed accursed and incapable of rest.

† *Dissertations on the History of Ireland*, by CHARLES O'CONOR, *Ballinagar*, Dis. 6.

aim, that the lays of Homer were first collected and authenticated from the recital of their oral depositaries—a task in which the greatest legislators of antiquity, Solon, Lycurgus, and Pisistratus, are all recorded to have been more or less concerned. It was a powerful tribute to the influence of the songs of a country.

Fortunately for England and Scotland, they have found able labourers in this field. Bishop Percy thought it no idle expenditure of his learned leisure to collect and elaborately improve and illustrate the early minstrelsy of his country—which produced such a marked effect upon its subsequent literature—and was ably followed by Ritson and Ellis. And a greater than Percy—Scott—was induced to play the truant with his legal pursuits, that he might, with his fellow-labourer Leyden, the linguist, accomplish the same good work for his country, by adding the old border ballads to the common stock of Scottish song. Well, indeed, might he exult in the lyric fame of his own "Caledonia, stern and wild"—in her Ramseys, her Fergusons, her immortal Burns, and others, whose productions shed such a charm of romance over the humble life and rugged features of that noble land—

> "Lift her low-rafted cottage to the clouds,
> Smile o'er her heaths, and from her mountain tops
> Beam glory to the nations."*

Ireland, with a minstrelsy in her ancient, venerable language, which, in point of antiquity, not to make any more

---

* *Gustavus Vasa*, a Tragedy, by HENRY BROOKE, father of Miss Brooke noticed later, and author of *The Earl of Essex*, and other dramas, and of *The Fool of Quality; or, History of Henry, Earl of Moreland*.

invidious comparison, that of the sister-countries cannot even approach, can boast of the works of Miss Brooke, Mr. Hardiman, and several more recent publications.*

The former of these, especially both as regards the importance of the originals, and the high talents displayed in rendering them into verse, notwithstanding the cold poetical mannerism of the period, is indeed a proud monument of the national genius, both as regards the originals and the translations.

---

* The *Reliques of Irish Poetry*, containing the originals, with elegant metrical versions, of Heroic Ballads, War Odes, Elegies, &c., was published by Miss Brooke in 1789, and was the first opportunity, with perhaps one exception, afforded the English reader of judging of the poetical merits of our ancient countrymen and their primitive language. The exception referred to is that of Charles Wilson, a young man of considerable poetical talents, who died early in London, and who, in the year 1782, according to Walker, but 1792, according to Mr. Hardiman, had published some poetical translations from the Irish. The writer has not been able to discover a copy of this work, which was never much known, and is not to be found even in our best public libraries, and was only made aware of its existence by a reference to its author in Walker's *Bards*, Scott's *Life of Swift*, and by a passage quoted by Mr. Hardiman, whose *Irish Minstrelsy*, with metrical versions by a variety of poetical contributors, including Furlong, Dr. Drummond, Mr. H. G. Curran, Mr. D'Alton, &c., was published in 1831. This work, with the *Jacobite Relics* and the *Poets and Poetry of Munster*, both edited by Mr. J. Daly, the Irish scholar, with metrical versions, in the former by the late Edward Walsh, and in the latter by the late J. C. Mangan, with the *Irish Popular Songs*, by Edward Walsh, the present work, and Dr. Drummond's *Minstrelsy*, all published about the middle of the present century, are all the small contributions that have been made in distinct collections to the invaluable labour of preserving and endeavouring to familiarize to the English reader the treasures of our ancient minstrelsy.

With regard to the future of our ancient literature, in reference to its being made to yield up more fully its treasures to the English reader, some might be inclined to take a desponding view, from the existing conditions of modern life—its railway speed and feverish excitement—the wonderful results of scientific discovery, tending to annihilate time and space—and the pressure of the increasing demands of material interests in the race of competition in all pursuits. But against the prospect of its being crushed out by these causes, it may be worthy of notice, that it was in the midst of a busy and active community, keenly alive to material interests, and absorbed in industrial pursuits, that the late Mr. (afterward Sir S.) Ferguson became one of a little band of students of the ancient language, literature, and antiquities of his country; and another of those students, himself practically engaged in industrial pursuits, became the originator and editor of a provincial archæological journal. Since then there have been professorships of Irish established in our colleges, including the provincial ones. From these, and from the students they will send out, some fruit may reasonably be expected; while the names of Dr. Todd, and Petrie, and Ferguson, and O'Donovan, and Reeves, will remain as a bright galaxy, to stimulate and guide and illuminate the way.

Many and various are the claims of our ancient poetry. A fanciful legend relates of our great Columba, that when his taper chanced to expire, whilst engaged in writing, a light was emitted from his fingers, by which he was enabled to pursue his occupation through the darkness of the night. This may afford a not inapt illustration of the illumination which "the light of song" is calculated to shed upon the dark places of a nation's history. And it has this additional advantage, that it will fix the interest and impress the memory of many a reader on whom the dry and elaborate details of the historian would fall with little effect. And considered merely with reference to their antiquity, the early ballads and songs of a country must possess great attractions for the curious as well as the historian. If our interest and veneration irresistibly attach themselves, like the ivy, to the mouldering ruins of a former age, and coins, and ornaments, and other relics of the past be highly prized and treasured up, how much higher and more rational is the regard which is justly due to even the smallest intellectual relic of an early age, than to the most elaborate workmanship of stone or metal.

But there is another point of view, by far the most important, in which our ancient poetry is to be considered—that is, as an exponent of the national sentiments, affections, passions, and feelings, or in one word, character. From this source we derive what may be compared to a photographic portraiture of a people, possessing, as it does, an unerring fidelity, and being embalmed in verse. In this view we regard our ancient poetry as deserving of the highest consideration. It will be found to present a plea for the national character, far more valuable and effective than all the studied vindications and special pleadings of the historian or the novelist. These songs and ballads form the fragments of a national autobiography, without the consciousness and deliberation of the self-historian—a cast taken from the life in the time of excitement and passion, when there was no concealment—an impression deeply stamped, in the plastic moment of intensest heat. And what are the salient points of this mental portraiture? They are such as would surely be highly honourable to any people—indicating as they do the highest development of the affections, the glorification of the sentiment of love, an undying devotion to freedom—in opposition to their persistent Danish invaders—a passionate love of nature, and at times a touching and intensely pathetic expression of the long-suppressed wailings of manly grief—sometimes for self, but oftener for country and people—welling up from the deep perennial fountains of sorrow, which had their source in the sad realities of the national story, and all the more affecting from the contrast with the natural joyousness of the national temperament.

Many of our ancient poems are also highly valuable as illustrations of the topography and natural scenery of the country, and, if more extensively known, would tend to render many a romantic glen, now little frequented, the picturesque banks of many a stream, whose waters now glide by unnoticed by the eye of the traveller, and many a one of the "fair hills of Ireland," no unclassic ground. This it was that Burns* longed to do for his "loved, his native soil," and which Scott, both in prose and verse, has so gloriously accomplished.

> " When tired at eve, the pilgrim leans
> Upon some rocky pile,
> Of days long gone the rude remains,
> Saved by their rudeness from the Vandal reigns,
> Which, red and ruthless, swept the plains
> Of this ill-fated isle,—

---

* "I have no dearer aim," he says, in one of his letters, "than to have it in my power, unplagued by the routine of business (for which, Heaven knows, I am unfit enough), to make leisurely pilgrimages thro' Caledonia; to sit on the fields of her battles, to wander on the romantic banks of her rivers, and to muse by the stately towers or romantic ruins, once the honoured abodes of her heroes."

> He little thinks the mossy stones
>   Beneath his feet
> Afford some hero's hallow'd bones
>   Their cold retreat ;
> Perhaps, e'en there, on Fingal's arm
>   A thousand heroes hung,
> While Ossian, music of the storm,
>   The battle anthem sung.
> Or there Emania's palace rose
>   In more than regal pride ;
> Ollam inhaled a nation's woes,
> Conn's fiery sceptre crush'd his foes,
>   Or noble Osgur died."
>
> PHILLIPS.

The following beautiful lines, entitled "Songs of our Land," by the late Frances Brown, a poetess of whom Ireland may well feel proud, are so peculiarly appropriate to the spirit of these pages, that we cannot resist the temptation of quoting them, in memory of many years of personal intimacy with the writer :—

> " Songs of our land, ye are with us for ever,
>   The power and splendour of thrones pass away,
> But yours is the might of some far-flowing river,
>   Through summer's bright roses, or autumn's decay.
> Ye treasure each voice of the swift-passing ages,
>   And truth which time writeth on leaves or on sand ;
> Ye bring us the bright thoughts of poets and sages,
>   And keep them among us, old songs of our land.
>
> " The bards may go down to the place of their slumbers,
>   The lyre of the charmer be hush'd in the grave,
> But far in the future, the power of their numbers
>   Shall kindle the hearts of our faithful and brave.
> It will waken an echo in souls deep and lonely,
>   Like voices of reeds by the summer breeze fann'd ;
> It will call up a spirit for freedom, when only
>   Her breathings are heard in the songs of our land.

" For they keep a record of those, the true-hearted,
    Who fell with the cause they had vow'd to maintain ;
They show us bright shadows of glory departed,
    Of love that grew cold, and the hope that was vain.
The page may be lost, and the pen long forsaken,
    The weeds may grow wild o'er the brave heart and hand,
But ye are still left, when all else hath been taken,
    Like streams in the desert, sweet songs of our land.

" Songs of our land, ye have follow'd the stranger,
    With power over ocean and desert afar ;
Ye have gone with our wanderers through distance and danger,
    And gladden'd their path like a home-guiding star.
With the breath of our mountains, in summers long vanish'd,
    And visions that pass'd like a wave from the sand,
With hope for their country, and joy for her banish'd.
    Ye come to us ever, sweet songs of our land.

" The spring-time may come, with the song of her glory,
    To bid the green heart of the forest rejoice,
But the pine of the mountain, though blasted and hoary,
    And the rock in the desert can send forth a voice.
It is thus, in their triumph o'er deep desolations,
    While ocean waves roll, or the mountains shall stand,
Still hearts that are bravest and best of the nations
    Shall glory and live in the songs of their land."

B.C. 500.   AMERGIN* is recorded as the first to whom was assigned the dignity of Arch-Druid and Ard-filea, or high priest

---

* The chronology of Irish history prior to Christianity is a dangerous subject to meddle with. Our historical antiquaries have generally placed this event about the year B.C. 1,000. Among these are O'Flaherty, O'Halloran, the elder O'Conor, and Walker. Keating and the *Psalter of Cashel,* with most of the metrical histories, make it three centuries earlier. But Tigernach, a learned annalist of the eleventh century, and the recent profound researches of Dr. O'Conor, concur in favour of a more moderate chronology, such as has been adopted in the text.

and chief bard of the realm. The duties of these offices of Amergin were to preside over the interests of philosophy, poetry, religion, history, and law; and thus was laid the foundation of an empire which has long survived, as if typical of its nature, that regal power with whose origin it was contemporaneous. The literary order thus instituted continued, in each succeeding age, to increase in importance and influence. To Amergin succeeded *Lugad*, the son of Ith, who, as we are told, is called in old writings, "the first poet of Ireland;" and there "still remain," according to a learned and zealous advocate of our ancient literature, "after a lapse of nearly three thousand years, fragments of these ancient bards. . . . The subject and language of these poems (he adds) afford internal evidence of an antiquity transcending that of any literary monument of the modern languages of Europe."* Though the originals of these curious ancient relics have been preserved, they have never been given to the public in an English dress; nor, indeed, do they possess much interest, save what they derive from their antiquity and philological value.

The ancient Celtic, the original language of a great portion of the west of Europe, consisted, like the ancient Greek, of several dialects. Of these, the Fenian was the most classic, and that adopted by the best writers. It is in this dialect that these fragments are composed. The natural changes of the language, however, in the course of centuries, and its gradual comparative discontinuance as a written medium,

---

* *Irish Minstrelsy*, by J. HARDIMAN, M.R.I.A., vol. i., pp. 4, 5.— A work which, notwithstanding much in its political tone and spirit to be regretted, may justly be regarded as one of the most valuable of the recent accessions to the stock of Irish literature.

have left between it and the oral language which has descended to our time, or even the later Irish writings, a chasm so wide, that, in a certain sense, it may be said these

"Bards speak in a language which hath perished."

The subject of the first of these antique relics is a description of the island by Amergin. The second also purports to have been written by the same bard. To Lugad, the successor of Amergin, is attributed the third piece, which is written upon the death of his wife Fial, under very singular circumstances.* In the first stanza he sadly exclaims:—

> "Here sit we on the strand,
> Fierce is our cold,—
> There is shivering on my teeth,—
> A great loss is the loss that has come on me." †

Many circumstances have been recorded, which serve to illustrate the high estimation in which the office and functions of the bard were held. Shortly after the institution of the order, a law was passed, requiring that the different classes in the state should be distinguished by a certain number of colours or stripes in their garments. In this practice, which

---

* "The writer himself," says Mr. Hardiman, "is fully convinced of the antiquity of these poems, and that they have been composed by the bards whose names they bear. To this conclusion he has arrived, after a scrupulous investigation of the language and contents of our earliest records, aided by whatever external evidence could be found to bear on the subject. . . . . *The language is so obsolete, that it cannot be understood without a gloss; and even the gloss itself is frequently so obscure as to be equally difficult with the text.*"—*Irish Minstrelsy*, vol. ii., pp. 348-9.

† For the translation of this stanza the editor is indebted to Mr. Curry of the R.I.A.

appears to have prevailed among the Celtic nations generally, originated the plaids, which have continued to be the national costume of Scotland. On this occasion, the Ollamhs, or chief bards, were allotted within one of the regal number. "Can any nation," adds their historian triumphantly, "be deemed barbarous in which learning shared the next honours to royalty?"* The colours which distinguished the bardic dress were blue, green, black, white, and red.

The time occupied by the education of the bards in the Druidic colleges† was no less a period than twelve years. When this term of probation was completed, they were admitted to all the honours of their order. They had estates settled on them, and lived free from all pressing worldly cares in perfect independence. Their persons were considered sacred; the murder of a bard was esteemed a crime infinitely more heinous than that of any ordinary citizen, and was visited on the descendants of the guilty party through successive generations. In fact, the principle of "divine right" appears to have been more attached to the profession than to the crown itself; for, while we have recorded the violent deaths of many of our kings, we have few examples of the murder of a bard, though exposed to the vengeance of their enemies by exerting their influence on the field of battle. To seize the estates which they held from the crown was deemed an act of sacrilege, which not even the necessi-

---

* Walker's *Hist. Mem.*, p. 5.

†" These institutions, intended for the quiet retreat of learning, were sunk in the bosom of deep woods of oak; 'the garish eye of day' was excluded from them, and their members studied by the light of tapers and lamps. Here the heart-corroding cares of life had no admission. Here genius was fostered and the soul sublimed."—*Ibid.*, p. 6.

ties of the public service could justify, in times of the greatest emergency.

At some unrecorded period, a division took place in the bardic office and duties. The order was ultimately divided into four classes, namely, the FILEAS, or chief bards; the BREHONS, whose duties were legislative; the SEANACHIES, whose functions were antiquarian, historical, and genealogical (somewhat similar to the present office of king-at-arms); and the ORFIDIGH, or instrumental performers. The Brehons assisted in framing, or at least in administering and promulgating, the laws, which, at certain times, seated upon some commanding eminence, they recited aloud for the public benefit, accompanied, as has been conjectured, by the sound of the harp.* These Brehon laws continued to be strictly observed long after the Anglo-Norman invasion, as recorded by contemporary English writers. The Fileas, or Ollamhain-re-dan, were the chief poets of the order. Of these, the provincial kings and chiefs had each one, and their retinue frequently consisted of as many as thirty inferior bards. The Filea ever attended the king or chief, both in public and private, in the capacity of counsellor, and, in his hours of ease, joined his retainers in cheering with his song, or lulling him to rest with a soothing tale. These tales, which were chanted to the sound of the

---

* "The history of the nation, all the placits of their legislators, and all their systems—philosophical, metaphysical, and theological—were conveyed in the harmonious measures of sound and verse. . . . . . The interval between stretching on their couches and the time of rest was employed in attending to soft music, to which were sung the loves of their heroes and the virtues of their heroines."—O'Conor's *Disserts. on Hist. of Irel.*, third edition, p. 55.

harp, were generally eulogiums on the valorous exploits of the king or chief; in order to detail which, the bard accompanied him to battle, animated the troops, and raised the martial song. We can conceive no sight more imposing than the bards, on such occasions, "marching at the head of their armies, arrayed in white flowing robes, harps glittering in their hands, and their persons surrounded with instrumental musicians. While the battle raged, they stood apart, and watched in security (for their persons were sacred) every action of the chief, in order to glean subjects for their lays."*

The reign of the great law-giver, Ollamh Fodhla (Ollav Foala), the Solon of Ireland, forms an important era as well in the civil as in the bardic annals of the kingdom.† This monarch was an illustrious patron of letters and the arts. To him we must ascribe the institution of those seminaries at Tara, the residence of the supreme monarch, which were celebrated for so many ages. The most notable act of his reign, however, which has rendered it, indeed, one of the great landmarks of our pagan annals, was the institution of the famous Teamorian Fes, or National Convention, at Tara, which makes such a conspicuous figure in our early chronicles. In this celebrated palace, which has been the theme of poets, the pride of historians, and whose fame has been bequeathed to all future time in the imperishable melodies of Moore, the bards basked in the sunshine of royal favour. Indeed, we are told in a very old MS.,

---

* Walker's *Bards*, quarto edition, p. 10.
† The date assigned to the reign of this monarch by Walker is B.C. 768, which nearly agrees with the chronology of O'Flaherty. According to the moderate scheme of chronology adopted, on the grounds previously stated in this work, it would be about B.C. 350 or 400, this monarch being the twentieth of the Milesian line.

that "*Temur* (Tarah) was so called from its celebrity for melody above the palaces of the world:—*Tea*, or *Te*, signifying melody, and *mur*, a wall—Temur, the wall of music." On the same authority, it is added, what, unfortunately, could be said of few subsequent periods of our history, that at this time "such peace and concord reigned among the people, that no music could delight them more than the sound of each other's voices."*

As we approach still more nearly the precincts of the Christian era, we find several bards, some of whose attributed remains have descended to our time. The first of these was ROYNE FILE, a poet of royal descent, who sung of the wanderings of the Scoti until their settlement in Ireland, of the division of the island among them, with the names of their leaders. FERCIERTNE was both a bard and herald, which offices, indeed, were frequently united. In a still extant poem, which is attributed to this bard, we have a panegyric on the great monarch, Ollamh Fodhla, who is represented as valiant in war, and illustrious in peace, as the founder of the Teamorian Fes, and the Druidic College at Tara. After describing him as reigning gloriously for forty years as Ard-Riogh, or supreme monarch, the poet proceeds to give an account of six succeeding sovereigns of the same line, and concludes with the origin of the grand divisions of the island. This bard, according to a romantic story, which is too long for insertion here, "evinced, in the manner of his death, a strength of affection for his patron, and a sublimity of soul, unparalleled in the history of any nation."† The productions of these bards,

---

* Hardiman's *Irish Minstrelsy*, vol. i., p. 6.
† Walker's *Hist. Mems.*, pp. 32, 33.

from whatever cause, like the still earlier fragments already mentioned, have unfortunately not yet become accessible to the English reader by translation. It is hoped they may not long remain so. The originals have, however, survived, and been lately published by the zealous advocate of our ancient literature, already so frequently quoted. "These hitherto unpublished fragments," he adds, in reference to those under consideration, and the others previously alluded to, "are considered as decisive evidence of the early cultivation of letters and the poetic art in Ireland. . . . . . The poems themselves are preserved in grave historical treatises, many centuries old. They are found preceded by the names and short notices of the several fileas to whom they are attributed. Their language is obsolete, and their idioms antiquated. Both are evidently of the earliest ages. Certainly they are very different from any compositions of the last thousand years. According, therefore, to the strictest rules of historic evidence, their antiquity must be allowed."*

The age immediately preceding the Christian era has been rendered illustrious not less in the annals of Ireland, than in song, as the bright period

> "When her kings, with banner of green unfurl'd,
> Led the Red-Branch Knights to danger,
> Ere the emerald gem of the western world
> Was set in the crown of a stranger."

Of all the romances of our ancient countrymen, who were keenly alive to the high delights of romance and song, the ancient historic tale of "Deirdre, and the lamentable

---

* *Irish Minstrelsy*, vol. ii., pp. 353, 355.

fate of the three sons of Usna," has ever taken precedence as one of their three famous tragic stories, and has served as the groundwork of the "Darthula" of Macpherson's *Ossian.* This famous tale relates to the palmy days of Ulster's ancient chivalry.

Of this renowned order of knights, whose mansion adjoined the palace of Emania, the seat of the Ulster kings, near the ancient city of Armagh,* the most distinguished in the days of their greatest splendour, in the reign of Conor MacNessa, were the celebrated Cuchullin, and his kinsman, Conal Cearnach (Kerna), the master of the order, and the three sons of Usna—Naisi, Ainli, and Ardan. When Naisi eloped with Deirdre, whom Conor the king had reared with the view of making her his bride, he fled, accompanied by his brothers, and a small band of faithful followers, into Alba, or Scotland, where he remained until Conor, professing to have become reconciled, sent for him to return with every assurance of safety. This he the more readily complied with, as he found himself exposed to the machinations of the Albanian king, in consequence of the rumour of the extraordinary beauty of Deirdre having reached him. Their departure thence gave occasion to—

DEIRDRE'S FAREWELL TO ALBA.

VERSIFIED BY WM. LEAHY.

Delightful land! yon eastern clime!
Fair Alba, with its scenes sublime;—
Its charming plains I ne'er would leave
But that I come with Naisi brave.

---

* For a notice of this celebrated palace, the erection and destruction of which form remarkable eras of Irish history, see Dr. Stuart's valuable *Hist. Memoirs of Armagh,* p. 578.

From Dunfy and Dunfin to fly,
Mansions belov'd! I'll ever sigh!
The fort that rears its tow'ring pile—
Swyno's high walls, and Drayno's isle.

O wood of Cona! in thy bow'rs
Did Ainly spend his sweetest hours;—
In Alba's west too short my stay!
For Naisi call'd me soon away.

O vale of Lay!—far now it lies!
Where balmy slumbers clos'd my eyes:
The luscious flesh of badger rare,
And fish, and ven'son were my fare.

Adieu to Masan's verdant vale!
Where herbage sweet perfum'd the gale;
My cares were often lull'd to rest,
Enroll'd in Masan's grassy vest.

With woe my bosom Archay fills;
The valley fair of flow'ry hills!
No youth was there more sprightly seen
Than Naisi, of majestic mien.

O Ety's vale! retreat divine!
Where first a house uprear'd was mine;
Amid thy groves, with golden gleam,
The sun spreads wide his rising beam.

* * * * *

Farewell to Drayno's sounding shore,
O'er crystal sand whose waters roar;
These charming scenes I ne'er would leave,
But with my love—my Naisi brave.*

---

* In the first of Mr. (afterwards Sir S.) Ferguson's series of picturesque tales, "The Hibernian Nights Entertainment," in

It formed part of the terms of the free conduct granted by Conor to the sons of Usna, that they should by no means detain anywhere to partake of hospitality until they had arrived and been entertained at Eman. At the instance

which he has followed closely the more romantic of the two versions of the story of Dierdre, is an elegant and condensed paraphrase of these verses, in which he has given all the spirit of them in a few stanzas which we cannot forego the pleasure of quoting. (*Dub. Univ. Mag.*, Dec., 1834.)

> Farewell to fair Alba, high house of the sun,
> Farewell to the mountain, the cliff, and the Dun,
> Dun Sweeny, adieu! for my love cannot stay,
> And tarry I may not when love cries away.
>
> Glen Vashan! Glen Vashan, where roe bucks run free,
> Where my love used to feast on the red deer with me,
> Where, rock'd on thy waters while stormy winds blew,
> My love used to slumber, Glen Vashan, adieu!
>
> Glendaro! Glendaro! where birchen boughs weep
> Honey dew at high noon o'er the nightingale's sleep,
> Where my love used to lead me to hear the cuckoo
> 'Mong the high hazel bushes, Glendaro! adieu!
>
> Glen Urchy! Glen Urchy! where loudly and long
> My love used to wake up the woods with his song,
> While the son of the rock,* from the depths of the dell,
> Laugh'd sweetly in answer, Glenurchy! farewell.
>
> Glen Etive! Glen Etive! where dapple roes roam,
> Where I leave the green sheeling I first call'd a home;
> Where, with me and my true love, delighted to dwell,
> The sun made his mansion—Glen Etive! farewell.
>
> Farewell to Inch Draynoch, adieu to the roar
> Of blue billows bursting in light on the shore;
> Dun Finch! farewell, for my love cannot stay,
> And tarry I may not when love cries away.

* The ancient Irish poetical name for echo.

of the king, however, Barach met them on the way, and invited them, along with Fergus, who conducted them, to a feast that he had prepared at his mansion, which lay in their route. The sons of Usna declined to tarry, but it appears there was something connected with the strict laws of hospitality, or of his order, which rendered it not consistent with honour for Fergus, who was very indignant at the occurrence, to refuse compliance. He sends, however, his two sons with them in his stead. Deirdre forebodes ill, and thus continues her lament at having departed from Alba:—

VERSIFIED BY WM. LEAHY.

DEIRDRE—From east how woeful to depart!
    The thought with anguish wrings my heart:
    Though true the son of Roy may be,
    To hold his plighted word to thee.

    O ne'er shall sorrow leave my breast,—
    No night shall give me soothing rest:
    Alas! brave youths, with grief I say,
    You rash approach your gloomy day!

NAISI—Nymph, brighter than the sun's bright beam,
    Why thus severe in woe you seem?
    Fergus would ne'er from westward come,
    Basely to lure us to our doom.

DEIRDRE—Oh! Usna's sons, of peaceful mien,
    'Tis sad to leave fair Alba green!
    'Tis lasting, never-ending woe
    From Alba's flowery plains to go!

Deirdre has afterwards a dream, which she thus relates to Naisi:—

THE DREAM OF DEIRDRE.

VERSIFIED BY WM. LEAHY.

DEIRDRE—Oh ! hear my visionary tale !
    I saw your bodies breathless, pale,
    Extended, headless, on the ground,
    And none to offer aid around !

NAISI—Fair woman, of resplendent mien,
    By thee, but evils, nought is seen ;
    May from thy ruby lips what flows
    Of vengeance fall upon our foes.

DEIRDRE—Then said the dame, I'd better know
    That half mankind were sunk in woe,
    Than you, renown'd and generous three,
    With whom I've travell'd land and sea.

    *   *   *   *   *

Deirdre then advises them to go to Dundalgan (Dundalk), the seat of their renowned kinsman, Cuchullin, to be under his safeguard, for fear of the treachery of Conor, until Fergus should return to them from the feast; but they decline to act upon that advice, and thus betray their suspicions. Deirdre continues her forebodings—

THE WARNING OF DEIRDRE.

VERSIFIED BY WM. LEAHY.

DEIRDRE—O Naisi! hither turn thine eye,
    And view yon cloud upon the sky !
    Direct above Emania green
    A cloud of blood is dreadful seen !

The awful sight my soul alarms—
A certain sign of pending harms!
The border's of a bloody hue!
So thin that I can see it through!

Oh, Usnach's sons! of matchless might,
Go not to Eman's walls to-night;
O let my well-judged word prevail!
With rest your weary limbs regale.

We'll to Dundalgan turn our course,
Where lives the chief of conq'ring force,
With day—from south we'll press the plain,
With great Cuchullin in our train.

NAISI—Then Naisi said, with angry air,
To Deirdre wise and heav'nly fair,
Our souls are not depress'd with fear—
We'll give to the advice no ear.

DEIRDRE—Thou famed descent from Rory's line,
Ere this, your will was always mine;
Naisi, before, obey'd my word—
Before we were of one accord.

On the arrival of Naisi and his companions at Emania, they took up their residence at the mansion of the Red Branch, of which they were such distinguished members; and Lavarcum, who had formerly been the companion of Deirdre, was sent by Conor to report if she still retained her incomparable charms. On visiting the fated party, she did not attempt to conceal her fears, but urged them and the sons of Fergus, with tears, to be on their guard against treachery, and uttered this lay :—

THE FOREBODINGS OF LAVARCUM.

VERSIFIED BY WM. LEAHY.

Treachery gives the deadly blow
To-night, and fills my soul with woe!
For which dire act it is decreed
That Eman will in future bleed.

The noblest three beneath the sky—
Nor braver earth sustain'd—must die!
By one rash woman's heedless thought,
Alas! to quick destruction brought.

Naisi, Ainli, Ardan's might,
Three youthful chiefs, renown'd in fight!
Their blood to-night in Eman flows,
And 'whelms me in a tide of woes!

When Lavarcum returned to Conor, her tender concern for the sons of Usna and Deirdre led her to use deceit, and she reported unfavourably of the charms of Deirdre, representing "the woman of most excellent visage and shape, at her departure from Eman, bereft of her own colour and countenance." Conor, however, was not to be satisfied with this, and sent another messenger, who reported differently—"that there was not in the world a woman possessed of superior visage and form." "When Conor heard this, he was filled of jealousy and envy, and proclaimed unto the troops to go and assault the mansion in which were the children of Usnach." Upon this, Illan the Fair, son of Fergus, who is described as a "generous youth, who refused not a person on the ridge of the world anything he might possess," indignantly remonstrated with Conor, saying—"It is like that it is Fergus' guaranty you mean to break." "By my troth," said Conor, "it will be a subject of regret to the children of Usnach to have my betrothed wife." The devoted party then prepared for a desperate resistance, and "made a firm phalanx of their shields, and put the links of their shields around Deirdre between them." But their valour was unavailing, and they were cruelly stricken down, though, the story intimates, not without magical intervention. Deirdre, only, was spared for a more miserable fate. The distraction of her grief is pathetically described; and after its first bursts, she thus gave expression to the anguish of her settled sorrow and the praises of the departed heroes:—

THE LAMENT OF DEIRDRE.

VERSIFIED BY WM. LEAHY.

Now weary rolls, to me, each gloomy hour—
   Now dimly shines, to me, earth's genial ray—
For Usna's noble sons—alas! no more
   Appear, to glad the rising beam of day!

Oh! let sorrow every breast inspire!
   With them, how sweet was life!—and I how bless'd!
The princely offspring of a royal sire,
   Who made th' unfriended stranger their free guest.

Three brindled lions, whose imperial roar
   Echo'd aloud from Huma's woody height!
But now the dreadful sound is heard no more,
   The falcons of the hill have wing'd their flight!

Three youths divine!—whom Britain's fair admir'd!
  Who ne'er up-reared the beamy shield in vain—
Receding valour shrunk, with fear inspir'd,
  And trembling heroes fled the crimson plain!

Three mighty leaders, who disdain'd to yield,—
  Who ne'er to mortal servile homage shew'd,
While their strong hand the brazen spear could wield!
  For whom, in love, the Ultonian bosom glow'd!

Three lordly bears that rang'd the forest wide,
  And tore th' opposing oaks with fury down!—
Three rocks unmov'd in battle's furious tide!
  Three chiefs, whose greatest riches was renown!

Three that to Caffa's daughter ow'd their source!—
  Tears for their treacherous fall shall ever pour!
Three powerful props of Cualnia's martial force!
  Three dragons fierce of Monad's lofty tow'r!

Three whom the RED BRANCH honour'd 'bove the rest:
  They're gone!—and with them all my joys are fled!
Three, that every bloody fray repress'd!
  Three that in Aife's warlike school were bred!

Three, whom tributary realms obey'd!
  Three adamantine pillars, that sustain'd
The slack'ning arm of war; who forceful stay'd
  The rushing foe,—and the dread fight maintain'd!

Three, that in Dunsky's learned halls were train'd,
  Whom Otha taught to break th' embattled line;
Whose reach of thought each noble art attain'd!
  In death's eternal sleep they now recline!

For Naisi's love I fled my royal lord,—
  I fled Ultonia's treasures, throne, and king!
For three for deeds of fame admir'd—ador'd!
  Their lamentable dirge I'll plaintive sing!

And let no earthly being vainly deem
    That after Naisi I could here delay!
To follow Ainli—Ardan, chief supreme!
    I'll quickly sink beneath the kindred clay!

Three that rush'd impetuous o'er the plain!—
    He's gone!—He's gone! my Naisi!—deathless name!
Whose shining blade heap'd high the hills of slain!
    O'er his cold corse shall woeful torrents stream!

Oh!—bending o'er the tomb, here let me stay!—
    Resume the spade and make the mansion wide,—
And when I weep my gloomy soul away,—
    Then, generous, place me by my Naisi's side!

With them each danger would I gladly share,
    And winter's cold and summer's heat endure;—
Now lamentations pierce the wounded air!
    No more upon their shields I lie secure!

No more their radiant spears shall be my bed!
    Upraise their steely falchions o'er the grave,
Yet reeking with the blood of hostile dead!—
    Around the field, no more they'll deathful wave!

No more the hound, unfetter'd, springs away;
    The hawk no more shall guide his deadly aim,
And cautious pounce upon the trembling prey;—
    They breathe no more, who lov'd the sportive game!

They breathe no more, who gloried in the chase!
    Whom Conall rear'd,—whom heav'nly Maia bore;
Of might the fury of the foe to face;—
    The thunder of the battle rolls no more!

Whene'er I cast around my wand'ring eye,—
    And the three slips of their three hounds I see,—
Forth from my bleeding heart it draws a sigh!
    For they,—alas!—were held in care by me!

Naisi!—my life existed but in thine!—
   And now thy gen'rous, mighty soul is flown!
Why should this body long imprison mine?
   Why does your Deirdre linger thus alone?

For though, full oft, from me did Naisi part,
   Yet had I then no real cause to mourn:
His bless'd existence fill'd with joy my heart—
   But now he's gone,—ah!—never to return!

Is Naisi, then, in earth's cold bosom laid?
   My sight grows dim,—woe stops my sobbing breath!—
Soon, joyful, will I follow his dear shade,—
   My fainting spirit courts the approach of death!

None—ah! none I leave to mourn my doom!—
   Now fate's impending stroke will not be long;—
Betray'd by me, they sank into the tomb!
   There will be none to sing my funeral song!

Ah! had the unhappy Deirdre been no more!—
   Ah! had she slept within her narrow cell!—
Ere, with false Fergus, she left Alba's shore,
   Ere Usna's noble offspring treacherous fell!

Oh! how beguil'd! how woefully deceiv'd!
   To the Red Branch by sweet persuasion brought!
The sacred, seeming, promise was believ'd!
   The sons of Usna harbour'd no base thought!

With thee, belov'd and generous chief, to go,
   I fled Ultonia's beauteous scenes—divine!—
In cheerless gloom and solitary woe,
   While painful life continues, now I pine!

No radiant beam of joy my soul receives!
   No friendly tongue can soothe my flowing grief!
No cold revenge my mighty loss retrieves!
   No human aid can give me now relief!

> Oh! death at length my sinking form invades!
> The vital blood my veins no longer warms;—
> Now—now I join the three great martyr'd shades!—
> Receive me, Naisi, in thy blood-stain'd arms!*

The story then relates that "Deirdre flung herself upon the grave of Naisi, and died forthwith, and stones were laid over their monumental heap; their Ogham name was inscribed, and their dirge of lamentation was sung." This is noted as the first breach of public faith in the Irish records, and its effects were very disastrous. Fergus, indignant at the breach of his guaranty and the perfidy of Conor, resorted to the Court of Oilioll and Mevia, who then reigned in Connaught, and had long been at enmity with Conor, and succeeded in uniting them in a league with the other provinces against the perfidious king of Ulster. This was the occasion of the seven, or, according to others, ten years' war between the Connacians and the Ultonians, which produced the greatest evils to both, and only terminated in the destruction of Emania.

The following is Mr. (Sir S.) Ferguson's beautiful version of Deirdre's Lament, which is here given at the risk of repetition:—

> The lions of the hill are gone,
> And I am left alone—alone;
> Dig the grave both wide and deep,
> For I am sick, and fain would sleep.

---

* *Dublin Gaelic Soc. Trans.*

THE LAMENT OF DEIRDRE.

The falcons of the wood are flown,
And I am left alone—alone;
Dig the grave both deep and wide,
And let us slumber side by side.

The dragons of the rock are sleeping—
Sleep that wakes not for our weeping;
Dig the grave, and make it ready,
Lay me by my true love's body.

Lay their spears and bucklers bright
By the warriors' sides aright;
Many a day the three before me
On their linked bucklers bore me.

Lay upon the low grave floor,
'Neath each head, the blue claymore;
Many a time the noble three
Redden'd these blue blades for me.

Lay the collars, as is meet,
Of their greyhounds at their feet;
Many a time for me have they
Brought the tall red deer to bay.

In the falcon's jesses throw
Hook and arrow, line and bow;
Never again by stream or plain
Shall the gentle woodsmen go.

Sweet companions, were ye ever
Harsh to me, your sister?—never.
Woods, and wilds, and misty valleys,
Were with you as good's a palace.

Oh! to hear my true love singing,
Sweet as sounds of trumpets ringing;
Like the sway of ocean swelling,
Roll'd his deep voice round our dwelling.

Oh! to hear the echoes pealing
Round our green and fairy shealing,
When the three, with soaring chorus,
Made the sky-lark silent o'er us.

Echo, now sleep morn and even—
Lark, alone enchant the heaven;
Ardan's lips are scant of breath,
Naisi's tongue is cold in death.

Stag, exult on glen and mountain,
Salmon, leap from loch to fountain;
Heron, in the free air warm ye,
Usnach's sons no more will harm ye.

Erin's stay no more ye are,
Rulers of the ridge of war;
Never more 'twill be your fate
To keep the beam of battle straight.

Woe is me! by fraud and wrong,
Traitors false, and tyrants strong,
Fell Clan Usnach bought and sold,
For Barach's feast and Conor's gold.

Woe to Eman, roof and wall!
Woe to Red Branch, hearth and hall!
Tenfold woe and black dishonour
To the foul and false Clan Conor.

Dig the grave both wide and deep,
Sick I am, and fain would sleep!
Dig the grave, and make it ready,
Lay me by my true love's body.

There is a very interesting poem written on Cuchullin by an unknown bard, which, though it cannot with certainty be traced to his own age, being anonymous, yet, from its undoubted antiquity and its relation to this period, may not improperly be introduced here. From the language and idiom, it has been pronounced by competent judges among the oldest heroic poems in the language.

The poem is founded on a tale of unfortunate love and female revenge. It appears that Cuchullin, with all his knightly qualities, was not distinguished for his fidelity to the fair. A Scottish lady, named Aifé, daughter of Airdgenny, who had been the victim of his infidelity during one of the knight's visits to her country, determined that his own son, the offspring of her ill-requited attachment, should be the instrument of the vengeance which she vowed against him. Instead, therefore, of sending the youth to Ireland, according to the wish expressed to her by Cuchullin, she had him carefully trained in the military science of the period, and in due time sent him upon the unnatural mission for which she had so long and carefully prepared him. The mansion of the RED-BRANCH KNIGHTS, to which Cuchullin belonged, adjoined the palace of EMANIA, the seat of the Ulster kings, near Armagh, and thither the young hero, on arriving in Ireland, accordingly directed his steps.

CONLOCH.

TRANSLATED BY MISS BROOKE.

Conloch, haughty, bold, and brave,
Rides upon Ierne's wave!
Flush'd with loud applauding fame,
From Dunscaik's walls he came—
Came to visit Erin's coast,
Came to prove her mighty host!

On his approaching the palace, a herald was despatched by the king (Conor Mac Nessa) to inquire the name and business of the knight, whom he thus courteously addresses:—

"Welcome, O youth of the intrepid mien,
  In glittering armour drest!
Yet *thus* to see thee come, I ween,
  Speaks a stray'd course, illustrious guest!*
But now that safe the eastern gale
  Has given thee to our view,
Recount thy travels, give the high detail
Of those exploits from whence thy glory grew."

The youth, inspired with feelings of the fiercest resentment, which his mother had taken care to instil into his mind, haughtily declines either to reveal his name, or pay the customary tribute which was exacted at the drawbridge, as an acknowledgment of the superior prowess of the Ulster knights, while his language and deportment evinced his hostile intentions so unequivocally, as at once to be construed into a challenge. The result was a recourse to single combat, when Conloch vanquished an incredible number of knights, which, as O'Halloran patriotically observes, "is all poetic fiction, in order to raise the character of the hero, who then falls the greater victim to the glory of his own

---

* "It is evident that the herald here only *affects* to mistake the meaning of Conloch's martial appearance, with a view perhaps to engage him to change his intention; or probably, through politeness to a *stranger*, he would not seem to think him an enemy until he had positively declared himself such."

It may here be mentioned that all notes marked with inverted commas, as above, throughout the volume, are by the translator—those not so marked, by the editor.

father." The king seeing his champions, hitherto deemed invincible, thus overcome by a stripling, despatches a courier for Cuchullin, who had not attended at the court since the perfidious slaughter of his kinsmen, the three sons of Usnoth, by order of the king, but who, finding the honour of his country at stake, nobly merges his private wrongs in the sense of his public duty. It appears that at the sight of Cuchullin, the youth was moved not only with the yearnings of natural affection towards the father, but with admiration at the commanding presence of the hero. The intervening stanzas, detailing the defeat of the knights, the consternation of the monarch, and the arrival of Cuchullin, are omitted, as are several other portions, in order not to swell the piece to too great length, without adding much to the interest.

> Then, with firm step and dauntless air,
> Cuchullin went, and thus the foe addrest:
> "Let me, O valiant knight (he cried),
>   Thy courtesy request;
> To me thy purpose and thy name confide,
> And what thy lineage, and thy land, declare!
> Do not my friendly hand refuse,
>   And proffer'd peace decline;
> Yet, if thou wilt the doubtful combat choose,
> The combat, then, O fair-hair'd youth be thine!"
>
>   "Never shall aught so base as fear
>   The hero's bosom sway,
>   Never, to please a curious ear,
>   Will I my fame betray;
>   No, gallant chief, I will to none
> My name, my purpose, or my birth, reveal;
> Nor, even from *thee*, the combat will I shun,
> Strong though thine arm appear, and tried thy martial
>   steel.

"Yet hear me own that, did the vow
  Of chivalry allow,
I would not thy request withstand,
But gladly take, in peace, thy proffer'd hand;
So does that face each hostile thought control!*
So does that noble mien possess my soul!"

Reluctant, then, the chiefs commenc'd the fight,
Till glowing honour rous'd their slumbering might!
Dire was the strife each valiant arm maintain'd,
And undecided long their fates remain'd;
For, till that hour, no eye had ever view'd
A field *so* fought, a conquest *so* pursu'd.
At length, Cuchullin's kindling soul arose:
  Indignant shame recruited fury lends;
With fatal aim, his glittering lance he throws,
  And low on earth the dying youth extends.

Flown with the spear, his rage forsook
  The hero's generous breast,
And, with soft voice and pitying look,
  He thus his brave, unhappy foe addrest—
  "Gallant youth! that wound, I fear,
  Is past the power of art to heal!
Now, then, thy name and lineage let me hear,
  And whence, and why we see thee here, reveal!
That so thy tomb with honour we may raise,
And give to glory's song thy deathless praise!"

  "Approach!" the wounded youth replied—
    "Yet—yet more closely nigh!
  On this dear earth—by that dear side
    O let me die!

---

*"Deeply as, it is evident, Conloch had been prepossessed against Cuchullin, yet nature here begins to work; and the sight of the paternal face raises strong emotions in his breast. This is finely introduced by the masterly poet to heighten the distress of the catastrophe."

Thy hand— my father!—hapless chief!
And you, ye warriors of our isle, draw near,
    The anguish of my soul to hear,
    For I must kill a father's heart with grief!

"O first of heroes! hear thy son,
    Thy Conloch's parting breath!
    See Dunscaik's* early care!
    See Dundalgan's cherish'd heir!
    See, alas! thy hapless child,
    By female arts beguil'd,
    And by a fatal promise won,
Falls the sad victim of untimely death!"

"O my lost son!—relentless fate!
    By this curst arm to fall!—
Come, wretched Aifé, from thy childless hall,
And learn the woes that thy pierc'd soul await!
    Why wert thou absent in this fatal hour?
    A mother's tender power
Might sure have sway'd my Conloch's filial breast!
My son, my hero, then had stood confest.
    But it is past!—he dies!—ah, woe!
Come, Aifé—come, and let thy sorrows flow!
Bathe his dear wounds!—support his languid head!—
Wash, with a mother's tears, away the blood a father
    shed!"

"No more," the dying youth exclaim'd—
    "No more on Aifé call—
Curst be her art!—the treacherous snare she fram'd
Has wrought thy Conloch's fall!

---

* "Dun-Sgathach (*i.e.*, the fortress of Sgathach), in the Isle of Skye, took its name from the celebrated Albanian heroine, who established an academy there, and taught the use of arms."

Curse on the tongue that arm'd my hand
    Against a father's breast—
That bound me to obey her dire command,
And with a lying tale my soul possest—
That made me think my youth no more thy care,
And bade me of thy cruel arts beware!

" Curst be the tongue to whose deceit
The anguish of my father's heart I owe.
  While thus to bathe his sacred feet,
    Through this unhappy side
  He sees the same rich crimson tide
That fills his own heroic bosom flow."

  *   *   *   *   *   *

" But, ah, Cuchullin!—dauntless knight!—
  Ah, hadst thou better mark'd the fight!
Thy skill in arms might soon have made thee know
    That I was only *half* a foe!
Thou wouldst have seen, for glory though I fought,
    Defence, not blood, I sought.
Thou wouldst have seen from that dear breast
Nature and love thy Conloch's arm arrest!
Thou wouldst have seen his spear instinctive stray ;
  And, when occasion dar'd its force,
Still from that form it fondly turn'd away,
    And gave to air its course."*

No answer the unhappy sire return'd,
  But wildly, thus, in frantic sorrow mourn'd—
"O my lov'd Conloch, beam of glory's light,
    O set not yet in night!

---

* " Here is one of those delicate strokes of nature and sentiment that pass so directly to the heart, and so powerfully awaken its feelings! Sympathy bleeds at every line of this passage, and the anguish of the father and the son are at once transfused into our hearts!"

Live, live, my son, to aid thy father's sword !
O live, to conquest and to fame restor'd !
Companions of the war, my son, we'll go,
Mow down the ranks, and chase the routed foe !
Ourselves an host, sweep o'er the prostrate field,
And squadrons to my hero's arm shall yield.

* * * * *

"Gone !—art thou gone ? O wretched eyes !
See where my child ! my murder'd Conloch lies !
Lo ! in the dust his shield of conquest laid !
And prostrate now his once victorious blade !
O let me turn from the soul-torturing sight !
 O wretch ! deserted, and forlorn !
 With age's sharpest arrows torn !—
Stript of each tender tie, each fond delight !

 " Cruel father ! cruel stroke !—
  See the heart of nature broke !
Yes, I have murder'd thee, my lovely child !
Red with thy blood this fatal hand I view !—
O from the sight distraction will ensue,
And grief will turn with tearless horror wild !

  "Reason !—whither art thou fled ?
  Art thou, with my Conloch, dead ?
  Is this lost wretch no more thy care ?
  Not one kind ray to light my soul ;
  To free it from the black control
   Of this deep, deep despair !

" As the lone skiff is toss'd from wave to wave,
  No pilot's hand to save !
 Thus, thus my devious soul is borne !
Wild with my woes, I only live to mourn !
 But all in death will shortly end,
And sorrow to the grave its victim send !

Yes, yes, I feel the near approach of peace,
    And misery soon will cease!
As the ripe fruit, at shady autumn's call,
Shakes to each blast, and trembles to its fall;
I wait the hour that shall afford me rest,
And lay, O earth, my sorrows in thy breast."

LAMENTATION OF CUCHULLIN
OVER THE BODY OF HIS SON CONLOCH.

Alas, alas! for thee,
    O Aife's hapless son!
And oh, of sires the most undone,
My child! my child! woe, tenfold woe, to me!
    Alas! that e'er these fatal plains
    Thy valiant steps receiv'd!
And oh, for Cualnia's* wretched chief
    What now, alas, remains!
What but to gaze upon his grief!
Of his sole son, by his own arm, bereav'd!

*   *   *   *   *   *

Could fate no other grief devise?
    No other foe provide?—
Oh! could no other arm but mine suffice
    To pierce my darling's side!—
My Conloch! 'tis denied thy father's woe
Even the sad comfort of revenge to know!
To rush upon thy murderer's cruel breast,
Scatter his limbs, and rend his haughty crest!

---

* "Cuchullin was called, by way of pre-eminence, the HERO OF CUALNIA, that being the name of his patrimony, which it still retains in the County of Louth."

While his whole tribe in blood should quench my rage,
And the dire fever of my soul assuage!*
The debt of vengeance then should well be paid,
And thousands fall, the victims of thy shade!

Ultonian knights!† ye glory of our age!
Well have ye 'scaped a frantic father's rage!
That not by *you* this fatal field was won!
That not by *you* I lose my lovely son!—
Oh, dearly else should all your lives abide
The trophies from my Conloch's valour torn;
And your RED BRANCH, in deeper crimson dy'd.
The vengeance of a father's arm should mourn!

O thou lost hope of my declining years!
O cruel winds that drove thee to this coast!
  Alas! could destiny afford
  No other arm, no other sword,
  In Leinster of the pointed spears
On Munster's plains, or in fierce Cruachan's‡ host,
  To quench in blood my filial light,
And spare my arm the deed, my eyes the sight?

  * * * * *

---

* "What a picture of a heart torn with sorrow is here exhibited, in these wild startings of passion! The soul of a hero pressed down with a weight of woe, stung to madness by complicated aggravations of the most poignant grief, and struggling between reason and the impatient frenzy of despair! How naturally does it rave around for some object whereon to vent the burstings of anguish, and the irritations of a wounded spirit."

† "These were the famous heroes of the RED BRANCH." Ultonia, the ancient name of Ulster.

‡ Cruachan (Croghan), the regal palace of Connaught.

Why was it not in Sora's barbarous lands
    My lovely Conloch fell ?
Or by fierce Pictish chiefs,* whose ruthless bands
    Would joy the cruel tale to tell ;
Whose souls are train'd all pity to subdue ;
Whose savage eyes, unmov'd, that form could view.

* * * * * * *

But what for me—for me is left !
Of more, and dearer far, than life bereft !
    Doom'd to yet unheard of woe !
A father doom'd to pierce his darling's side !
    And, oh ! with blasted eyes abide
To see the last dear drops of filial crimson flow !

* * * * * * *

Alas !—my trembling limbs !—my fainting frame !
    Grief, is it thou ?—
    O conquering grief, I know thee now !
Well do thy sad effects my woes proclaim !—
Poor Victor !—see thy trophies where they lie !—
Wash them with tears !—then lay thee down and die !

* * * * * * *

Alas, I sink !—my failing sight
    Is gone ! 'tis lost in night !
Clouds and darkness round me dwell,
Horrors more than tongue can tell !

* * * * * * *

---

* "The period when the Picts first invaded North Briton has not, I believe, been exactly ascertained. We here find that country divided between the Picts and the Albanians, and the former mentioned as a bloody and cruel people. It was not until two centuries after this that a third colony from Ireland was established there under Carby Riada."

Lo, the sad remnant of my slaughter'd race,
Like some lone trunk, I wither in my place!
No more the sons of Usnoth to my sight
Give manly charms, and to my soul delight;
No more my Conloch shall I hope to see,
Nor son nor kinsman now survives for me!
O my lost son, my precious child, adieu,
No more these eyes that lovely form shall view;
No more his dark-red spear shall Ainle wield,*
No more shall Naoise thunder o'er the field;
No more shall Ardan sweep the hostile plains,
Lost are they all, and nought but woe remains!
Now, cheerless earth, adieu thy every care—
Adieu to all but horror and despair.

Cuchullin probably did not long survive his son, his death being recorded in the second year of the Christian era.† The name of Cuchullin has, indeed, been rendered in some degree familiar to English readers by the famous literary imposture of Macpherson, the Scottish writer, in the productions which, with so much ability, he has dressed up into a species of rude epic grandeur, under the title of Ossian's Poems. In these, he brings the hero, Cuchullin, and their reputed author together, by a stretch of poetic licence, without any reference to the period of better than two centuries which dull prosaic chronology had interposed between them. The age of Ossian himself, however, will afford a more suitable opportunity for any further remarks on this subject.

---

* "Ainle, Naoise, and Ardan were the three sons of Usnoth."

† O'Halloran places the incidents of this poem about the year B.C. 54; but as Cuchullin is here represented in the decline of life, it is not a probable supposition that he should have survived his grief fifty or sixty years, and he then at an advanced age. From this period the chronology becomes much more certain, however.

A.D. 9.
We now come to the opening of the Christian era, about which time flourished the bards, LUGAR and CONGAL, whose remains, like those previously noticed, have not hitherto been translated. Scarcely fifty years had elapsed from that period, when a storm gathered over the heads of the bards, which threatened destruction to their whole order. With that tendency to abuse which clings to all, even the best, human institutions, and in which the possession of great and undefined authority by any body of men is almost certain to result, the Brehons came in time so grossly to pervert their judicial influence, that the popular indignation was roused to such a pitch of fury as threatened the expulsion of the whole order from the kingdom. By the timely interference, however, of Concovar, one of the provincial monarchs, such a reformation was effected, by limiting their power and reducing their number, from the great magnitude to which it had swelled, to about two hundred, as pacified the popular clamour and prevented so desperate an alternative.

A.D. 174-177.
One of the most curious relics connected with Irish literature is the Testament of Cathaoir Mor (*i.e.*, the Great), King of Leinster, and afterwards elevated to the supreme monarchy, which he enjoyed three years (174-177). This singular document is preserved in the *Book of Rights*, published by the Celtic Society, with a translation and Notes by Dr. O'Donovan, the eminent Irish scholar. Of its authenticity there can, therefore, be no question, though some doubt may exist as to its having originally been written in the precise form in which it has come down to us. The editor and translator of that work—to whose learning and research Irish literature is deeply indebted—expresses his "opinion that it *was*

drawn up in its present form some centuries after the death of Cathaeir Mor, when the race of his more illustrious sons had definite territories in Leinster."* In a subsequent note to the document itself, he informs us that "the words of Cathaeir's will are in that peculiar metre called by the Irish 'Rithlearg,' an example of which occurs in the Battle of Magh Rath, &c."† The following metrical version was made by the late ingenious author of the *Anthologia Germanica*, &c.

THE TESTAMENT OF CATHAEIR MOR.

METRICAL VERSION BY JAMES CLARENCE MANGAN.

My Sovereign Power, my nobleness,
My strength to curse and bless,
My royal Privilege of Protection,
I leave to the son of my best affection,
Ros Failghe, Ros of the Rings,
Worthy descendant of Eire's Kings!
To serve as memorials of succession
For all who yet shall claim their possession
  In after ages.
Clement and noble and bold
  Is Ros, my son.
Then let him not hoard up silver and gold,
 But give unto all fair measure of wages.

Victorious in battle he ever hath been;
 He therefore shall yield the green
And glorious plains of Teamhair to none,
  No, not to his brothers;
   Yet these shall he aid
  When attack'd or betray'd.

---

* *Introd. to Book of Rights*, p. xxxv.
† *Book of Rights*, p. 193.

This blessing of mine shall outlast the tomb,
And live till the day of doom.
    And a prosperous man above
    And beyond all others
    Ros FAILGHE shall prove!

Then he gave him ten shields and ten rings and ten swords,
And ten drinking-horns*—and he spake him these words:
  "Brightly shall shine the glory,
    O Ros, of thy sons and heirs.
  Never shall flourish in story
    Such heroes as they and theirs!"

Then, laying his royal hand on the head
Of his good son, DAIRE, he bless'd him and said:
  "MY VALOUR, my daring, my martial courage,
    My skill in the field, I leave to DAIRE,
    That he be a guiding torch and starry
  Light and lamp to the hosts of our age.

---

* "As to the golden ornaments, swords, shields, &c., mentioned in this will, it appears that such articles were in great abundance in Ireland in the early ages, as sufficiently demonstrated by the fact that, in various parts of the country, there have been found in bogs, ramparts, and ancient fortresses, golden crowns worn by ancient kings and queens—torques, or golden collars, golden gorgets and bracelets, crescents, large hollow golden balls, fibulæ, breast-pins or brooches, golden-hilted swords, and a variety of other ornaments, the uses of which are unknown at the present day. Some of these articles were from half a pound to two pounds weight [of the finest and purest gold], and many of them are still to be seen in museums and private collections; but vast quantities of these interesting antiquities have been barbarously *sold to goldsmiths and melted down!*"—*Annals of the Four Masters* (Connellan's Trans.), note, p. 220.

A hero to sway, to lead, and command,
Shall be every son of his tribes in the land!
O Daire, with boldness and power
    Sit thou on the frontier of Thuath Laighean,*
And ravage the lands of Deas Ghavair.†
    Accept no gifts for protection of thine,
And so shall Heaven assuredly bless
Thy many daughters with fruitfulness,
    And none shall stand above thee,
For I, thy sire, who love thee
    With deep and warm affection,
I prophesy unto thee all success
    That warlike men may covet or boast
    Over the great Gailian‡ host."
And he gave him, thereon, as memorials and meeds,
Eight bondsmen, eight handmaids, eight cups, and eight steeds.

    The noble monarch of Eire's men
      Spake thus to the young Prince of Breasal, then:
"My Sea, with all its wealth of streams,
    I leave to my sweetly speaking Breasal,
To serve and to succour him as a vassal—
    And the land whereon the bright sun beams
Around the waves of Amergin's Bay§
As parcell'd out in the ancient day;
By free men, through a long, long time,
    Shall this thy heritage be enjoy'd—
    But the chieftainry shall at last be destroy'd
Because of a Prince's crime.

---

    * "North Leinster."   † "South Leinster."
‡ "An ancient designation," according to O'Donovan, "of the Laighnigh, or Leinstermen."
§ "Originally the estuary of the Blackwater, or Avonmore, in the County of Wicklow, said to derive its name from Amergin."

And though others again shall regain it,
   Yet Heaven shall not bless it,
   But power shall oppress it,
And weakness and baseness shall stain it."
And he gave him six ships, and six steeds, and six shields,
Six mantles, and six coats of steel,
And the six royal oxen that wrought in his fields—
These gave he to Breasal the Prince for his weal.

     Then to Ceatach he spake:
     "MY BORDER-LANDS
Thou, Ceatach, shalt take,
But, ere long, they shall pass from thy hands,
   And by thee shall none
   Be ever begotten, daughter or son!"

     To Fearghus Luascan spake he thus:
     "THOU, FEARGHUS, also, art one of us,
   But over-simple in all thy ways,
   And babblest much of thy childish days.
   For thee have I nought, but if lands may be bought,
     Or won hereafter by sword or lance,
       Of those perchance
   I may leave thee a part,
All simple babbler and boy as thou art!"

     Of goods young Fearghus, therefore, had none,
   And the monarch spake to another son:
   "To my BOYISH HERO, Crimthan the mild,
    Who loveth to wander in woods and wild,
     And snare the songful birds of the field,
     But shunneth to look on spear and shield,
   I have little to give of all that I share.
   His fame shall fail, his battles be rare,
   And of all the kings that shall wear his crown,
   But one alone shall win renown!"
And he gave him six cloaks, and six cups, and seven steeds,
And six harness'd oxen, all fresh from the meads.

But on Aenghus Nic, a younger child,
   Begotten in crime and born in woe,
The father frown'd, as on one defiled,
   And with lowering brow he spake him so:
"To Nic, my son, that base-born youth,
   Shall nought be given of land or gold;
He may be great and good and bold,
But his birth is an agony all untold,
Which gnaweth him like a serpent's tooth.
     I am no donor
       To him or his race—
     His birth was dishonour;
     His life is disgrace!"*

And to EOCHAIDH TIMINE spake he with pain:
"WEAK SON OF MINE, thou shalt not gain
   Waste or water, valley or plain.
From thee shall none descend save cravens,
   Sons of sluggish sires and mothers,
     Who shall live and die,
But give no corpses to the ravens!
     Mine ill thought and mine evil eye †
   On thee beyond thy brothers
     Shall ever, ever lie!"

And to Oilioll Ceadach his words were these:
   "O OILIOLL, great, in coming years,
Shall be thy name among friends and foes
   As the first of *Brughaidhs*‡ and Hospitaliers!

---

* "The reader may, perhaps, here be reminded of the lines in Byron's *Parisina*, addressed by Hugo to his father, Count Azo:—
   "'And with thy very crime, my birth,
     Thou tauntest me as little worth,
       A match ignoble for thy throne.'"
† Literally, "My weakness, my curse."
‡ "Public victuallers."

But neither noble nor warlike
Shall show thy renownless dwelling;
Nevertheless
Thou shalt dazzle at chess,
Therein supremely excelling
And shining like somewhat starlike!"
And his chess-board, therefore, and chessmen eke,
He gave to Oilioll Ceadach the Meek.

Now Fiacha,—youngest son was he,—
Stood up by the bed of his father, who said,
The while caressing
Him tenderly:
"My Son! I have only for thee my blessing,
And nought beside—
Hadst best abide
With thy brothers a time, as thine years are green."

Then Fiacha wept, with a sorrowful mien;
So Cathaeir said with cheerful speech:
"Abide one month with thy brethren each,
And seven years long with Ros Failghe, my son.
Do this, and thy sire, in sincerity,
Prophesies unto thee wealth and prosperity,
And a renown surpass'd by none."

And further he spake, as one inspired:
"A chieftain flourishing, fear'd and admired,
Shall Fiacha prove!
The gifted man from the Bearoa's* borders,
His brother tribes shall obey his orders.
Proud Aillinn and Alwain his forts shall remain;
In Carman,† too, he shall rule and reign:

---

* "*Anglicè*, the River Barrow."

† "The localities here mentioned were principally residences of the ancient kings of Leinster. The latter was on the site of the present town of Wexford."

The highest renown shall his palaces gain,
When the ruins of others bestrew the plain.
His power shall broaden and lengthen,
   And never know damage or loss ;
The impregnable N'as he shall strengthen,
   And govern in Ailve and Airgead Ros.
Yes ! O Fiacha, foe of strangers,
     This shall be thy lot !
   And thou shalt pilot
Ladhraun* and Liamhan, with steady and even
Heart and arm, through perils and dangers !
   Overthrown by thy mighty hand
     Shall the lords of Teamhair lie ;
And Taillte's† fair, the first in the land,
     Thou, son, shalt magnify,
And many a country thou yet shalt bring
To own thy rule as Cean and King.
   The blessing I give thee shall rest
    On thee and thy seed,
      While time shall endure,
Thou grandson of Fiacha the blest !
   It is barely thy meed,
     For thy soul is child-like and pure !"

Here ends this curious testament; but the narrative adds‡:—"He (Fiacha) abode then with his brothers, as Cathaeir had ordered. . . . And he remained seven years with Ros (Failghe) in that manner, and it was from him that he took arms, and it is from the descendants of Ros that every man of his descendants is bound to receive his first arms. Cathaeir afterwards went to Taillte, and fought the

---

* "This was another fort of the kings of Leinster, situated on the sea-coast in the territory of Kinsela and county of Wexford."

† "Taillte (*Anglicè*, Teltown), a village between Kells and Navan, in Meath."

‡ *Book of Rights*, p. 203.

Battle of Taillte, and was killed there by the Fian of Luaighne. . . . . Whence Lughair, the complete poet, said :

> "A world-famed, illustrious, honourable man,
> The light of his tribe and their law,
> King Cathaeir, the glory and prop of each clan,
> Was kill'd by the Fians, in Magh Breagh."

It appears that the prophetic anticipation of Cathaeir respecting his son Fiacha was not disappointed, for we are assured that "the branch of this youngest prince of the family obtained the government of the province of Leinster, and were kings of that country for many ages."*

Conn, the illustrious hero of the Hundred Fights, who succeeded to the supreme monarchy, attempted to set aside the sovereignty of the line of Cathaeir in Leinster; but Eogan More (commonly called Modha Nuagat) having been disobliged by the monarch lending his aid in opposing his claim to the throne of Munster, strengthened the hands of the Cahirians, and not only restored their supremacy in Leinster, but by a series of the most brilliant successes obliged the monarch to make a division of the kingdom with him. This territorial division was marked by a line running from Dublin to Galway, and was long known by the names of *Leath Cuin* and *Leath Modha*, or Conn's half and Modha's half—or the northern and southern divisions.

One of the most desperately contested conflicts between these rival heroes was the Battle of Cnucha,† which, owing principally to the prowess of Goll, the

A.D. 190.

---

* *Keating* (Duffy's ed.), vol. i., p. 254.

† O'Halloran makes this battle fought A.D. 155; but the editors of the *Four Masters*, with much greater probability, place it under the date adopted above. The scene of this battle is supposed to have been at Castleknock, near Dublin. See *Annals of Four Masters* (Connellan's Translation), note, p. 221.

son of Morna, the great leader of the Conacht legions, was decided in favour of Conn. It was on this occasion that Cumhal, the great father of a greater son, Fion MacCumhal, the master of the Leinster knights, who was joined in the confederacy against Conn, fell in single combat with Goll, which was a principal cause of the implacable enmity that so long subsisted between the *Clanna Morna* and the Finns. There is preserved an ode or rhapsody addressed to Goll on this occasion by his bard, according to the custom which was prescribed as one of the leading duties of the bards—their attendance upon the king or chief in the hour of battle, to lend the aid of their inspiring art to sustain the ardour of the warrior, and afterwards to record his exploits. Though only a literal version, and with all the transitions of an extempore rhapsody, it may perhaps here be given as a specimen, though by no means the best, of the *Ros Catha*, or War Songs of our ancient Celtic countrymen. The translation is by O'Halloran, the historian.*

WAR ODE TO GOLL, THE SON OF MORNA.

Goll, vigorous and warlike, chief of heroes!
Generous and puissant hand: meditator of glorious deeds.
Bulwark, dreadful as fire: terrible is thy wrath!
Champion of many battles: royal hero!

Like a lion, rapid to the attack: ruin to the foe.
Overwhelming billow: Goll, frequent in action,

---

* The plan of "notes with a poem" does not appear to have been altogether a modern book-making invention, and these verses were exhumed from a mass of learned comment, in which they were shrouded. Those who wish to peruse the notes may find them in Walker's *Armour, Dress, Weapons, &c., of the Ancient Irish*, octavo edition.

Invincible in the most dreadful conflicts.

   *   *   *   *   *

Great in the conflicts : warrior of increasing glory.
Hero of mighty deeds. Lion, furious in action ;
Animating harmonious bards. Destroyer of councils.
Puissant, all-victorious !

Subduer of fierce legions. Ruin to the renown'd.
In anger impetuous. Admired by mighty monarchs.
Chief of heavy tributes : of all-persuasive eloquence.
Bold and intrepid warrior. Unbiass'd legislator.

Goll, of martial pride. Strong in body, great in arms.
Courteous and polite to the legions. Fierce and powerful in
  action.
Shield of great lustre : flower of unfading beauty :
Rapid as the mountain flood is the force of your strong arm.

   *   *   *   *   *

Patron of bards ! respite to champions.
A tribute on Septs. Ruin of invaders.
Prince of sure protection. Subduer of nations.
Conspicuous in regal laws. Imposer of heavy tributes.

   *   *   *   *

Sea of resounding billows. Lord of high cultivations.
Companion of gallant feats. Mighty are the strokes of the
  illustrious Goll !
Vigilant commander of the legions. Deviser of exalted
  deeds.
Fierce, all-victorious. In words graceful and nervous.

Goll, of fierce and mighty blows. Hero of rigid partition.
Despoiler of the Ernains. Sword of rapid and severe execu
  tion.

Hero of heavy contributions. Constant benefactor of Munster.
A swift-flowing stream, fair as the snowy foam.

Protector of Connaught. Of unbounded enterprise.
Generous hero of the long-flowing hair. Shield to the retreating.
Commander of mighty legions. Unrivall'd prowess.
Solid and extensive support. Great in the rout of battle.

Great is the majesty of my Goll; his glory is unsullied.
My Goll is a bulwark. The spirit of close conflict.
Goll, vigorous and warlike, &c.

A.D. 213. The reign of Cormac Ulfada (Longbeard) the son of Art the Melancholy, and grandson of Con, the illustrious hero of the Hundred Fights—comprising a period of forty years*—was the most brilliant and well-authenticated era of our pagan annals. This royal sage, who ascended the throne as supreme monarch of Ireland in the first quarter of the third century, was possessed of every princely quality that could give lustre to the crown. The nobility of the man eclipsed the dignity of the monarch. Losing the sight of one of his eyes, he became incapacitated, according to an absurd law, which, however, is found to coincide with the custom of some eastern nations, from holding the reins of government; he therefore vacated the throne, and like Charles V., in later times, spent the remainder of his life in philosophic retirement. Among many important acts of his reign was the founding of three additional academies at Tara, for the study of jurisprudence,

---

* Tigernach, one of the most learned, candid, and trustworthy of the annalists, makes it forty-two years, commencing A.D. 218; but the above seems the most reconcilable with general chronology.

history, and military science. Cormac's own writings, combined with his military fame and the splendour of his court, have shed a lustre round his age.

The meeting and subsequent marriage of this distinguished royal sage with Eithne Ollavada, daughter of Dunluing,* and foster-child to Buicioy Brugha, a wealthy Leinster grazier of the most princely hospitality, would form an interesting chapter in the romance of Irish history.

This generous herdsman, Buicioy, kept open house, and was visited frequently by the gentry of the surrounding country, with their retinues, till at last he was almost totally ruined by the shocking rapacity and ingratitude of his guests, who, at their departure, are said to have made no scruple often of carrying off large quantities of his flocks. At length, he resolved, with the small remnant of his substance, to leave the scenes of his former munificence; and, taking his journey by night, accompanied by his wife and foster-child Eithne, he found a secluded retreat in the midst of an extensive wood in the plains of Meath. Here he erected an humble sheeling and accommodation suitable to his altered fortunes. It chanced that this spot, solitary as it appeared, was not far distant from one of the occasional residences of the young prince Cormac, who, on a certain occasion, riding out in that direction, was surprised to find there a human habitation, and still more astonished to observe a young and lovely creature, of the most graceful deportment—a flower in this wilderness, apparently

"———born to blush unseen
And waste its sweetness on the desert air."

Concealing himself among the foliage, he watched her

* See p. 58, *note*.

movements, tending her little flock, and was charmed with the skill and alacrity with which she delighted to return the care and tenderness of her foster-parents in their adversity. At length, approaching the damsel, who was somewhat startled from her propriety by the unexpected apparition, he addressed her with the utmost courtesy, and entered into conversation on the subject of her pastoral duties. He appeared to take the greatest interest, and evinced the utmost curiosity, in learning from her the most minute particulars of the mysteries of the dairy, and inquired who was the happy person for whom she seemed so cheerfully to perform these simple labours. Having heard the name, he immediately remembered the well-known generous, and once wealthy herdsman. Cormac ultimately made the offer of his hand to the beautiful Eithne, whose discretion seemed to equal her external charms, and restored her worthy foster-parents to a state of ease and affluence.

It appears from the following verses, ascribed to Cormac, the authenticity of which is believed to be unquestioned, that this marriage was not happy in its results. He alludes to the fact of his never having evinced any symptom of jealousy, as an aggravation of his desertion by Eithne; but there is reason to believe that he had not been equally careful of not giving *her* ground for that feeling.* Cormac, in his wisdom and sagacity, and the aphorisms he has left behind him in his writings, resembled Solomon; and the comparison derives additional aptness from the similarity of their foibles. Whether the flight of Eithne was owing to this circumstance it is impossible to say; but it appears that while Cormac bore this severe domestic calamity with the spirit of a philosopher, he, nevertheless, felt it as a man.

* See Keating (Dub. ed., 1841), i. 298.

LAMENT OF KING CORMAC.

VERSIFIED BY J. CLARENCE MANGAN.

I, Cormac MacConn,*
   The Ard-Riagh† of Teamor,
Am lost and undone,
   And my heart is in tremor
From morning till e'en!
   For two who should aid me—
My Brehon and Queen—
   Have deceived and betray'd me!

She hath given herself up
   Unto him as her lover;
And the black-beaded cup
   Of mine anguish flows over!
He is Falvey the Red,
   She is Eithne of Leinster:
King Cathal‡ is dead,
   Or his wrath had unprinced her!

Three causes there be
   That have wreck'd my ship's anchor
Of wedlock for me—
   Lies, Coldness, and Rancour!

Three things, too, suffice
   For a wife's highest pleasure—
Kind smiles—good advice—
   And love without measure!

---

* The poet has here sacrificed the reason to the rhyme. He was Cormac MacArt, or else O'Con.
† "The Chief Monarch."
‡ "Her father," according to Mr. Mangan; but this must be a mistake. She is called the daughter of Dunluing. See p. 56.

> My queen had all three,
>   And, ah! why should she leave me?
> Why scorn me and flee,
>   Why betray and deceive me?
>
> Enough! I and Peace
>   Must eternally sever—
> But here I will cease
>   My lamentings for ever.
>
> I have heard from my bards that the only four crown'd,
>   Of all that have sprung from the race of the Gael,
> Who never knew jealousy all their lives long,
>   Were Oilioll and Fergus and Conn the Renown'd,
> And he who now pens this deplorable tale
>   Of disaster and wrong!

The age of Cormac derived additional lustre from the military fame of Fion MacCumhal (the Fingal of Macpherson's Ossian), and his son, Oisin or Oshin, and grandson, Osgur, or Oscar.*

---

* Dr. Shaw, the author of the Gaelic Dictionary, whose love of truth rose superior to a false patriotism—if patriotism it can be called, that would seek an empty triumph of having produced some windy, unmeaning epics, or whatever they may be, at the expense and cost of another country—though at first inclined to attach some credit to the productions of Mr. Macpherson, yet, after the most careful investigation, the result of which he published in the year 1781, he was forced to acknowledge the poems of Ossian to be an imposture. "Fion," he says, "is not known in the Highlands by the name of Fingal. He is universally supposed to be an Irishman. . . . This is the universal voice of all the Highlanders, excepting those who are possessed of abilities and knowledge to peruse the work of Macpherson, and are taught by nationality to support an idle controversy."—*Inquiry into the Authenticity of the Poems ascribed to Ossian*, p. 65.

The names of Finn and his son Oisin, or Ossian, are intimately connected with the subject of Irish poetry. The first of these celebrated heroes was the son of Cumhal, and lineally descended from the royal family of Leinster. He was commander-in-chief of the famous Fianna Eireann, or Fenian Militia, whose exploits were such a favourite theme with the bards of the middle ages. Finn was instrumental in founding the colony of Scoti, from this country, in Argyleshire, North Britain* (afterwards known as Dalriada), which ultimately changed the name of that country from its ancient titles of Caledonia and Albania to that of Scotia, and from which, as the Scottish historians themselves are obliged to acknowledge, was derived the royal line of the Stuarts.†

But though Finn bore a high character for proficiency in the various accomplishments of his age, especially poetry

---

* "Cormac (says Walker) at the head of the Fiann, and attended by our hero (Finn), sailed into that part of North Britain which lies opposite to Ireland, where he planted a colony of Scots (the name which the Irish then bore) as an establishment for Carbry Riada, his cousin-german. This colony, which the Irish monarch fostered with the solicitude of a parent, was often protected from the oppressive power of the Romans by detachments of the Fiann, under the command of Finn, whom one of their writers has dignified with the title of ' King of Woody Morven,' and hence the many traditions concerning him which are still current on the west coast of Scotland."—*Hist. Mems. Irish Bards*, pp. 37-8.

† Sir WALTER SCOTT (*History of Scotland*, vol. i., chap. ii.) acknowledges that in the Scoto-Irish chiefs of Argyleshire "historians must trace the original roots of the royal line;" and James I., in a speech which he made at Whitehall in 1613, said that "there was a double reason why he should be careful of the welfare of that people (the Irish)—first as king of England, ... and also as king of Scotland, *for the ancient kings of Scotland were descended of the kings of Ireland.*"—Cox's *Hibern. Anglican.*

and music, in which indeed all the Fenii were required to be skilled, yet it appears he was outshone in those arts, if not in all others, by his son Oisin, whose name has descended with the united wreaths of the hero and the bard.

Though no well authenticated specimens of the remains of Oisin have survived the devastations of time and of civil war, yet his name, coupled with the productions of a variety of anonymous bards of the middle ages, known by the name of the Fenian poems, in which he is made, with great art, the narrator of the exploits of his Fenian compeers, have served as the groundwork of one of the most singular literary impostures of modern times. As the historical affinities existing between Scotland and Ireland in early times, joined to the original similarity of their language, and the profound ignorance of the history of the latter country which generally prevailed, can alone account for the remarkable fact of these poetic fragments, and the traditions concerning Oisin and the Fenian heroes, having, by means of oral recitations, become naturalized in the Highlands of Scotland, a few explanatory remarks are here requisite to set the matter in its true light.

It has already been stated, that in the course of the age now under consideration, an Irish colony was led into Argyleshire by Carbry Riada (the kinsman of King Cormac), from whom the settlement took the name Dalriada. This historical connection between Scotland and Ireland, though for a long period overlooked, is distinctly recognised by Bede, the early English historian. Previous to this event the name of *Scotia* belonged exclusively to Ireland, Scotland being then only known as Caledonia and Albania. In course of time, however, as the Scotic colony extended its boundaries, it came to be designated *Scotia Minor*, while

Ireland, by way of distinction, was called *Scotia Major*. This distinction was so well known on the Continent in the middle ages, that we frequently find the distinguishing appellations of "Scots of Albany," and "Hibernian Scots," applied to the natives of each in the seventh, eighth, and ninth centuries, and it was not until about the tenth century that Ireland ceased to participate in the name.*

That Ireland was the ancient Scotia would be a matter of small consequence to show, were it not that the possession of this title in common, and the connection subsisting for so long a period with the Highlands of Scotland, have served as a pretext for a most extensive system of literary depredation, and of this country being rifled of many of its early ornaments. The Dalriadian colonists carried with them their own historical traditions, and as the intercourse between the countries continued for many centuries, the later romances and poems were conveyed thither by wandering bards from time to time, and handed down in a mutilated and corrupted form by oral recitations. Thus the colonists came in time to adopt what was originally the property of the mother country. Hence, they have borrowed many

---

* 4th century.—"*Scotorum* cumulos flevit glacialis Ierne."—*Claudian.* "Hibernia a *Scotorum* gentibus colitur."—*Ethicus Cosmog.* "Hæc insula proprior Britanniæ, &c., colitur a *Scotis.*"—*Paul. Orosius.* 7th century.—"Gens *Scotorum* incolit Hiberniam."—*Bede, Vita St. Columb.* "Hibernia dives lactis et mellis insula, nec vinearum expers, &c. Hæc proprie patria *Scotorum* est."—*Ibid., Hist. Gent. Anglicanæ.* 17th century.—"*Scoti* omnes Hiberniæ habitatores initio vocabantur."—*Buchanan, Hist. rerum Scoticarum.*

Whoever wishes for more ample information may find it in the last edition of Sir James Ware's *Antiquities of Ireland.*—HAMILTON's *Letters on North Coast of Antrim,* pp. 61-2.

names from the Irish regal list, many saints from her calendar, and to complete this extensive system of plagiarism, the productions of some nameless Irish bards of the middle ages,* in connection with the name of Oisin, were in the last century made the groundwork of an imposture, so plausibly fabricated, that it went forth to Europe on the wings of fame, and obtained for Scotland the unfounded claim of having produced the earliest epics perhaps in existence, with the exception of those of Homer and Virgil—a claim which by many is not even yet disallowed.† This daring and ingenious attempt of Mr. Macpherson to impose upon public credulity, was favoured by the ignorance which generally prevailed of this twilight period of Irish history; and by corrupting, falsifying, and clothing in an inflated and mock-heroic diction, which with many might pass for a species of barbaric sublimity suitable to the age of the bard, those oral versions of the Fenian poems and romances which had found their way to the Highlands of Scotland, he has certainly made his epics almost sufficiently different from the originals to warrant the claim of Scotland (though not of Oisin) to their authorship. The argument founded on the impossibility of their having been orally

---

* "There are numberless Irish poems still extant," says Miss Brooke, "attributed to Oisin, and either addressed to St. Patrick, or composed in the form of a dialogue between the saint and the poet. In all of them, the antiquary finds traces of a later period than that in which Oisin flourished; and most of them are supposed to be the compositions of the eighth, ninth, and tenth centuries."—*Reliques of Irish Poetry*, quarto edition, p. 73. Specimens of these Fenian poems will be found in another part of this volume.

† See the commencement of Lamartine's *Pilgrimage to the Holy Land*, where he speaks of Ossian with undoubting faith.

transmitted through so many ages, is not quite conclusive,* when we consider that the epics of Homer were similarly preserved (though certainly among a more refined people) for about five hundred years, until collected by Pisistratus; but the glaring defiance of chronology and geography by which these pretended translations are so strongly marked, the total absence of genuine simplicity, the introduction of manners and customs incompatible with their reputed age, and numerous other grounds of internal evidence, are fatal to the idea of their authenticity as the works of the bard to whom they are assigned. On the other hand, the very names of the heroes, Cuchullin, Fingal, Osgar, McMorne, &c., and many of the localities being undoubtedly Irish, are significant evidences of their genuine source, of which the so-called translator was unable wholly to divest them, without sapping the very foundation on which the whole structure of his imposture was to be reared. It is worthy of remark, that the very chronological errors of Mr. Macpherson afford an argument no less against the authenticity of these productions as the writings of Ossian, than in favour of their being derived in substance, though not in form, from the Fenian tales and poems. These Fenian

---

* Hume applies the same argument to them as he has used against the evidence of miracles. "It is indeed strange that any man of sense could have imagined it possible that above twenty thousand verses, along with numberless historical facts, could have been preserved by oral tradition during fifty generations, by the rudest, perhaps, of all the European nations, the most necessitous, the most turbulent, and the most unsettled. *Where a supposition is so contrary to common-sense, any positive evidence of it ought ever to be disregarded."*— *Corresp. with Gibbon.* It would certainly have been as well to inquire if there were any positive evidence before resorting to such a general and doubtful proposition.

writings, which, it has been already stated, are supposed to have originated with a number of Irish bards in the course of the ninth, tenth, and eleventh centuries, bear on the very face of them the same chronological inaccuracy, many of them being in the form of a dialogue between Oisin, who flourished about the middle of the third, and St. Patrick, whose mission did not commence till nearly the same period of the fifth, century. The bards who composed these poems were doubtless aware of the anachronism of which they were guilty, and merely adopted it as an artifice to add to the reality and heighten the dramatic effect of their poetical descriptions, by making their favourite hero, Oisin, the narrator of the exploits of his companions in arms, thus giving to their tales a living and personal interest, which makes it difficult, in reading them, not to be sometimes persuaded that they were written by one who had witnessed what he describes. Such a coincidence in error on the part of Mr. Macpherson, could scarcely have been accidental. To enter here into the long-contested discussion as to the genuineness of the poems of Ossian, further than appeared necessary to elucidate the subject, would indeed be a work of supererogation, after Hume, Gibbon, O'Conor, Young, Drummond, O'Reilly, and others, have successively and successfully lent their talents to destroy the imposing but unsubstantial fabric.

To return to our narrative. Though Oisin, according to tradition, was not unskilled

"Himself to sing, and build the lofty rhyme."

yet he was probably more enamoured of the sword, and, consequently, the dignity of chief bard to the Fenii fell to his brother Fergus, called Fionbell, or the sweet-voiced— "a bard on whom successive poets have bestowed as many

F

epithets as Homer has given to his Jupiter. . . . . So persuasive was his eloquence, that, united with his rank, it acquired an almost universal ascendancy."*

Of this extraordinary power possessed by Fergus—as well in virtue of his office as of his personal character—there is a notable example on record, evincing that, if the bardic influence was frequently exerted in fanning the flames of war, it was also employed in evoking the halcyon of peace. It appears that the unanimity of the Fenian militia, when not cemented by opposing the common enemies of their country, was sometimes disturbed by the heart-burnings of the rival septs of Morni and Boishne, of which Goll (or Gaul) and Finn were the respective leaders. Of this contention for precedence the cause has never been distinctly assigned. On one occasion, near the palace of Finn, at Almhaim (Allwin), when it rather appears that the chief was in fault, it assumed such a serious aspect, and threatened such consequences, that the bards required to use their utmost authority to soothe the chafed spirits of the chiefs, and pour oil upon the troubled waters. "To effect this, they shook the *chain of silence*,† and flung themselves among the ranks, extolling the

---

* "Several admirable poems, attributed to Fergus," continues Mr. Walker, "are still extant. . . . . Dargo, a poem written on a foreign prince of that name, invading Ireland. Dargo encountered the Fenii, and was slain by Goll, the son of Morni; and Cath Gabhra (the battle of Gabhra). . . . Besides these, there is a *Panegyric on Goll*, the son of Morni, and another on Osgur. . . . The diction of these panegyrics is pure, nervous, and persuasive, and to each the name of Fergus, the poet, the son of Fin, is prefixed."—*Hist. Mems. Irish Bards*, pp. 43, 44.

† The reader will recollect Moore's beautiful allusion to this custom :—

"Dear harp of my country! in darkness I found thee,
  The *cold chain of silence* had hung o'er thee long,
When proudly, my own island harp, I unbound thee,
  And gave all thy chords to light, freedom, and song."

sweets of peace, and the achievements of the combatants' ancestors. Immediately both parties, laying down their arms, listened with attention to the harmonious lays of their bards, and in the end rewarded them with precious gifts."*

The ode from which the following passages are taken, is supposed by the translator—and, indeed, the internal evidence is such as to admit little doubt of the fact—to be the one which Fergus "composed, or rather recited extempore, on the occasion" † of this memorable contest:—

ODE TO GAUL, THE SON OF MORNI.

TRANSLATED BY MISS BROOKE.

High-minded Gaul, whose daring soul
Stoops not to our chief's‡ control!
Champion of the navy's pride!
   Mighty ruler of the tide!
   Rider of the stormy wave,
   Hostile nations to enslave! §

---

* Walker's *Hist. Mems.*, p. 44.
† *Reliques of Irish Poetry*, 4to ed., p. 163.
‡ "Finn Mac Cumhal, then general of the Irish militia."
§ "Besides their standing armies, we find the Irish kept up a considerable naval force, whereby, from time to time, they poured troops into Britain and Gaul, which countries they long kept under contribution. To this, however, many objections have been made, ... whilst, at the same period of time, no objections have been made to the accounts of the Phœnicians, the Tyrians, and, after them, the Greeks, having very considerable fleets, and making very distant settlements."—O'Halloran's *Introd. to Hist. and Antiq. of Ireland.*

Shield of freedom's glorious boast!
Head of her unconquer'd host!
Ardent son of Morni's might!
Terror of the fields of fight!
Long renown'd and dreadful name!
Hero of auspicious fame!
Champion in our cause to arm!
Tongue, with eloquence to charm!
With depth of sense, and reach of manly thought;
With every grace and every beauty fraught!

Girt with heroic might,
When glory, and thy country, call to arms,
Thou go'st to mingle in the loud alarms,
   And lead the rage of fight!
  Thine, hero!—thine the princely sway
   Of each conflicting hour;
Thine ev'ry bright endowment to display,
The smile of beauty, and the arm of pow'r!
  Science, beneath our hero's shade,
Exults, in all her patron's gifts array'd:
Her chief, the soul of every fighting field!
The arm, the heart, alike unknown to yield!

  Hear, O Finn! thy people's voice!
  Trembling on our hills,* we plead—
O let our fears to peace incline thy choice!
Divide the spoil,† and give the hero's meed!

---

* "This alludes to a custom which prevailed among the early Irish of holding all their public meetings, and frequently their feasts, on the tops of lofty eminences."

† "Possibly, it might have been about the division of the booty gained in some British or, perhaps, continental expedition, that the tribes of Morni and Boishne were at variance; at least, it appears, by this passage, that a part of their discontents arose from some such occasion."

For bright and various is his wide renown,
And war and science weave his glorious crown!

Did all the hosts of all the earth unite,
　From pole to pole, from wave to wave,
　　Exulting in their might :
　　His is that monarchy of soul
　To fit him for the wide control,
　　The empire of the brave !

　　Friend of learning! mighty name !
　　Havoc of hosts, and pride of fame !
Fierce as the foaming strength of ocean's rage,
　When nature's powers in strife engage,
　　So does his dreadful progress roll,
　　And such the force that lifts his soul !

　　　*　　*　　*　　*　　*

Finn of the flowing locks,* O hear my voice !
　　No more with Gaul contend !
　Be peace, henceforth, thy happy choice,
　　And gain a valiant friend !
　Secure of victory, to the field
　　His conquering standard goes ;
　'Tis his the powers of fight to wield,
　　And woe awaits his foes.

---

* "The natural and beautiful ornament of *hair* was much cherished and esteemed amongst the ancient Irish. . . . . . The epithets 'flowing, curling, waving locks,' perpetually occur, and are apparently esteemed as essential to the beauty of the warrior as to that of the fair."

Not to mean, insidious art*
Does the great name of Gaul its terrors owe;
But from a brave, undaunted heart
His glories flow!

* * * * *

Finn of the dark-brown hair! O hear my voice!
No more with Gaul contend!
Be peace sincere henceforth thy choice,
And gain a valiant friend!
In peace, though inexhausted from his breast
Each gentle virtue flows:
In war, no force his fury can arrest,
And hopeless are his foes.

* * * * *

Spirit resolute to dare!
Aspect sweet beyond compare,
Bright with inspiring soul! with blooming beauty fair!
Warrior of majestic charms!
High in fame and great in arms!
Well thy daring soul may tow'r—
Nothing is above thy pow'r!

---

* "Indeed, for a spirit of honour and a natural rectitude of mind, the Irish were remarked even by the writers of a nation once their bitter enemies. Their love of justice and attachment to the laws was thus acknowledged in the days of Henry VIII.: 'The laws and statutes made by the Irish on their hills (called Brehon laws), they keep firm and stable, without breaking them for any favour or reward.'—BARON FINGLAS' *Breviate of Ireland.* Sir John Davies, too (attorney-general in the reign of James I.), acknowledges that 'there is no nation under the sun that love equal and indifferent justice better than the Irish.'—DAVIES' *Hist. of Ireland.*"

ODE TO GAUL.

Hear, O Finn! my ardent zeal,
While his glories I reveal!
Fierce as ocean's angry wave,*
When conflicting tempests rave;
As still, with the increasing storm,
Increasing ruin clothes its dreadful form;
Such is the chief, o'erwhelming in his force,
Unconquer'd in his swift, resistless course!

Tho' in the smiles of blooming grace array'd,
And bright in beauty's every charm;
Yet think not, therefore, that his soul will bend,
Nor with the chief contend;
For well he knows to wield the glittering blade,
And fatal is his arm!
Bounty in his bosom dwells—
High his soul of courage swells!
Fierce the dreadful war to wage,
Mix in the whirl of fight, and guide the battle's rage!
Wide, wide around triumphant ruin wield,
Roar through the ranks of death, and thunder o'er the field

Many a chief of mighty sway
Fights beneath his high command;
Marshals his troops in bright array,
And spreads his banners o'er the land.

Champion of unerring aim!
Chosen of kings, triumphant name!
Bounty's hand, and wisdom's head,
Valiant arm, and lion soul,
O'er red heaps of slaughter'd dead,
Thundering on to glory's goal!

---

* "Here we find a repetition of the same image that occurs a few stanzas before. . . . . . But an extemporaneous composition like this ought to be exempt from the severity of criticism which may, with justice, be exercised on the productions of study and the labours of time."

Pride of Finian fame, and arms!
Mildness* of majestic charms!
Swiftness of the battle's rage!
Theme of the heroic page!
Firm in purpose, fierce in fight!
Arm of slaughter, soul of might!

Glory's light! illustrious name!
Splendour of the paths of fame!
Born bright precedent to yield,
And sweep with death the hostile field!

Leader of sylvan sports; the hound, the horn,
   The early melodies of morn!—
Love of the fair, and favourite of the muse!†
In peace, each peaceful science to diffuse:
Prince of the noble deeds! accomplish'd name!
Increasing beauty, comprehensive fame!

   *   *   *   *   *

Hear, O Gaul, the poet's voice!
O, be peace thy gen'rous choice!
Yield thee to the bard's desire!
Calm the terrors of thine ire!
Cease thee here our mutual strife,
And peaceful be our future life!

---

* "The knowledge of arms was but a part of the education of the Celtic warrior. In Ireland, they were well informed in history, poetry, and the polite arts; they were sworn to be the protectors of the fair, and avengers of their wrongs; *and to be polite in word and address, even to their greatest enemies.*"— O'HALLORAN.

† "Irish history informs us that those of their monarchs, or chiefs, who, besides the accustomed patronage of science and song, were *themselves* possessed of the gifts of the muse, obtained, on that account, a distinguished portion of honour, respect, and celebrity."

GAUL—I yield, O Fergus, to thy mild desire;
    Thy words, O bard! are sweet;
    Thy wish I freely meet,
    And bid my wrath expire.
No more to discontent a prey,
I give to peace the future day:
    To thee my soul I bend,
    O guileless friend!*
The accents of whose glowing lips well know that soul to sway.

BARD—O swift in honour's course! thou generous name!
    Illustrious chief, of never-dying fame!

A.D. 296.

Another ode by Fergus, which has survived the wreck of time, affords a fine specimen of the WAR SONGS of our ancient Celtic countrymen. The language and idiom of these odes are considered, by the accomplished translator, as conclusive evidence of their antiquity. "The military odes of the ancient Celtæ," remarks that lady, "have been noticed by numberless historians. . . . . . One of the duties of the bard was to attend his chief to battle, and there exert his poetic powers, according to the fluctuations of victory, and the fortunes of the fight. This fact is well attested by ancient Greek and Roman writers, ... and historians affirm that this custom continued amongst the Gauls many centuries after their dereliction by the Romans. Even at the Battle of

---

* "A character without *guile* or *deceit* was esteemed the highest that could be given amongst the ancient Irish; and the favourite panegyric of a bard, to his favourite hero, would be, that he *had a heart incapable of guile.*"

Hastings the troops of Normandy were accompanied by a bard, animating them to conquest with warlike odes."* The following interesting ode was addressed by Fergus to Osgur, the son of Oisin, and nephew of the bard, on occasion of the fatal Battle of Gabhra (Gaura), one of the most tragic civil strifes which our early history records, and which formed one of the most favourite themes of the bards and romances of the middle ages.† The immediate cause of this battle is involved in much uncertainty. It appears that Cairbre, the supreme monarch of Ireland, had long been jealous of the formidable power, and consequent overweening arrogance, of the Fenian militia; and, taking advantage of the absence of their renowned commander, who,‡ with a large detachment, was aiding the British in resisting the encroachments of their Roman invaders, united with some of the provincial monarchs in crushing this celebrated legion. On this occasion, Osgur, the son of Oisin, commanded, and achieved incredible but fruitless feats of heroism with his little band. Urged on by the inspiriting harangues of the bard, which mingled with the storm of battle, he singled out the monarch Cairbre, who fell beneath his arm. It was impossible, however, to resist the force of numbers, and Osgur himself at length sunk exhausted upon the field. The enemy, then, redoubling their efforts, rushed on like an overwhelming flood, bore down the Fenii, who opposed a feeble bulwark to

---

* *Reliques of Irish Poetry*, 4to ed., p. 137.

† The various poems on this battle are asserted to have formed the ground-work of Mr. Macpherson's "Temora."—See *O'Reilly's Essay*.

‡ Walker represents Finn as having fallen (A.D. 294) two years previous to the battle of Gabhra, in an engagement at Rathbrea. From this the poetical accounts, which are here followed, differ.

the undulation of its waves, and swept over the ranks with resistless fury."*

WAR ODE

TO OSGUR, THE SON OF OISIN.

At the Battle of Gaura,

TRANSLATED BY MISS BROOKE.

Rise, might of Erin! rise!†
O! Osgur of the generous soul!
Now on the foe's astonish'd eyes
Let thy proud ensigns wave dismay!
Now let the thunder of thy battle roll,
And bear the palm of strength and victory away.

---

* "The ANNALS OF INNISFALLEN, and other ancient records and poems," says Miss Brooke, "inform us that the Battle of Gabhra was fought in the year A.D. 296. . . . It would be tedious to relate the various causes assigned, by different writers, for the discontents which occasioned this battle. Historians, in general, lay the chief blame upon the Fenii; and the poets, taking part with their favourite heroes, cast the odium upon Cairbre, monarch of Ireland. The fault, most likely, was mutual, and both parties severely suffered for it. Cairbre himself was killed in the action, and a dreadful slaughter ensued among his troops; but those of the Fenii were almost totally destroyed; for, relying upon the valour which they proudly deemed invincible, they rushed into the field against odds which madness alone would have encountered."—*Reliques of Irish Poetry*, pp. 146, 147.

† "Literally, *arise*. It means here—*rouse thyself*—*exert all thy powers.*"

Son of the sire whose stroke is fate,
  Be thou in might supreme ;
Let conquest on thy arm await
  In each conflicting hour ;
Slight let the force of adverse numbers seem,
  Till o'er their prostrate ranks thy shouting squadrons pour !

    O hear the voice of lofty song !
        Obey the bard !—
    Stop—stop M'Garai ! check his pride,
And rush resistless on each regal foe !
Thin their proud ranks, and give the smoking tide
    Of hostile blood to flow !
    Mark where Mac Cormac* pours along !
        Rush on—retard
His haughty progress ! let thy might
    Rise, in the deathful fight,
    O'er thy prime foe supreme,
        And let the stream
        Of valour flow,
    Until thy brandish'd sword
Shall humble ev'ry haughty foe,
    And justice be restor'd.

  * * * * *

Resistless as the spirit of the night,
  In storms and terrors drest ;
Withering the force of every hostile breast,
  Rush on the ranks of fight !

* "Cairbre, monarch of Ireland. He was son to Cormac, the preceding monarch ; and it was in his quarrel that the allied princes were assembled in this day's battle against the little band of the Fenii."

Youth of fierce deeds and noble soul!
  Rend—scatter wide the foe—
Swift forward rush,—and lay the waving pride
  Of yon high ensigns low!
  Thine be the battle—thine the sway!
On—on to Cairbre hew thy conquering way,
And let thy deathful arm dash safety from his side!
  As the proud wave, on whose broad back
    The storm its burden heaves,*
    Drives on the scatter'd wreck,
    Its ruin leaves;
So let thy sweeping progress roll,
  Fierce, resistless, rapid, strong;
Pour, like the billow of the flood, o'erwhelming might
    along!

From king to king,† let death thy steps await,
  Thou messenger of fate,
Whose awful mandate thou art chosen to bear:
  Take no vain truce, no respite yield,
  Till thine be the contested field;
O thou, of champion'd fame the royal heir!
  Pierce the proud squadrons of the foe,
And o'er their slaughter'd heaps triumphant rise!
Oh, in fierce charms and lovely might array'd!
Bright, in the front of battle, wave thy blade!
Oh, let thy fury rise upon my voice!
Rush on, and glorying in thy strength, rejoice!
  Mark where yon bloody ensign flies!
Rush!—seize it!—lay its haughty triumphs low!

---

* "It is impossible that the utmost stretch of human imagination and genius could start an image of greater sublimity than this! Had Fergus never given any further proof of his talents than what is exhibited in the ode now before us, this stanza alone had been sufficient to have rendered his name immortal."

† "The monarch and provincial kings who were united against the Fenii."

>   Wide around the carnage spread!
>   Heavy be the heaps of dead!
>   Roll on thy rapid might,
> Thou roaring stream of prowess in the fight!
>   What though Finn be distant far,*
>   Art thou not thyself a war?
>   Victory shall be all thine own,
> And this day's glory thine, and thine alone!
> Be thou the foremost of thy race in fame!
> So shall the bard exalt thy deathless name!
> So shall thy sword supreme o'er numbers rise,
> And vanquish'd Teamor's† groans ascend the skies!
>
>
>   Though unequal be the fight,
>   Though unnumber'd be the foe,
>   No thought on fear or on defeat bestow,
> For conquest waits to crown thy cause, and thy successful
>   might!
>   Rush, therefore, on amid the battle's rage,
>   Where fierce contending kings engage,
>   And powerless lay thy proud opponents low!

* * * * *

---

* "A beautiful and most affecting poem (ascribed to Oisin) informs us that Finn arrived just time enough to take a last adieu of his dying grandson. . . . . . The poet adds, that Finn never after was known to smile. Peace, after that, had no sweets, nor war any triumphs that could restore joy to his breast, or raise one wish for ambition or for glory."

† "Teamor was the royal seat of the kings of Ireland, and the principal court of legislation, from the days of Ollamh Fodhla down to the reign of Dermod M'Cervail; so that the Feis of Teamor continued, from time to time, through a series of more than eleven hundred years."—*Disserts. on Hist. of Ireland*, p. 108.

Wide the vengeful ruin spread!
Heap the groaning field with dead!
Furious be thy gleaming sword,
Death with every stroke descend!
Thou whose fame earth can no match afford;
That fame which shall through time, as through the world,
 extend!

Shower thy might upon the foe!
Lay their pride, in Gabhra, low!
Thine the sway of this contested field!
To thee for aid the Fenii* fly;
On that brave arm thy country's hopes rely,
From every foe thy native land to shield!

Aspect of beauty! pride of praise!
 Summit of heroic fame!
O theme of Erin! youth of matchless deeds!
Think, think on thy wrongs! now, now let vengeance raise
 Thy valiant arm! and let destruction flame,
Till low, beneath thy sword, each chief of Ulster lies!
 O prince of numerous hosts and bounding steeds!
 Raise thy red shield, with tenfold force endu'd!
Forsake not the fam'd path thy fathers have pursu'd,
 But let, with theirs, thy equal honours rise!

Hark! Anguish groans—the battle bleeds
Before thy spear! its flight is death!—
 Now, o'er the heath,
 The foe recedes!

---

* "The Irish in general were frequently called *Fenians* or *Phenians*, from their great ancestor, *Phenius Farsa*, or, perhaps, in allusion to their Phœnician descent. But the Leinster legions proudly arrogated that name entirely to themselves, and called their celebrated body, exclusively, *Fenii*, or *Fiana Eirean*."

And wide the hostile crimson flows!—
See how it dyes thy deathful blade!
See, in dismay, each routed squadron flies!
Now, now thy havoc thins the ranks of fight,
And scatters o'er the field thy foes!—
O still be thy increasing force display'd!
Slack not the noble ardour of thy might!
Pursue—pursue with death their flight!
Rise, arm of Erin—rise.

From these fine specimens of the age of Oisin, and by the brother of that hero-bard, it will be seen that, like all productions of real antiquity, they are characterized by great simplicity, forming a remarkable contrast with the turgid, stilted, and mock-heroic diction of those productions which Mr. Macpherson has imposed upon the world, as the translated remains of Ossian. It is left to the reader to compare the respective productions, and from the internal evidence to pronounce which carry with them more strongly the stamp of the genuine antique.

Nothing more is known with certainty of the history of Oisin. According to popular tradition, which, indeed, some credulous writers have allowed to discredit their pages, he lived till the arrival of the national apostle, to whom he communicated the exploits of his Fenian compeers. This absurd popular error has evidently arisen from those suppositious productions of the middle ages, called the Fenian Poems, being conducted, in many cases, in the form of a dialogue between Oisin and St. Patrick, with so much art as to give them a great appearance of reality. By all accounts, however, he survived the death of his son Osgur; and, perhaps, the lament for the loss of his sight, to which Mr. Macpherson, in the poem of *Carthon*, makes him give

expression, may not have been contrary to the fact:—
"When the world is dark with tempests, when thunder rolls, and lightning flies; thou [addressing the sun] lookest in thy beauty from the clouds, and laughest at the storm; but to Ossian thou lookest in vain; for he beholds thy beams no more, whether thy yellow hair floats on the eastern cloud, or thou tremblest at the gate of the west."

A.D. 400. The list of pagan bards closes with TORNA EGEAS, some of whose later productions, indeed, almost verge upon the very period when the Christian faith burst upon the land in a blaze of light so pervading and irresistible as to penetrate to the remotest recesses of the kingdom with a celerity equally surprising and unprecedented.

Torna was chief doctor and arch-bard of the kingdom, and several of his poems have survived. Among the latest of these was a lament written on the death of the two princes to whom he had been preceptor—Core, King of Munster, and Niall the Great. These princes had been rival candidates for the supreme monarchy, on the ground of their descent respectively from different branches of the royal line—a contest which resulted in favour of Niall, though descended of the Heremonian, or younger, branch. On this occasion the bard successfully exerted his influence as mediator between them. To both he was attached by one of the strongest bonds of the peculiar society which then existed—that of fosterage—the life-long devotion and almost sacred obligations of which are scarcely conceivable. This was one of the chief of those aboriginal customs, which proved so powerful in making the Norman barons, as well as their vassals, *ipsis Hibernis Hiberniores*, more Irish than the Irish themselves, as they proverbially became, in the course of a very few generations after the invasion.

Niall, one of the princes celebrated by the bard, was the famous hero of the Nine Hostages—one of the most accomplished and ambitious warriors of all the Irish monarchs, who attained the supreme dignity about the year A.D. 379. He derived his surname from the number of princes from whom he obtained hostages. After defeating the Picts, who had menaced destruction to the Irish colony of North Britain, which, on this occasion, adopted the Scotic title from the mother country, Niall carried his arms into the territories of the Romans in the south, and plundered the coasts of Wales and Lancashire—an exploit of such notoriety as to have been recorded by the poet, Claudian, thus translated :—

> "When Scots came thundering from the Irish shores,
> And th' ocean trembled, struck with hostile oars."

Urged by the inordinate thirst of conquest, which "grows by what it feeds on," he likewise made a memorable descent on the coast of Brittany, in France; from whence, along with various spoils, he carried off a number of youths as captives—one of whom, then in his sixteenth year, Providence had destined to be the author of one of the greatest moral revolutions ever achieved by a single individual. In the moral world, Providence has ever ordained some concomitant good to be depurated from the darkest evils by which His creatures can be visited, as in that of nature, the thunder-storm, the tempest, and the whirlwind, when their devastations have ceased, are the means of carrying off taint and contagion from the infected atmosphere, and of restoring its salubrity and equilibrium. And the youthful captive, Patrick, on whom was inflicted one of the severest calamities, in his loss of liberty, was privileged to make a glorious return of good for evil, in giving freedom to his masters from the dark and sanguinary superstitions of Druidism, and conferring upon them the boon of a purer and more elevating faith. Thus did the slave become the giver of liberty, and the horrors of war herald the halcyon of peace. Niall, however, fulfilled the destiny predicted of those who destroy with the sword, having been assassinated at Liege by one of his own followers, in revenge for a long-remembered injury.

The present version of the following ancient relic, like most of those by the same talented translator, is as nearly literal as possible, and expressly made in deprecation of that spirit of refining upon the original by which many of the poetical translations of the bards are characterized. In its native simplicity, it presents a touching picture of mingled affection, devoted loyalty, and desolate bereavement. With what natural touches the bard pourtrays the character of the royal youths, and dwells with justifiable pride on the honour of his own position—placed between them—Niall on the right side, the seat of dignity; and Corc, to whom pride was unknown, on his left, appropriately nearer his heart.

TORNA'S LAMENT FOR CORC AND NIALL.

TRANSLATED BY S. (AFTERWARDS SIR S.) FERGUSON, M.R.I.A.

My foster-children were not slack;
Corc or Neal ne'er turn'd his back;
Neal, of Tara's palace hoar,
Worthy seed of Owen More;

Corc, of Cashel's pleasant rock,
Con-ccad-cáhá's* honour'd stock.
Joint exploits made Erin theirs—
Joint exploits of high compeers;
Fierce they were, and stormy strong;
Neal, amid the reeling throng,
Stood terrific; nor was Corc
Hindmost in the heavy work.
Neal Mac Eochy Vivahain
Ravaged Albin, hill and plain;
While he fought from Tara far,
Corc disdain'd unequal war.
Never saw I man like Neal,
Making foreign foemen reel;
Never saw I man like Corc,
Swinging at the savage work;†
Never saw I better twain,
Search all Erin round again—
Twain so stout in warlike deeds—
Twain so mild in peaceful weeds.

These the foster-children twain
Of Torna, I who sing the strain;
These they are, the pious ones,
My sons, my darling foster-sons!
Who duly every day would come
To glad the old man's lonely home,

---

* Conn of the Hundred Battles.

† In the paraphrase of this elegy, by Mr. D'Alton, in the *Minstrelsy*:—

> "The eye of heaven ne'er look'd on one
> So God-like in the field as Tara's lord,
> Save him the comrade of his youth alone—
> Brave Corc, terrific wielder of the sword."

TORNA'S LAMENT FOR CORC AND NIALL.

Ah, happy days I've spent between
Old Tara's Hall and Cashel-green !
From Tara down to Cashel ford,
From Cashel back to Tara's lord.
When with Neal, his regent, I
Dealt with princes royally.
If with Corc perchance I were,
I was his prime counsellor.

Therefore Neal I ever set
On my right hand—thus to get
Judgments grave, and weighty words,
For the right hand loyal lords ;
But, ever on my left hand side,
Gentle Corc, who knew not pride,
That none other so might part
His dear body from my heart.
Gone is generous Corc O'Yeon—woe is me !
Gone is valiant Neal O'Con—woe is me !
Gone the root of Tara's stock—woe is me !
Gone the head of Cashel rock—woe is me !
Broken is my witless brain—
Neal, the mighty king, is slain !
Broken is my bruised heart's core—
Corc, the Righ More, is no more !*
Mourns Lea Con, in tribute's chain,
Lost Mac Eochy Vivahain,

---

* The beautiful definition of the different feeling experienced by the loss of each, here conveyed—his reason being affected by the great national loss sustained by the death of Niall; while his *heart* is bruised by the loss of Corc, his favourite—is thus expressed in Mr. D'Alton's version :—

"In Niall's fall my reason felt the shock ;
But, oh, when Corc expired, my heart was broken."

And her lost Mac Lewy true—
Mourns Lea Mogha,* ruined too!

Three poems, attributed to Torna, refer to one or both of his princely wards, Core and Niall. There is another preserved by Keating, which refers to the cemetery of Croghan, the most famous of the two royal burial-places in Ireland, which is here given, with an attempt to Anglicise the names.

THE ROYAL CEMETERY OF CROGHAN.

BLANK VERSE TRANSLATION.

This sepulchre preserves the royal dust
Of the renowned monarchs of the isle.
Here Dathy† lies, whose acts were sung by fame,

---

* Leath Cuin, or Con, and Leath Mogha—the names of the great northern and southern divisions of the island, of which these princes were the respective representatives. This territorial division was made in the reign of Conn of the Hundred Battles, A.D. 180, and marked by a great wall which extended from Galway to Dublin.

† Dathy, the last pagan king of Ireland, and one of the few Irish princes whose ambition led him to undertake foreign expeditions, is recorded to have lost his life by a stroke of lightning at the foot of the Alps. His remains were carried to Croghan, the bearers, it is stated, still keeping his face turned toward the enemy, and the spot of his interment marked by a red pillar-stone. The tradition respecting him has been made the subject of a fine ballad by the late Mr. Davis. In Dr. O'Donovan's most interesting and valuable account of the forts and other ancient remains still visible, Croghan is described as presenting the appearance of "the ruins of a town of Raths." "About two hundred paces to the north of the circular enclosure, called *Reilig na Riogh*, is to be seen a small circular enclosure, with a tumulus in the centre, on the top of which is a very remarkable red pillar-stone, which marks the grave of Dathy, the last pagan monarch of Ireland."—*Notes to* Connellan's *Trans. of the Annals of the Four Masters*, p. 122.

Near Croghan's pensive walls, close by whose side,
For great exploits in war and equal arms,
Dreaded Duncalach sleeps; who from his foe
Wrested, by greater might, to his own sway,
Numbers of captived hosts, in fetters bound,
Witnessing thraldom. Near the mournful shade
These weeping marbles cast, are also laid
The great remains of Conn, who sway'd with fame
Hibernia's royal sceptre; nor deny
To hold the kindred dust, in love since join'd,
Of Thuathal and Tumulta, who their sire,
While mortal, Achy Feylioch own;
He, too, great parent of three sons as brave,
Mingles his dust with those he once inspir'd
With happy life; nor does the grave refuse
To keep the breathless dust, by death disjoin'd,
Of Achy Airiav, who his fate
Ow'd to Mormaol's sword, with blood distain'd.
Nor could thy beauty, lovely once, secure
Thee, Clothro, or from death's subduing arm
Guard thy all-conquering eyes, whose lance destroy'd
(With thee in blood alike and charms allied)
Thy sisters Meyv and Murasg; here entomb'd,
They rest in silence, near three royal queens
(Forgetful now in death they ever reign'd),
Eire, Fola, Banba, from the sceptred line,
Sprung of the Thualtha de Dananns, far renown'd
For dire enchanting arts and magic power.
In this repository sleep in peace
Karmada's royal sons; three warlike names,
While life and vigour could their arms inspire,
Now lifeless each, nor more intent on fame.
Here valiant Myer rests, to death a prey,
While the still monument seems proud to hold
The relics of great Caol and Ugaine,
Mix'd with the brother dust, which lies entomb'd,
Of Cootha and Bayocha, who, in happier times
Were born, now sleep near Oilioll's princely urn.

A.D. 432.

The introduction, in the early part of the fifth century, of the light of Christianity, which spread with unprecedented rapidity, far from proving prejudicial to the bardic order or art, only served to give a more exalted direction to their powers, and

"Imp their wings to heaven."

DUBTACH (DUVACH) MAC LUGHAIR, the chief bard of the kingdom, became a zealous disciple, and converted the pæans which he had composed to the false deities, into hymns in praise of the new faith. Among others who followed his example was Fiech, afterwards Bishop of Sletty, to whom is attributed a hymn in honour of the national apostle.* The former was appointed one of the famous committee of nine appointed to revise the national records, the result of their labours being entitled *Seanchus Mor*, or the Great Antiquity. A poem attributed to Duvach, on the privileges of the bards, is preserved in the *Book of Rights*.†

The hymn or poem on the life of St. Patrick, attributed to Fiech, gives, in the space of thirty-four verses, the principal events of the life of the great apostle. Some doubts have been entertained of its genuineness, and it is altogether repudiated by Ledwich, as inconsistent with his absurd incredulity of the existence of the apostle. The ground of the objection to the authenticity of this piece, which was first urged by the Bollandists, rests on its reference to previous histories. It is preserved by Colgan, with

---

* *Hist. Mems. of the Irish Bards*, p. 46, quarto edition.
† Published by the Celtic Society (1847), p. 237.

a Latin translation. An imperfect English translation was made by General Vallancey, the eminent Irish scholar and antiquary, in his Irish Grammar; but a much better one is given in the Appendix to Lynch's Life of St. Patrick, a work of considerable research, in which all the arguments in its favour are adduced. From that work we take the first verse:

> "Patrick was born at heavenly Tours,
> As it is ascertain'd in stories;
> A youth of sixteen years
> At the time he was brought under bondage."

It must be confessed that, except with regard to its subject, it is scarcely deserving of the interest that has been attached to it. It deals much in the marvellous, from which the writings respecting St. Patrick, which approach his own time, are considered to be the most free. The judgment of Ledwich, indeed, respecting this piece does not appear to be altogether unjust.

In the peculiar rhythmical structure adopted by our bards, which is stated to have included a variety of nearly a hundred different species of verse, is to be found the earliest example of rhyme in any European language. Dr. O'Conor remarks on this peculiarity in the poetry of the Irish bards, that "their metre and their jingle are national."[*] This metrical method, though used by them in a variety of forms, generally consisted in making the syllable in the middle of the line rhyme with that at the end; sometimes they made the final syllable of one line rhyme with that in the middle of the line following, and the middle syllable of the first line with the final one of the next, thus making two

---

[*] Quoted by Mr. Hardiman, vol. ii., p. 368.

rhymes or coincident terminations in each two lines. Among others, the famous poet, SHIEL, or, as his name was Latinized (Cœlius), Sedulius, who flourished about the middle of the fifth century, has adopted this metrical structure in his fine Iambic verses on the life of Christ, written in Latin. A more perfect or double rhyme was also frequently adopted, as in the following lines of Columbanus :—

A.D. 450.

> "Dilexerunt tenebras tetras magis quam *lucem*.
> Imitari contemnunt vitæ Dominum *Ducem*,
> Velut in somnis regnent, unâ horâ lætan*tur*,
> Sed æterna tormenta adhuc illis paran*tur*."

Shiel was well known on the Continent, like many of the early poets of Ireland, and a full account of him may be found in Bayle's Historical Dictionary. The Italian Church has adopted from him some of her most exquisite hymns.

The dates respecting this eminent man vary greatly in different accounts, and his history and writings have been confounded with those of another Sedulius, who flourished some time in the ninth century, and who therefore may be termed Sedulius Secundus. This latter was an eminent commentator and theological writer. The sacred Latin poems are indisputably the compositions of the earlier Shiel. His principal work was the *Paschale Carmen*, in four books of heroic verse,* which he afterwards converted

---

* A ludicrous anecdote is told by Bayle, on the authority of another writer, that, through the negligence or ignorance of a transcriber either of a catalogue or the MS. writings of Sedulius, instead of being described as *heroicis versibus*, they were slandered as *hereticis versibus*, which threw the poet into great discredit at Rome. Bayle does not, however, attach much credit to the story. —*Hist. & Crit. Dict.*, vol. v., p. 105.

into prose, under the title of *Paschale Opus*. He was also the author of several beautiful Latin hymns, which have been adopted in the Italian Church service. Two of these, commencing, the one, "A solis ortus cardine," the other, "Hostes Herodes impie," have been particularly admired.

What Sedulius is supposed to have been the first to introduce into Latin poetry,* is recorded to have existed long previously among the bards of Ireland in their native tongue. In some cases (perhaps the earliest attempts) it consisted merely of a coincident termination, as in this hymn of Sedulius, either in the middle of the line, or at the end, or both. If we may place any dependence on the *Precepts of the Poets*— one of the earliest relics of Irish literature, attributed to Forchern (Forthern)—the variety of the lyric measures of the bards must have been astonishingly great, as directions are therein given for the composition of no less than a hundred different species of verse. However, it is admitted that this ancient piece was interpolated by the Poet Kinfiela, who flourished about the middle of the seventh century; and perhaps

---

* This anterior indeed to the generally received era of the first introduction of rhyme into Europe. Sharon Turner seems struck with astonishment at meeting with an example of middle-line rhymes in the writings of Adhelm—the earliest Anglo-Saxon who wrote Latin verse—and remarks: "Here, then, is an example of rhyme in an author who lived before the year 700, and he was an Anglo-Saxon. Whence did he derive it? Not from the Arabs: they had not yet reached Europe. I would rather refer it to the popular songs in his own language, *or in the language of his neighbours.*"—*Hist. Anglo-Saxons.* Now, as Turner had referred to the practice of this art at an earlier age by Sedulius, whom he terms an Irishman, and alludes to a rhyme quoted from him by Albinus, it would have been more candid to have stated the fact that Adhelm derived it from his preceptor Maidulf, an Irish scholar.

this may have been one of his additions, in reference to what then existed. There is every reason to conclude indeed, that the mediæval bards departed greatly from the simplicity of their predecessors, and taxed their invention in rendering more elaborately artificial and intricate the rules of their art, as the sophists endeavoured to atone by the introduction of their rhetorical rules for the decline of Grecian eloquence. " The rhythm consisted (we learn) in an equal distance of intervals and similar terminations, each line being divisible into two, that it may be more easily accommodated to the voice and music of the bards; it is not formed by the nice collocation of long and short syllables, but by a certain harmonic rhythm, adjusted to the voice of song, by the position of words which touch the heart, and assist the memory. In every ancient Irish verse, a pause in the middle of it may be discerned from which the succeeding clause of the same verse commences, and, making harmony with the preceding, is completed in the same space of time, and with similar terminations. Hence, each verse consists of two lines, terminating with a like cantilena, and making two verses as to sound."* Thus in the hymn of Sedulius—one of the most ancient existing examples in Latin verse—

"A solis ortus card*ine*, ad usque terræ lim*item*,
Christum canamus princip*em*, natum Maria virg*ine*."

Bayle inclines to the opinion that he was not an Irishman, in which he is followed by Ledwich; but he assigns no reason for his opinion, nor adduces any authority in support of it. He is

---

* Rev. Dr. Drummond's *Essay on the Authenticity of Ossian*, p. 112, vol. xvi., *Trans. R. I. Acad.*

doubtless correct in the opinion that the Sedulius called in the notes to St. Paul's Epistles, *Sedulii Scoti Hiberniensis*, was the later writer of the same name; but it is natural to infer that, the one being an acknowledged Irishman, the name was also Irish. Ussher claims him, and adduces numerous authorities to prove him an Irishman. Besides, we have no proof of the existence of this rhymed style, which was afterwards adopted from the Irish poets by the Anglo-Saxons, having existed on the Continent, and we have clear evidence that it did exist in Ireland. This is an argument in favour of our claim to him which has not hitherto been noticed. The only fault found with his verse by Bayle is an occasional slip in point of prosody.* It is admitted that there was something noble in his great poem, and Bayle quotes some laudatory verses, with which we shall close this notice :—

> "The learn'd Juvencus in heroic verse
> Does the great work of majesty rehearse;
> Hence, too, Sedulius chose his radiant theme,
> And grew conspicuous in the book of fame."

We come now to the sixth century, in the latter part of which flourished two eminent poets, EOCHY EIGEAS (or the Wise), better known as DALLAN FORGAIL, chief laureate in his day, and SEANCHAN TORPEST, a Connaught bard, who succeeded him and commemorated him in a fine elegy. The

---

* Dr. Drummond's account of the poetic licence claimed by our *lyric* poets at least is :—" And though neither the same number of syllables occurred, nor the same sounds were observed in the finals, the art itself, and the skill of the musician, in lengthening or shortening the time, claimed the privilege of producing what was short and abbreviating what was long. . . . . It was made long by dwelling on it a double space of time."—*Ibid.*, p. 113.

principal production of Dallan was a poem in honour of St. Columba, who himself has been numbered among the sons of Apollo, though the authenticity of the productions attributed to him has been much questioned. The following pieces by Dallan, independent of their antiquity and poetic merit, are interesting from the glance which they afford into the manners and spirit of the age. It appears that Aodh, son of Duach, King of Orgiall,* was possessed of a shield as renowned in its day as that of Achilles. This shield, which had got the appellation of Dubh-Ghiolla, had long excited the envy of the Prince of Breifne, who, after many efforts, promises, and flatteries, at length prevailed on the bard to use his influence in obtaining it for him.† With this view he proceeded to Orgiall, and recited to the young prince the following flattering odes:—

ODE TO AODH, SON OF DUACH.
A.D. 580.

TRANSLATED BY HENRY GRATTAN CURRAN.

Bounteous and mighty Aodh! whose potent shield
Glares like a fatal star upon the field—
Fierce as the stooping hawk, or following hound,
Resistless as the ocean-billow's bound—
Thy shield I sing—the warrior's best relief—
Avenger of the fall of sept and chief;
Brighter than foam that shrouds the bursting wave,
That glorious shield that heroes, monarchs crave,
Renown'd o'er all that warlike arm may wield
Amid the failing ranks! dread speckled shield;

---

* A district comprehending the present counties of Louth, Monaghan, &c.

† *Irish Minstrelsy*, vol. ii., p. 358.

That guardian shield where Duach's son up-rears,
Awe-struck, the daring heart no longer dares.
Oh, would the prince our bardic spell requite
With that proud shield—dread portent of the fight;
Aodh's glorious name through Erin's plains should ring,
While Dallan's hand could wake the trembling string.

ODE TO DUBH-GHIOLLA, THE SHIELD OF AODH.

TRANSLATED BY HENRY GRATTAN CURRAN.

Bright as the speckled salmon of the wave!
Dubh-Ghiolla! panic of the branded brave;
With thee would I combine, in deathless praise,
Proud Aodh, whose arm of might thy burden sways,
Fenced with its thorny mail the holly stands—
So, round the prince the guardian shield expands:
The bull's strong hide the needle's point defies—
Thus vainly round him baffled ranks arise:
That shield at once his panoply and blade,
He scorns the spear, the falchion's feebler aid.
As chafing storms, too long in durance pent,
Sweep through the forest, finding sudden vent;
Such is the voice of Aodh when with his shield
Compass'd he stands, bright terror of the field!

Notwithstanding, however, the influence which at all times the bards possessed, and the dread which, in this age, they inspired, by the excessive insolence that again characterized the order, the prince thought proper to decline the modest request of Dallan. "Your poem is good," said he, "and I will reward thee with gold and silver, and precious gems; stately steeds and cattle I will likewise give, but not the shield—that thou canst not have." The pitch of insolence to which the bards had arrived, and which, as we shall see, at length recoiled upon themselves, is strikingly evinced in the reply of Dallan, thus baffled in his object. "I will satirize the king," said he, "and make his name odious throughout the wide-extended regions of Alba and Ireland." How greatly the order stood in need of reformation, will be obvious from an instance of such wanton arrogance in one of their leading members. Indeed, their number had now swelled so incredibly, and their presumption, even towards the throne, increasing in proportion—that from being idolized by all ranks, from the king to the peasant, they came at length to be regarded as a crying national evil. Besides having become burdensome to the state, from their incredible number, they had rendered themselves odious to the nobility, whom they did not scruple to lampoon; and to such a height did their arrogance at length arrive that, we are assured, they even dared to demand some of the immunities and privileges of the crown itself.*

To put a stop to a grievance so intolerable, a convention of the states-general was called at Drumceat, in County Donegal (A.D. 580), at which the question of their suppression, or banishment, was discussed and almost decided upon, when St. Columba, who had just arrived from his settlement in Iona, entering the convention, proposed such a reformation of abuses in the bardic order, and such a reduction of their number, as, with the great influence of the advocate, satisfied all parties. It was on this occasion that Dallan commenced his *Amhra* in eulogy of Columba, reserving the completion till the time of Columba's death, at the saint's own request. The death of the bard, which occurred about seventeen years after this convocation, was commemorated in the following fine elegy by his friend and successor, SEANCHAN TORPEST.

* *Hist. Mems.*, p. 53.

LAMENT

OVER THE DEAD BODY OF DALLAN.
A.D. 597.

TRANSLATED BY HENRY GRATTAN CURRAN.

The soul is fled, but still that brow, tho' cold, its transcript wears;
And the hearts that loved him ache, above each record that it bears.
Of mighty mould, yet courteous,—henceforth who the bards shall lead,
That honour'd him, their gifted chief, for whom our bosoms bleed?

Thrice fifty bards, of passing skill, attended in his train,
But the fleetest hand that swept the harp would pause amid the strain,
And slumber on the silent chord, beneath the wakening swell
Of Dallan's harp—a thousand more had own'd the potent spell!

As wintry torrents, when along their channell'd depths they rave,
Was Dallan's song—'twas as the strength of Easroe's bounding wave.
His wit was as the winged shaft as rapid, and as deep
As ocean, where, beneath the tide, the silent waters sleep.

From chaos as the sun appear'd, through clouds asunder riven,
When the mighty one's behest had mark'd his pathway in the heaven;
The stars grew feeble in his light, transcendent as he shone,
So Dallan, 'mid surrounding bards, stood glorious and alone.

His glowing lip, oh, King supreme, Thy power with wisdom bless'd,
And the minstrels hail'd him for their chief—the brightest and the best;
Our reverence, our love were his; but death the arrow sped,
And wounded, through his comely side, each heart that mourns him dead.*

---

* The following is a more literal version, which has since appeared, by a late gifted writer:—

SEANCHAN'S LAMENT FOR DALLAN.†

METRICAL VERSION BY J. C. MANGAN.

Dear, dear, unto me is his body in the winding-sheet,
   Ulla! Ullalu!
Gigantic he was, yet an active man, alert and fleet,
   Ulla! Ullalu!
 Light in frame, he yet dealt heavy blows;
 Mortal man couldn't resist his blows;
 He sang sweetly, too, as when the south wind blows,
   Ulla! Ullalu!

A fine host and brave was he master of and governor,
   Ulla! Ullalu!
We, thrice fifty bards, we confess'd him chief in song and war.
   Ulla! Ullalu!
 Had we all been ten for every one,
 He could still have taught us, every one.
 Praise, and fame, glory, daily ever he won!
   Ulla! Ullalu!

O! like was this man to the Deluge in the days of Noh,
   Ulla! Ullalu!
O! like to the war of the cataract of Assa-roe,‡
   Ulla! Ullalu!

---

† *Dublin University Mag.*, vol. xxxi., p. 250.
‡ *Eas-Ruadh*, the red cataract; or Ballyshannon Waterfall.

Scanchan was the author of an historical poem preserved in the Book of Lecan. He survived till somewhere about the middle of the seventh century.

We now proceed to notice some pieces of the Latin poetry of two illustrious ecclesiastics who adorned this period, Columba and Columbanus. Of them also we shall say little, as any account of these eminent men, to be satisfactory, would occupy a disproportioned space in these pages.

 Like the thunder and the stormy sea,
 Cowering those who would put out to sea,
 O! like an embodied hurricane to see!
    Ulla! Ullalu!

Search worlds upon worlds! pass the universe's outer sphere,
    Ulla! Ullalu!
And none shall you find like to him whose bones are buried here.
    Ulla! Ullalu!
Kingly he was, both in speech and mien,
Much abhorring all things false and mean,
What *he* spoke, *that* truly ever did he mean.
    Ulla! Ullalu!

  * * * * *

 Never yet saw earth a grander bard—
 Never a sublimer warrior-bard—
 Yet his last low bedroom's door, alas! is barred!
    Ulla! Ullalu!

This is given by way of contrast to the foregoing, being much more literal and less paraphrastical.

Columba, the great apostle of the Western Islands, and founder of the famous order of the Culdees, who flourished in the middle and latter part of the sixth century,* was a distinguished friend and patron of the bards; nor does his admiration of their art appear to have been merely theoretical. Several pieces of sacred poetry attributed to him, both in Latin and Irish, are still extant, and there are many others, now probably lost, noticed by Colgan, who states that he had in his possession ten of the Irish pieces, of each of which he quotes the first line.† The only one of the Irish poems we have seen is an ode addressed to his monastery in Ireland, at his departure for Hy, or Iona, the imagery of which is singular. Seven angels are supposed to take charge alternately of the monastery during each day of the week, each making his report in turn to the recording angel, a fancy well calculated to preserve discipline and keep alive the vigilance of the members. As it is of considerable length, and in some places rather obscure and prolix, the first few verses only are here given from the *Transactions of Dublin Gaelic Society.*

A.D. 521-597.

---

* There is a difference of five years between the *Annals of the Four Masters* and those of Tigernach, in the year of his death—the former making it 592, the latter, 597.

† *Trias Thaum.*, p. 472.

COLUMBA'S FAREWELL TO ARRAN.

BLANK VERSE TRANSLATION FROM THE IRISH
BY T. O'FLANAGAN.

Farewell from me to Arran—
A sad farewell to my feelings;
I am sent eastward to Hy,
And it separated since the flood.

Farewell from me to Arran;—
It anguishes my heart
Not to be westward at her waves,
Amidst the groups of the saints of heaven!

Farewell from me to Arran;—
It has anguish'd my heart of faith,
It is the farewell lasting;—
Oh, not of my will is the separation!

*   *   *   *

 Of Columba's Latin poetry Colgan has published three hymns, of which Dr. Smith * has furnished metrical translations. One of these is stated to have been composed during a thunder-storm at Durrough, one of the religious houses he had established in Ireland; another is on the fall of angels and the final judgment; and the third in praise of the Redeemer. These pieces, as the reader will perceive from the lines of the original quoted below, are written in rhyme "agreeably to the form and measure of Irish poetry," as Dr. Smith states, "to which his disciples were

---

* *Life of Columba*, Edinburgh, 1798, Appendix.

so much accustomed."* The two first are here selected as affording the most favourable poetical specimens.

VERSES WRITTEN DURING A THUNDER-STORM, ABOUT THE YEAR 550.

Gracious Father! bow Thine ear,
And our request in mercy hear:
O bid the thunder cease to roar,
And let the lightnings flash no more;
Lest long in terror we remain,
Or by its stroke we should be slain.
  The pow'r supreme to Thee belongs,
Archangels laud Thee in their songs;
The wide expanse of heav'n above
Resounds Thy glory and Thy love.
  O Saviour of the human race!
Whose pow'r is equal to Thy grace,
For ever be Thy name ador'd
As King supreme, and only Lord!
To all Thy people Thou art nigh,
And oft Thy grace prevents their cry.

* * * *

May love and zeal to Thee, my God!
Have in my heart a firm abode:
O that the casket may be such
As fits a gem so very rich!

---

* "Noli Pater indulgere
Tonitrua cum fulgere," &c.

ON THE CREATION, FALL OF ANGELS, FINAL JUDGMENT.

The God omnipotent, who made the world,
Is subject to no change. He was, He is,
And He shall be : th' ETERNAL is His name.
    *   *   *   *   *

This God created all the heav'nly hosts,
Archangels, angels, potentates and pow'rs,
That so the emanations of His love
Might flow to myriads, diffusing good.
But from this eminence of glory fell
Th' apostate Lucifer, elate with pride
Of his high station and his glorious form.
Fill'd with like pride, and envy'ng God Himself
His glory, other angels shar'd his fate,
While the remainder kept their happy state.
Thus fell a third of the bright heav'nly stars,
Involv'd in the old serpent's guilt and fate,
And with him suffer, in th' infernal gulf,
The loss of heav'n, in chains of darkness bound.
God then to being call'd this lower world,
According to the plan form'd in His mind.
He made the firmament, the earth and sea,
The sun, the moon, and stars ; a glorious host !
The earth He clad with herbs for food, and trees,
And then to ev'ry living thing gave birth,
And last to man, whom He made lord of all.
When angels (the first morning stars) beheld
The wondrous fabric, with glad songs they hymn'd
The praise of the Almighty Architect,
For such displays of wisdom, pow'r, and love.
But our first parents, from their happy state
Seduc'd by Satan, were with terror fill'd,
With dreadful sights appall'd, till God with grace
Consol'd their hearts, and Satan's pow'r restrain'd.

His providential care He also show'd,
And bade the humid clouds distil their rains,
And times and seasons in their order run.
Rivers and seas (like giants bound in chains)
He forced to keep within the limits fix'd,
And flow for ever for the use of man.
 Lo! earth's vast globe, suspended by His pow'r,
On nothing hangs, as on a solid base.
   * * * * *

 O happy they who love His holy law,
And in the blessings of the saints partake!
Who, in the paradise of God above,
Drink of the living stream, and eat the fruit
Of that life-giving tree, ordain'd by God
To heal the nations, and to feed the soul.
 Thrice happy is the soul that shall ascend
To this abode of God, when the last trump
Shall sound, and shake the earth, more than of old,
When Sinai shook, and Moses was afraid.
 This awful day of God the Lord draws nigh,
When earthly objects shall have lost their charm,
And joy or terror fill each human soul:
Then shall we stand before the judgment seat,
To render an account of all our deeds:
Then shall our sins before our face be set,
The books be open'd, and the conscience heard.
None shall be missing; for the dead shall hear
The voice of God, and from their graves come forth
To join their souls, and stand before the bar.
 Time runs his course no more; the wand'ring orbs
Through heaven lose their course: the sun grows dark,
Eclipsed by the glory of the Judge;
The stars drop down as, in a tempest, fruit
Is shaken from the tree; and all the earth,
Like one vast furnace, is involved in flames.
See! the angelic hosts attend the Judge,
And, on ten thousand harps, His praises hymn.

Their crowns they cast before His feet, and sing—

* * * * *

But we who have believ'd, and kept His word,
Shall enter into glory with the Lord;
And there, in diff'rent ranks, we shall receive,
Through grace, rewards proportion'd to our deeds,
And dwell in endless glory with our Lord.
 Almighty Father, Son, and Holy Ghost,
Thou ONE Eternal, ever-blessed God!
To me, the least of saints, vouchsafe Thy grace!
O may I join the thousands round Thy throne!

The Culdee College of Columba at Iona or Icolmkille, justly called by Dr. Johnson "the luminary of the Caledonian regions," from the admirable discipline and character imparted to it by its venerable founder, continued for ages after his decease to be one of the most distinguished seats of learning and religion in Europe. "From this nest of Columba," says O'Donnell, one of his biographers, in reference to his name, signifying a dove, "these sacred doves took their flight to all quarters." Besides his establishment at Iona, the number of houses for religion and learning said to have been founded by him in Ireland, the land of his princely sires,* almost exceeds belief. The name Culdee is merely a corruption of the Irish *Ceile-De*, or servants of God. Almost the only relic of Columba remaining in his own

---

* St. Columba was descended of Conal Gulban, son of Niall of the Nine Hostages, the distinguished Irish monarch in the early part of the fifth century. Many of his disciples, likewise, were of royal and noble descent.

country, is the magnificently illuminated MS. copy of the Gospels preserved in the University of Dublin, which is traditionally ascribed to him. Perhaps it is unequalled for the beauty of its penmanship and illumination.

Another poetical ecclesiastic of this period, of more extended European reputation than the former, with whom he has been not unfrequently confounded, was COLUMBANUS, the glory of his age and country. For the reason previously stated, we mean not to dwell upon his history. After residing for a considerable time at the celebrated monastery of Bangor, in Down, where he received his education, he passed over to France, from thence to Germany, and at last to Italy, filling all these regions with houses of religion and learning. It appears to have been in the latter country, where he founded the famous monastery of Bobbio, in which, after his various wanderings, he quietly spent the residue of his days, that he composed the principal of his poetical pieces. In one of them, addressed to Fœdolius, Bishop of Treves, he alludes to the advanced age he had attained. Several of them are addressed to a favourite disciple named Hunaldus, cautioning him against the snares and vanities of the world—one of them forming, in the original, an acrostic—COLUMBANUS—HUNALDO—commencing—"Casibus innumeris decurrint tempora vitæ." The following translation of an epistle to the same person is given by Dr. Smith. In some copies, however, the name is Sethus, and not Hunaldus.*

A.D. 543-615.

---

* Taylor's *Biog. Britannica Literaria*, p. 158, Anglo-Sax. Era. The remainder may be seen in Smith's *Life of Columba*, though he admits that it was probably the production of Columbanus, of which there cannot be the smallest doubt.

EPISTLE TO HUNALD, AGAINST AVARICE.

Hunald! the counsel of Columban hear,
And to thy friend give now a willing ear;
No studied ornament shall gild my speech,
What love shall dictate, I will plainly preach.
 Have faith in God, and His commands obey,
While fleeting life allows you here to stay;
And know, the end for which this life is giv'n
Is to prepare the soul for God and heav'n.
Despise the pleasures which will not remain,
Nor set thy heart on momentary gain;
But seek for treasures in the sacred page,
And in the precepts of each saint and sage.
These noble treasures will remain behind
When earthly treasures fly on wings of wind.
 Think of the time when trembling age shall come,
And the last messenger to call thee home.
'Tis wise to meditate betimes on death,
And that dread moment which will stop the breath,
On all the ills which age brings in its train,
Disease and weakness, languor, grief, and pain.
The joints grow stiff, the blood itself runs cold,
Nor can the staff its trembling load uphold.
And need I speak of groans and pangs of mind,
And sleep disturb'd by ev'ry breath of wind?
What then avails the heap of yellow gold,
For years collected, and each day re-told?
Or what avails the table richly stored
To the sick palate of its dying lord?
The sinful pleasures which have long since past,
Are now like arrows in his heart stuck fast.
 He who reflects that time, on eagle-wing,
Flies past, and preys on every earthly thing,
Will scorn vain honours, avarice despise,
On nobler objects bent, beyond the skies.

Alas! vain mortals, how misplac'd your care,
When, in this world, you seek what is not there!
True lasting happiness is found above,
And heav'n, not earth, you therefore ought to love.
The rich enjoy not what they seem to have,
But something more their souls incessant crave.
The use of riches seldom do they know;
For heirs they heap them, or they waste in show.

O! happy he, to whose contented mind
Riches seem useless, but to help mankind;
Who neither squanders what should feed the poor,
Nor suffers avarice to lock his store.
No moths upon his heaps of garments feed,
Nor serves his corn to feed the pamper'd steed.
No cankering care shall take his peace away;
No thief, nor flame, shall on his substance prey.
His treasure is secure beyond the skies,
And there he finds it on the day he dies.

This world we enter'd naked at our birth,
Naked we leave it and return to earth;
Silver and gold we need not much, nor long,
Since to this world alone such things belong.
Life's little space requires no ample store;
Soon heaven opens to the pious poor;
Whiles Pluto's realms their gloomy gates unfold,
Those to admit who set their souls on gold.

Our Saviour bids us avarice avoid,
Nor love those things which can't be long enjoy'd.
Short, says the Psalmist, are the days of man,
The measure of his life a narrow span.
Time flies away; and on its rapid wing
We fly along with ev'ry earthly thing.
Yet time returns, and crowns the spring with flow'rs,
Renews the seasons and repeats the hours.
But life returns not with revolving years,
And man, once gone, on earth no more appears.
Wise, then, is he who makes it his great care,
In this short space, for heaven to prepare.

The poem addressed to Fœdolius, Bishop of Treves, is a very curious one, written in a sort of verse then very uncommon, but afterwards adopted, probably from him, by several writers, and the origin of which he attributes to Sappho. The metre is pentesyllabic, with a hexametrical conclusion of six lines. It is chiefly on the same subject as the foregoing—a subject on which he seems never tired of expatiating, though in a much more playful style, appealing to various classical subjects tending to dissuade from the love of money. It is too long for insertion.

The following beautiful verses, which appear to have been addressed to some of the youthful nobles whom the fame of the sanctity and learning of the great missionary gathered round him, are on much the same general subject as the preceding pieces—a homily against the love of the world :—

THE RHYTHMICS OF COLUMBANUS.*

The world itself rolls daily to its wane ;
If, then, it fades, shall man, vain man, remain ?
Whom equal birth but equal honour gave,
Claims he exemption from the common grave ?
Hopes he that law of nature to defy,
By which the dead have died, the living die ?
On what presumption—hath the bravest breath'd
Beyond the space creation first bequeath'd ?
Of all their boasted triumphs point me one
O'er death, to swell the list of their renown.
Alas ! not one—when he descends to strike,
The bravest, proudest—all—submit alike.

---

* The translation is given by Dr. Campbell in his *Ecclesiastical Strictures*, merely with the initials " the Rev. J. W."

Vainly the miser toils to heap a store,
Vainly he starves himself, and cheats the poor.
Forc'd to be lib'ral at his latest breath,
And what he sav'd from God—resign to Death;
Some spendthrift riots in his ill-got gold,
And dissipates the hoard before he's cold.
Fondly the pleasures of this life we prize,
Fondly the terrors of the next despise;
Grasping at that which glides, and mocks our hold,
And, where we should be cautious, blindly bold;
We leave the guide of day to plunge in night,
And love the foulest darkness more than light.
An hour of sway—a transitory reign,
A dream of bliss—are all we here can gain,
And yet for these we hazard endless pain;
Braving the pangs that on the wicked wait,
And all the horrors of an unknown state.
Not so thy choice—though vice herself array
In ev'ry splendour—take the virtuous way:
Believe Isaiah's hallow'd words, which say,
"Flesh is as grass," and feels a like decay—
The fairest flow'r, whose beauty tempts the eye,
Blooms but a short existence ere it die—
The fairest forms that yet of earth were made
Share the same fate—and, like the flow'r, fade;
As shrinks the flow'r beneath the scorching ray,
So droops the youth whom vice hath taught to stray;
Though others drink her poison'd cup and smile,
Let not their mirth thine appetite beguile;
False is the joyous semblance that appears,
The cup of vice is still the cup of tears.
Search not her haunts, to happiness unknown—
True happiness is virtue's gift alone.
Warn'd by the wrecks thou seest on ev'ry side,
Trust not her dang'rous hand thy course to guide;
Let no temptation thy pure soul entice
To one base action which thy thoughts despise

Raise thy mind's eye to scenes of bliss above,
Where angels dwell in never-ending love.
Where age its groans—its weakness youth resigns,
Where the soul ne'er in thirst or hunger pines :
Where feeds the crowd on heav'nly food alone—
Where pangs of birth and death are both unknown :
Where the true life, for ever green, appears—
Nor chang'd by sorrows, nor consum'd by years.

In the latter part of the sixth, and the course of the seventh, century, the academies of Ireland had attained such reputation as to draw students not only from England, but from many of the continental states. With respect to the former we have the authority of Bede, Camden, and Lord Lyttleton—some of the very highest authorities with regard to early English affairs.* Lyttleton even assures us that the Anglo-Saxon students brought from thence the first knowledge of letters possessed by their countrymen, in which opinion Dr. Johnson also coincides. Indeed, that the Saxons brought no alphabet with them to England, appears a matter of almost absolute certainty.

Among the Anglo-Saxon students thus resorting to Ireland, we find Prince Aldfrid, afterwards king of the Northumbrian Saxons. This event, which occurred about A.D. 684, is corroborated by Bede in his " Life of St. Cuthbert." Aldfrid appears to have spent several years in Ireland, and there is still extant in the Irish language a poem attributed to this prince, descriptive of the various provinces and cities of the kingdom, of which the public are here presented, for the first time, with the only metrical version that has appeared.

---

* *Beda, Hist. Gent. Angl.*, lib. iii., c. 27 ; *Camden's Britannia ;* and *Lyttleton's History of Henry II.*

PRINCE ALDFRID'S ITINERARY THROUGH IRELAND.

TRANSLATED BY JAMES CLARENCE MANGAN.*

I found in Inisfail† the fair,
In Ireland, while in exile there,
Women of worth, both grave and gay men,
Many clerics and many laymen.

I travell'd its fruitful provinces round,
And in every one of the five‡ I found,
Alike in church and in palace hall,
Abundant apparel and food for all.

Gold and silver I found, and money,
Plenty of wheat and plenty of honey;
I found God's people rich in pity,
Found many a feast and many a city.

---

* The present version, like most of those by the same veteran translator, was made specially for this volume by Mr. Mangan, well known to the literary world, though perhaps not by name, by the *Literæ Orientales* and *Anthologia Germanica* in the *Dublin University Magazine*. The original was first printed, without any translation, in the *Irish Minstrelsy*, by Mr. Hardiman. An admirable literal translation, by Mr. O'Donovan, appeared in the *Dublin Penny Journal*, vol. i., p. 94, to which the reader is referred in proof of the rigid fidelity of the present version.

† Inisfail— one of the ancient titles of Ireland—signified the island of Destiny, from the *Lial Fail*, or Stone of Destiny, on which the monarchs were crowned.

‡ Three of the provinces have undergone little change except in name. Their ancient titles were Ultonia, Ulster; Mononia, Munster; Connacia, Connaught; Lagenia, Leinster; but the two Meaths then formed a fifth, now merged into the latter province.

I also found in Armagh, the splendid,
Meekness, wisdom, and prudence blended,
Fasting, as Christ hath recommended,
And noble councillors untranscended.

I found in each great church moreo'er,
Whether on island or on shore,
Piety, learning, fond affection,
Holy welcome and kind protection.

I found the good lay monks and brothers
Ever beseeching help for others,
And in their keeping the holy word
Pure as it came from Jesus the Lord.*

I found in Munster, unfetter'd of any,
Kings and queens, and poets a many —
Poets well skill'd in music and measure,
Prosperous doings, mirth and pleasure.

I found in Connaught the just redundance
Of riches, milk in lavish abundance;
Hospitality, vigour, fame,
In Cruachan's† land of heroic name.

I found in the country of Connall‡ the glorious
Bravest heroes, ever victorious;
Fair-complexion'd men and warlike,
Ireland's lights, the high, the starlike!

---

* Some fine specimens of the skill and ingenuity expended by the early Irish Christians upon their copies of the sacred writings and theological works are still extant. The beautiful illuminated copy of the Four Gospels, attributed to St. Columba, now preserved in the library of Dublin University, is worthy of particular admiration.

† Cruachan, or Croghan, was the name of the royal palace of Connaught.

‡ Tyrconnell, the present Donegal.

I found in Ulster, from hill to glen,
Hardy warriors, resolute men ;
Beauty that bloom'd when youth was gone,
And strength transmitted from sire to son.

I found in the noble district of Boyle
      [*MS. here illegible*]
Brehons, Erenachs,* weapons bright,
And horsemen bold and sudden in fight.

I found in Leinster, the smooth and sleek,
From Dublin to Slewmargy's† peak ;
Flourishing pastures, valour, health,
Long-living worthies, commerce,‡ wealth.

I found, besides, from Ara to Glea,
In the broad rich country of Ossorie,
Sweet fruits, good laws for all and each,
Great chess-players,§ men of truthful speech.

I found in Meath's fair principality
Virtue, vigour, and hospitality ;
Candour, joyfulness, bravery, purity,
Ireland's bulwark and security.‖

---

* The Brehons were the judges and promulgators of the law. The signification of *Erenach* is not distinctly known, except that it was a ruler of some kind, and has sometimes been interpreted as synonymous with the office of archdeacon.

† Ath-Cliath was the ancient name of Dublin. Slewmargy, a mountain in Queen's County, near the river Barrow.

‡ Tacitus, in his Life of Agricola, states that the harbours of Ireland were better known by means of commercial navigators than those of Britain. (Melius aditus portusque, per commercia et negociatores, cogniti.)

§ There are frequent allusions to the game of chess in most of the Irish poems.

‖ The allusion here is to the palace of Temur or Tara, the residence of the supreme monarch.

> I found strict morals in age and youth,
> I found historians recording truth;
> The things I sing of in verse unsmooth,
> I found them all—I have written sooth.

The inroads of the Norsemen, or Danes, which began by a descent on the island of Rathlin, on the northern coast, at the close of the eighth century, though ultimately productive of some advantage, produced, for a long period, the most disastrous effects upon the peaceful arts of life—and literary pursuits shared in the general disasters of the period. To these adventurous northern sea-kings of Scandinavia—variously termed in our annals and poems *Lochlanach*, or people of Lochlan, *Gals*, or strangers, and *Ostmanni*, or Eastmen—the establishment of the principal sea-ports is attributed. Under their rule, at least, they first rose to importance.

<small>A.D. 795.</small>

Donat, or Donatus—according to the custom prevalent in the middle ages of Latinizing the names of the learned—flourished about A.D. 840. Like many Irish scholars of the period, he proceeded to the Continent, and in the latter part of his life was made Bishop of Fesulæ, near the famed city of the Medici, in Tuscany. He has left some elegant Latin verses, which, though not strictly admissible, are here introduced. They are not only highly eulogistic of his country, but contain, perhaps, the earliest allusion on record to those peculiarities connected with it vulgarly attributed to the agency of St. Patrick.

> Far westward lies an isle of ancient fame,
> By nature bless'd, and Scotia* is her name—
> Enroll'd in books—exhaustless in her store
> Of veiny silver and of golden ore.

---

* See p. 62.

Her fruitful soil for ever teems with wealth ;
With gems her waters, and her air with health ;
Her verdant fields with milk and honey flow ;
Her woolly fleeces vie with virgin snow ;
Her waving furrows float with bearded corn ;
And arms and arts her envied sons adorn.
No savage bear with lawless fury roves ;
No rav'ning lion through her sacred groves ;
No poison there infects—no scaly snake
Creeps through the grass, nor frogs* annoy the lake :
An island worthy of its pious race,
In war triumphant, and unmatch'd in peace.

About the middle of the tenth century flourished an eminent poet, CORMACAN EIGEAS (or the wise), son of Maolbrigid, chief laureate of Ulster. His principal production was *The Circuit of Ireland*,† a poem written in celebration of the great exploit of the renowned warrior, Murkerta, or Murtagh, MacNeill, commonly surnamed of the *leather-cloaks*, whose friend and follower he was. This chief, who was prince of Aileach, in the north, was also heir to the crown of Ireland, and, in order to strike terror into any secret rival claimants, he set forth in the depth of winter, and made the circuit of the kingdom, exacting hostages of all the principal chiefs. These, as a pledge of his loyalty, and a proof of the injustice of some latent feelings of jealousy with which he had reason to

A.D. 940.

---

* However fabulous this may appear, it is said that frogs were formerly unknown in this country, and were first propagated here from spawn introduced as an experiment by a Fellow of Trinity College, Dublin, in 1696.

† Published in the *Archæological Society's Tracts.*

believe he was regarded, he presented to the monarch. The poem commences—

> "Muircheartach, son of valiant Niall,
> Thou hast taken the hostages of Innisfail;
> Thou hast brought them all into Aileach,
> Into the stone-built Grainan (palace) of steeds.
> Thou didst go forth from us with a thousand heroes,
> Of the race of Eoghan of red weapons,
> To make the great circuit of all Erin,
> O Muircheartach of the yellow hair!"

From this period the country became subject to the predatory incursions of the Danes and Northmen, the blighting influence of which soon became visible in the decline of the literary spirit. The temerity of these ruthless invaders continued for a long period to increase, and threatened to destroy lastingly the peace and tranquillity of the kingdom. Fresh swarms of them were continually arriving. Like an overwhelming torrent, they poured over the land—marring the very face of nature, destroying the institutions of learning, and sweeping away almost every trace of literature, civilization, and art from the island. We may well imagine the bard, in his place of refuge from the fury of the storm, in the mountain caves or deep recesses of the forest, having recourse to his beloved harp to soothe the anguish of his spirit, or chant a deep imprecation on the desolators of his country—realizing the noble picture of the poet—

> "Robed in sable garb of woe,
> With haggard eyes the poet stood
> (Loose his beard and hoary hair
> Stream'd like a meteor to the troubled air);
> And, with a master's hand and prophet's fire,
> Struck the deep sorrows of his lyre."
>
> GRAY.

The reign of the celebrated monarch, Brian Boru, in the tenth century, served, like that of Alfred in England, to check this great national calamity, and restored the kingdom, in some degree, to its former prosperity and peace. While, by his military prowess, he subdued these lawless invaders of his kingdom, he was not less careful in improving the peace thus procured by the wisest civil measures and most judicious legislation. Soon, however, the Danes, taking advantage of a favourable opportunity, and aided by some of the dastardly native chiefs, appeared in arms doubly strong. The venerable monarch, then in his eighty-third year, hastened to meet those old foes whom he had so often quelled before. A fierce engagement took place at Clontarf, near Dublin, 23rd April, 1014, in which the invaders were defeated with great slaughter; but the good and aged monarch was himself treacherously slain in his tent, after having defeated the Danes, as historians assure us, in no less than fifty separate engagements. Thus died the illustrious Brian Boru, almost the last distinguished native monarch of Ireland, equally celebrated as an enlightened statesman, an able soldier, and an accomplished musician and bard.* The following elegiac composition

---

* The following account of the fine old harp *supposed* to have been that of Brian, is from the first volume of the *Dublin Penny Journal*, which, notwithstanding its unassuming title, is enriched with the contributions of some of the first Irish scholars and antiquarians of the day:—"These regalia were kept in the Vatican, till the Pope sent the harp to Henry VIII., but kept the crown, which was of massive gold. Henry gave the harp to the first Earl of Clanricarde, in whose family it remained until the beginning of the eighteenth century, when it came, by a lady of the De Burgh family, into that of M'Mahon, of Clenagh, in the

was written on his death, and on witnessing the desolation of his palace of Kincora, in Munster, by his secretary and biographer, McLiag: —

LAMENT OF M^cLIAG FOR KINCORA.

TRANSLATED BY JAMES CLARENCE MANGAN.

Oh, where, Kincora, is Brian the Great?
And where is the beauty that once was thine?
Oh, where are the princes and nobles that sate
At the feast in thy halls, and drank the red wine?
    Where, oh, Kincora?

---

county of Clare; after whose death, it passed into the possession of Commissioner M'Namara, of Limerick. In 1782, it was presented to the Right Hon. William Conyngham, who deposited it in Trinity College museum, where it now is. It is thirty-two inches high, and of good workmanship; the sounding-board is of oak, the arms of red sally; the extremity of the uppermost arm, in part, is capped with silver, extremely well wrought and chiselled. It contains a large crystal, set in silver; and under it was another stone, now lost. The buttons, or ornamented knobs, at the side of this arm, are of silver. On the front arm, are the arms, chased in silver, of the O'Brien family—the bloody hand, supported by lions. On the sides of the front arm, within two circles, are two Irish wolf-dogs, cut in the wood. The holes of the sounding-board, where the strings entered, are neatly ornamented with an escutcheon of brass, carved and gilt; the larger sounding-holes have been ornamented, probably, with silver. The harp has twenty-eight keys, and as many string-holes; consequently, there were as many strings. The foot-piece, or rest, is broken off, and the parts round which it was joined are very rotten. The whole bears evidence of an expert artist."

Oh, where, Kincora, are thy valorous lords?
　Oh, whither, thou hospitable, are they gone?
Oh, where are the Dalcassians of the golden swords,*
　And where are the warriors that Brian led on?
　　　　　　Where, oh, Kincora?

And where is Morogh, the descendant of kings—
　The defeater of a hundred—the daringly brave,
Who set but slight store by jewels and rings—
　Who swam down the torrent and laugh'd at its wave?
　　　　　　Where, oh, Kincora?

And where is Donogh, King Brian's worthy son?
　And where is Conaing, the beautiful chief,
And Cian and Core?　Alas! they are gone—
　They have left me this night alone with my grief?
　　　　　　Left me, Kincora!

And where are the chiefs with whom Brian went forth,
　The never-vanquish'd son of Erin the brave—
The great King of Onaght, renown'd for his worth,
　And the hosts of Baskinn, from the Western wave?
　　　　　　Where, oh, Kincora?

Oh, where is Duvlann, of the swift-footed steeds?
　And where is Kian, who was son of Molloy?
And where is King Lonergan, the fame of whose deeds
　In the red battle-field no time can destroy?
　　　　　　Where, oh, Kincora?

And where is that youth of majestic height,
　The faith-keeping prince of the Scots?　Even he,
As wide as his fame was, as great as was his might,
　Was tributary, oh, Kincora, to me!
　　　　　　Me, oh, Kincora!

---

　* *I.e.*, "Of the golden-hilted swords." The Dalcassians were Brian's body-guard.

They are gone, those heroes of royal birth,
   Who plunder'd no churches and broke no trust ;
'Tis weary for me to be living on the earth,
   When they, oh, Kincora, lie low in the dust !
            Low, oh, Kincora !

Oh, never again will princes appear
   To rival the Dalcassians of the cleaving swords !
I can never dream of meeting afar or anear,
   In the east or the west, such heroes and lords !
            Never, Kincora !

Oh, dear are the images my memory calls up
   Of Brian Boru !—how he never would miss
To give me, at the banquet, the first bright cup !
   Ah, why did he heap on me honours like this ?
            Why, oh, Kincora ?

I am McLiag, and my home is on the lake :
   Thither often, to that palace whose beauty is fled,
Came Brian to ask me, and I went for his sake.
   Oh, my grief ! that I should live, and Brian be dead !
            Dead, oh, Kincora !

There is also extant another piece of McLiag's on the same subject, which possesses considerable pathos, and was written by the bard in the Hebrides, to which he had retired shortly after the events which he so deeply deplores.

M^cLIAG IN EXILE REMEMBERS BRIAN.

TRANSLATED BY REV. W. H. DRUMMOND, D.D.

Tedious and sad lag the joyless hours—
   Ah, ne'er did fancy bode a change so dire !
What time I dwelt in sweet Kincora's bowers,
   I little fear'd the barbarous spoiler's ire.

Had Brian lived, munificent and good,
   Or Morragh, in his stately mansions fair,
Ne'er in the isle of strangers black and rude,
   Whelm'd had I sunk beneath a flood of care.

If Conaing lived, the guardian of our coasts,
   The chief of thousands, hero great in might
As dauntless Hector of the Trojan host,
   Long had I ne'er been exiled from his sight.

Grief and despair my anxious bosom fill,
   To hear my prince's joyous voice no more;
Oh, how unlike this journey, drear and chill,
   Was that to Cian in the days of yore!

To Cian of the Cairn—to Cian, high
   In wealth and power, I went with bounding speed;
With him could none but royal Brian vie,
   In every generous thought and glorious deed.

M'Liag, who, besides these and other poetical effusions, was the author of several historical pieces, did not long survive his munificent patron, having died in 1016.

A.D. 1015. There is yet another piece preserved on a kindred subject, written by one of the bards who frequented the famed court of Kincora, situated on the Shannon, near the present Killaloe. It was the chief seat of the heroic Brian as king of Munster, previous to his usurpation of the supreme sovereignty,* where the bardic order were munificently patronised.

---

* Mr. C. G. (now Sir C.) Duffy, in a note to one of his clever ballads, "The Irish Chiefs," informs us that "our great Brian is *called* a usurper, inasmuch as he combined, by force and policy, the scattered and jealous powers of the island into one sovereignty, and ruled it himself, by the true divine right of being the fittest

This piece of MAC GIOLLA CAOIMII (Mac Gilly Caw or Kew, as the bard's name may be Anglicised), though belonging to a class which we esteem as amongst the most interesting of the relics of our ancient poetry, created some hesitation as to its admission, on account of the misconstruction which might be put upon it by some readers. To many, the munificent gifts mentioned might appear incredible, and tend to throw contempt upon the poem, though

---

ruler." "Save me from my friends," wisely saith the old proverb. The artist who painted Hannibal in profile omitting the blind eye, displayed a delicate tact which was handsomely acknowledged; but Mr. Duffy has made a point of bringing prominently into view the only blemish which tarnishes the fair fame of King Brian. We cannot think so meanly of Mr. Duffy's understanding, as to believe that he could himself have been convinced by his own profound logic; yet why he should have written a note expressly to inculcate such doctrine, appears rather remarkable. We fear it would work ill in the world generally if everyone were to act upon "the true divine right," of taking by combined force and policy the place which he might consider himself better qualified to fill than his neighbour. We do not remember to have anywhere seen a better plea for the Anglo-Norman invasion, or any other practical assertion of

"The good old rule, the simple plan—
For him to take who has the power, and him to keep who can."

Never before have we heard of the regal dignity being degraded to a tenure during pleasure or good conduct, except in the case of persistence in some violent infraction of the implied compact between king and people—and then it is on *the people* that devolves the right of dethroning. Even in an elective government, the throne should be vacant before it could be an object of legitimate ambition. Weakness, or want of ability, could no more afford a justification of usurpation, than it would justify a man to seize on the estate of another, because he thought he could manage it to greater advantage. That Brian made the best atonement for his crime by the wisdom of his policy, is very true, and there is the most credible historical evidence of such munificence having been exercised in other countries than Ireland, especially among the Scandinavians. The philosophic bards and historians of the O'Donnells and the O'Briens, in long subsequent times, dwelt in baronial castles, to which a handsome patrimony was attached. Well might Dr. Petrie

---

what may equally be said of Cæsar or Cromwell; but it can surely never afford a justification for it that, in the language of his panegyrist, Mac Daire—

"Through him the nation's power obtain'd a giant's growth."

Surely it is more consistent with truth and manliness, if his errors are to be mentioned at all, instead of covertly justifying them, to confess them frankly, while we proudly acknowledge his merits.

Certainly Brian accomplished the act of usurpation in the spirit of a gentleman or of a prince. He offered the unhappy king, who in his extremity acted with great and even touching dignity, fair fight for his crown; he scorned anything mean or underhand, and even allowed him a fair time to muster his strength, on condition that, in the event of not being able to meet him on its expiration, he should quietly resign in his favour. He well knew, however, that it was of no use, though it had the great advantage of preventing bloodshed.

It was only a consideration of policy that prevented O'Neill, to whom Brian had applied for aid, from trying with Brian whether he did not possess "the true divine right" of being the stronger. If he had done so, such another scene must inevitably have ensued as the descendants of these princes enacted in the year 1252, when they met with a general convention of the clans for the purpose of electing a successor to Roderick O'Conor as Ard Righ. It was no poetical contest for precedence, such as the bards afterwards waged, that then ensued between the chiefs of *Leith Mogha* and *Leith Con*, but one that prostrated for an age the powers of both, and effectually established the sway of the Anglo-Norman dynasty.

remark in reference to the former—in the case of the distinguished family of the O'Clerys of Donegal—"Ah, it will be long till learning in the history and literature of our country be again thus nobly recompensed." But in addition to this, the very grief of the poet appeared liable to misapprehension, dwelling, as he does, so prominently on the loaves and fishes, though perhaps, only in the simplicity of his heart, to display the generosity of the princes whose loss he mourns. These verses are said to have been written by the bard during a pilgrimage he made to the east, after the Battle of Clontarf, on a retrospect of the happy days he had spent at the court of Kincora.

THE BARD MOURNFULLY REMEMBERS BRIAN AND HIS NOBLES.*

METRICAL VERSION BY REV. W. H. DRUMMOND, D.D.

In a far foreign land, on a pilgrimage wending,
    A bard of green Erin pass'd cheerless along;
On the dark barren heath gloomy night was descending,
    He thought of past pleasures, and thus grieved in song:
"Sad and gloomy the night that now gathers around;
No door opens friendly with sweet welcome sound;
For poesy here no calm shelter is found;
    No repose for the bard these wild regions among.

---

* Hardiman's *Irish Minstrelsy*, vol. ii., p. 203, where, by an oversight, the poem is attributed to McLiag, Brian's secretary and biographer, who has also written some pieces on the same subject.

Since Heaven so wills, be its ordinance blest,
    That verse in this land no reward shall enjoy:
Once with gifts it was honour'd—the bard was caress'd
    With a love that hereafter his peace may annoy.
Ah! well I remember—to Brian of old,
When foam'd the red wine in the goblet of gold,
As with Cian he feasted, the hours slowly roll'd
    If he heard not the songs of the son of Molloy.

"Welcome, bard," said the monarch, his face beaming
        gladness,
    When he saw me return from the hall of O'Neill:
"Thy consort is pining, forlorn, and in sadness,
    To think thou hast left her for ever to wail.
Bard, long was thy absence—what tidings of worth
Dost thou bring from the black, cloudy lands of the north?"
"As the raven's," cried Morrogh, "what time she flew forth
    From the ark, well, I wot, is our wanderer's tale."

"But come, tell what gifts and rare treasures you bring
    From him who bears sway o'er the Carn-i-neid host:
To Innisfail's nobles, and first to our king—
    Swear true, by this hand, not to flatter or boast."
"By heaven," I cried, "all the truth I'll unfold:
Twice ten gallant steeds—ten rich ounces of gold,
And of kine, ten the choicest, twice ten times well told,
    Such the treasures I bring from the fair northern coast."

"With presents," said Cian of generous deeds,
    "More noble, O Morrogh, his song we'll reward—
With more numerous kine, and more swift-footed steeds,
    Beside what the monarch shall give to the bard."
And true (to remember, my griefs fresh arise)
Ere the banquet was finish'd or sleep closed the eyes
Of munificent Brian, I shared a rich prize,
    E'en ten times more worthy the poet's regard.

Seven herd-cover'd plains, spreading fertile and wide,
  Gift worthy a monarch, the king gave to me;
And a district for aye, where his court loves to bide,
  In sweet summer sojourn, by mountain or sea.
Said Morrogh the pious, nor spake he in vain,
" Whate'er the rich gifts thou to-night shalt obtain,
To-morrow their equal from me shalt thou gain,
  With the love of a prince, bard, devoted to thee."

The character and exploits of this illustrious monarch need not be more minutely dwelt upon. The sceptre which he had acquired by such questionable means, he wielded with rare sagacity, and in the spirit of a patriot king. He was distinguished as the scourge of the Danes, whose power he completely annihilated after many sanguinary conflicts—though he had not disdained their aid in attaining the object of his ambition—and was also an eminent friend of learning and of the Church. Among many wise regulations attributed to him, was the establishment for the first time of surnames in Ireland. There is a strong parallel between this monarch and Alfred of England, as well in his personal character as in the circumstances of his reign.

Bereft of its illustrious monarch, the kingdom continued for a long period a prey to the Danish marauders and the spirit of internal faction and discord. Such a period was but little suited to the cultivation of the gentler arts. Learning, which had perceptibly declined since the eighth century, when the piratical incursions of the Danes and Northmen first commenced, had almost totally disappeared, and with it, in a great measure, " the light of song."

This will be the most suitable place to introduce some

specimens of the Fenian poems already noticed in these pages, in addition to those previously given under the dates of the events to which they referred.

Among the ancient literary remains of Ireland, as previously stated, are to be found numerous poems and tales of great antiquity, beauty, and interest, of which there is a distinct class known as the *Fenian* poems and tales. These derive their name from the heroes of the Fianna Eireann, or Fenian legion, the celebrated body of Leinster warriors under the command of Fion MacCumhal, who was son-in-law to the Irish monarch, Cormac O'Con. These productions form a large and most interesting class of historical ballads and romances, possessing such unity of design and execution as to justify, in some degree, the supposition of their being the fragments of a great epic poem and historical romance. At the same time, their great uniformity and separate completeness appear to forbid that supposition. It is not a little remarkable that the name of the author, or authors, of productions so extensive, and possessed of so much beauty and merit, should not have survived; and though, perhaps, the most interesting monuments of our ancient literature, yet that, like the pillar-towers, there should exist nothing but vague conjecture as to their origin.

They bear internal evidence of not being of the earliest age of Irish literature, and of having been produced much later than the time of Oisin, or Ossian, who flourished in the third century. That they were produced after the introduction of Christianity, in the fifth century, is apparent from the mention of St. Patrick, to whom the warrior-bard, Oisin, is represented as narrating the exploits of his companions in arms; and their general subject being an account of the descent of some chiefs of Scandinavia, or Lochlin, upon the Irish coast, places them two or three centuries, at least, later than the time of the national apostle, the earliest recorded incursions of the Norsemen not having occurred prior to that period.

It is impossible to tell with certainty to what precise age they belong; but they are generally considered to have been the productions of a series of bards between the eighth and twelfth centuries. They are chiefly devoted to the celebration of the Fenian warriors, whose exploits have been already noticed, and many of them are conducted in the form of a dialogue between Oisin and St. Patrick. The authors, thinking it important to usher their productions into the world under the sanction of these celebrated names, paid little regard to the anachronism of making contemporaries of the bard and the saint, who had flourished at periods separated by two or three centuries. However, it afforded the poet a good opportunity of pourtraying the change of manners and feeling from the chivalrous days of the pagan Fenii to those of Christianity. The saint and the bard sometimes find it difficult to preserve their equanimity of temper, for while the latter, with the querulous spirit of age, cannot restrain his indignation at the comparison of the saint and his "psalm-singing clerks" with his old companions in arms, the saint in turn is shocked at the impiety and profanity of Oisin. Thus the poet represents them as alternately indulging in mutual compliments and plain speaking, of which the latter, though not over-courteous, becomes sometimes rather amusing. The following extracts afford a not unfavourable specimen of these poems:—

THE CHASE.*

TRANSLATED BY THE REV. W. H. DRUMMOND, D.D.

OISIN.

O son of Calphruin! thou, whose ear
Sweet chant of psalms delights to hear,
   Hast thou e'er heard the tale,
How Fionn urged the lonely chase
Apart from all the Fenian race,
   Brave sons of Innisfail?

PATRICK.

O royal born, whom none exceeds
In moving song, or hardy deeds,
   That tale, to me as yet untold,
Though far renown'd, do thou unfold
   In truth severely wise,
From fancy's wanderings far apart;
For what is fancy's glozing art
   But falsehood in disguise?

OISIN.

Oh, ne'er on gallant Fenian race
Fell falsehood's accusation base;
By faith of deeds, by strength of hand,
By trusty might of battle-brand,

---

* The translation of this poem by Miss Brooke, like her other translations, is admirable, and the editor should be sorry to make any invidious comparisons, but there is in the present a peculiar felicity of vigorous compression. This version having originally appeared anonymously, the above remarks, and others now omitted, were written while ignorant of the translator's name. It may be added that a comparison will serve to vindicate the general fidelity of Miss Brooke's versions.

We spread afar our glorious fame,
And safely from each conflict came.
Ne'er sat a monk in holy chair,
Devote to chanting hymn and prayer
   More true than the Fenians bold;
No chief like Fionn, world around,
Was e'er to bards so gen'rous found,
   With gifts of ruddy gold.
If lived the son of Morné fleet,
Who ne'er for treasure burn'd,
Or Duiné's son, to woman sweet,
   Who ne'er from battle turn'd,
But fearless, with his single glaive,
A hundred foemen dared to brave;
If lived Macgaree, stern and wild,
   That hero of the trenchant brand;
Or Caoilte, Ronan's witty child,
   Of liberal heart and open hand;
Or Oscar, once my darling boy,
Thy psalms would bring me little joy.
If lived, the Fenian deeds to sing,
   Sweet Fergus, with his voice of glee,
Or Daire, who trill'd a faultless string,
   Small pleasure were thy bells to me;
If lived the dauntless little Hugh,
   Or Fillan, courteous, kind, and meek,
Or Conan bald, for whom the dew
   Of sorrow yet is on my cheek,
Or that small dwarf, whose power could steep
The Fenian host in death-like sleep—
More sweet one breath of theirs would be
Than all Thy clerks' sad psalmody.

      PATRICK.

Thy chiefs renown'd extol no more,
O son of kings, nor number o'er,

But low on bended knee record
The power and glory of the Lord;
And beat the breast, and shed the tear,
And still His holy name revere—
Almighty, by whose potent breath
Thy vanquish'd Fenians sleep in death.

OISIN.

Alas! for Oisin—dire the tale!
* * * * *
Where now are the royal gifts of gold,
The flowing robe with its satin fold,
　And the heart-delighting bowl?
Where now the feast and the revel high,
And the jocund dance, and sweet minstrelsy,
And the steed loud neighing in the morn,
With the music sweet of hound and horn,
And well-arm'd guards of coast and bay?
All, all, like a dream have pass'd away;
And now we have clerks with their holy qualms,
And books, and bells, and eternal psalms,
And fasting, that waster, gaunt and grim,
That strips of all beauty both body and limb.

PATRICK.

Oh, cease this strain, nor longer dare
Thy Fionn or his chiefs compare
With Him who reigns in matchless might,
The King of kings, enthroned in light.
'Tis He who frames the heaven and earth;
　'Tis He who nerves the hero's hand;
'Tis He who calls fair fields to birth,
　And bids each blooming branch expand:
He gives the fishy streams to run,
And lights the moon and radiant sun.
What deeds like these, though great his fame,
Canst thou ascribe to Fionn's name?

OISIN.

To weeds and grass his princely eye
    My sire ne'er fondly turn'd ;
But he raised his country's glory high,
    When the strife of warriors burn'd.
To shine in games of strength and skill,
To breast the torrent from the hill,
To lead the van of the banner'd host—
These were his deeds and these his boast.

  *   *   *   *   *

PATRICK.

Here let this vain contention rest,
For frenzy, bard, inspires thy breast.

  *   *   *   *   *

OISIN.

  *   *   *   *   *

This arm, did frenzy touch my brain,
    Their heads from thy clerks would sever,
Nor thy crozier here, nor white book remain,
    Nor thy bells be heard for ever.*

PATRICK.

O son of kings, adorn'd with grace,
    'Twere music to my ear,
Of Fionn and his wondrous chase
    The promised tale to hear.

---

* " Let it be remembered that Oisin is no convert to Christianity ; on the contrary, he is opposed to it, principally because it had put an end to his favourite pastimes." It is some excuse for this burst of passion in Oisin, that the saint had more than insinuated that the Fenian heroes were now in limbo.

OISIN.

Well, though afresh my bosom bleeds,
    Remembering days of old,
When I think of my sire and his mighty deeds,
    Yet shall the tale be told.

OISIN'S TALE.

While the Fenian bands, at Almhain's towers,*
In the hall of spears passed the festive hours,
The goblet crown'd, with chess-men played,†
Or gifts for gifts of love repaid,
From the reckless throng Fionn stole unseen,
When he saw a young doe on the heath-clad green,
    With agile spring draw near;
      On Sceolan and Bran, his nimble hounds,
      He whistles aloud, and away he bounds
    In chase of the hornless deer.

With his hounds alone and his trusty blade,
    The son of Luno's skill,
On the track of the flying doe he strayed
    To Guillin's pathless hill.
But when he came to its hard-won height,
    No deer appear'd in view;
If east or west she had sped her flight,
    Nor hounds nor huntsmen knew.
    *   *   *   *   *

There, while he gazes anxious round,
Sudden he hears a doleful sound,

---

* Almhain, pronounced Alwin, the palace of Finn McCumhal, was situated on the hill of Allen, to which it gave its name, in Co. Kildare.

† "The game of chess is repeatedly noticed in connection with various historical incidents in the early history of Ireland."

And by a lake of crystal sheen,
Spies a nymph of loveliest form and mien :
Her cheeks as the rose were crimson bright,
   Her lips the red-berry's glow ;
Her neck as the polish'd marble white,
   Her breast the pure blossom's full blow ; *
Downy gold were her locks, and her sparkling eyes
Like freezing stars in the ebon skies.
Such beauty, O sage, all cold as thou art,
Would kindle warm raptures of love in thy heart.

   Nigh to the nymph of golden hair,
     With courteous grace he drew—
"O hast thou seen, enchantress fair,
     My hounds their game pursue?"

NYMPH.—"Thy hounds I saw not in the chase,
     O noble prince of the Fenian race ;
     But I have cause of woe more deep,
     For which I linger here and weep."

FIONN.—"O hast thou lost a husband dear?
     Falls for a darling son thy tear,
      Or daughter of thy heart?
     Sweet, soft-palm'd nymph, the cause reveal
     To one who can thy sorrows feel,
      Perchance can ease thy smart."

---

* Miss Brooke's description runs thus:—

  "On her soft cheek, with tender bloom,
    The rose its tint bestowed,
  And in her richer lip's perfume
    The ripened berry glow'd.

  "Her neck was as the blossom fair,
    Or like the cygnet's breast,
  With that majestic, graceful air,
    In snow and softness drest."

The maid of tresses fair replied—
"A precious ring I wore
Dropp'd from my finger in the tide;
 Its loss I now deplore;
But by the sacred vows that bind
 Each brave and loyal knight,
I now adjure thee, chief, to find
 My peerless jewel bright."

He feels her adjuration's ties,
 Disrobes each manly limb,
And for the smooth-palm'd princess hies
 The gulfy lake to swim.
Five times deep diving down the wave,
Through every cranny, nook, and cave,
With care he searches round and round,
Till the golden ring at length he found;
But scarce to the shore the prize could bring,
 When by some blasting ban—
Ah! piteous tale—the Fenian king
 Grew a withered, grey old man!*

Meanwhile the Fenians passed the hours
In the hall of spears, at Almhain's towers;
The goblet crowned, with chessmen play'd,
Or gifts for gifts of love repaid,
When Caoilte rose and asked in grief,
"Ye spearmen, where is our gallant chief?

---

* "We learn from Irish romance," says Miss Brooke, "that the Fenii and the chiefs of the Dananian race were enemies; and these people were supposed to be skilful in magic. Most of the Irish romances are filled with Dananian enchantments, as wild as the wildest of Ariosto's fictions, and not at all behind them in beauty."

Oh, lost, I dread, is the Fenian's boast—
Then who shall lead our bannered host?"*

*　　　*　　　*　　　*　　　*

To urge the quest we then decree,
Of Finn and his hounds, the joyous three
　　That still to triumph led;

And soon from Almhuin's hall away,
With Caoilte, I, and our dark array,
　　North to Slew Guillin sped.
There, as with searching glance the eye
　　O'er all the prospect roll'd,
Beside the lake a wretch we spy,
　　Poor, withered, grey, and old.
Disgust and horror touched the heart,
To see the bones all fleshless start,
　　In a frame so lank and wan;
We thought him some starved fisher, torn
From the whelming stream, by famine worn,
　　And left but the wreck of man.

We ask'd if he had chanced to see
　　A swift-paced chieftain go,
With two fleet hounds, across the lea,
　　Behind a fair young doe.

---

* "The heroes of Finn," Miss Brooke remarks, "were naturally alarmed for the safety of their general when they missed him from the feast, and recollected the determined enmity and supernatural power of the Thuatha de Danans. Caoilte, in the passage before us, seems to apprehend that Finn was snatched away by enchantment from amongst them. For a particular account of these Thuatha de Danan, the reader is referred to the ancient history of Ireland."

He gave us back no answer clear,
But in the nimble Caoilte's ear
He breathed his tale—O tale of grief!—
That in him we saw the Fenian chief!

Three sudden shouts, to hear the tale,
   Our host raised, loud and shrill—
The badgers started in the vale,
   The wild deer on the hill.

*   *   *   *   *

Of Cumhal's son then Caoilte sought
What wizard Danan foe had wrought
Such piteous change, and Finn replied,
  "'Twas Guillin's daughter—me she bound
By a sacred spell to search the tide
   Till the ring she lost was found."

Then Conan spoke in altered mood—
  "Safe may we ne'er depart
Till we see restored our chieftain good,
  Or Guillin rue his art!"
Then close around our chief we throng,
And bear him on our shields along.

Eight days and nights the cavern'd seat
Where Guillin made his dark retreat,
  We dig, with sleepless care;
Pour through the windings close the light,
Till we see, in all her radiance bright,
  Spring forth the enchantress fair.

A chalice she bore of angled mould,*
  And sparkling rich with gems and gold;

---

* "Quadrangular—the ancient cup of the Irish, called *meadar*. Specimens of it may be seen in the Antiquarian Museum of the Royal Irish Academy."

Its brimming fount in the hand she placed
Of Finn, whose looks small beauty graced;
Feeble he drinks—the potion speeds
   Through every joint and pore;
To palsied age fresh youth succeeds—
Finn, of the swift and slender steeds,
   Becomes himself once more.
His shape, his strength, his bloom returns,
And in manly glory bright he burns!

We gave three cheers that rent the air;
   The badgers fled the vale;
And now, O sage of frugal fare,
   Hast thou not heard the tale?

Another of these poems describes the descent of a Norwegian prince upon the Irish coast. The invasion of a prince of the same name is recorded in our history to have occurred at the close of the eleventh century. There is nothing but conjecture to determine whether this poem alludes to that event or one of an earlier date. Here the anachronism again occurs of introducing Oisin and St. Patrick as contemporaries, still further exaggerated by bringing Finn and his warriors back to life to contend with the host of Magnus. The dialogue previous to the tale is very similar to that in "The Chase." The bard, grown old and querulous, is very testy in his humour, and at the recollection of his Fenian compeers, like Rachel mourning for her children, refuses to be comforted.

MAGNUS THE GREAT.*

TRANSLATED BY MISS BROOKE.

* * * * *

PATRICK.

O son of Finn, the Fenii's fame
  Thou gloriest to prolong,
While I my heavenly King proclaim
  In psalms' diviner song.

---

* A naval engagement is recorded as having taken place at Dundalgin, the present Dundalk, in the tenth century, with the Danes and Northmen, under the command of Magnus, Sitric, and Tor, in which the invaders were completely routed. Whether this Magnus was the same with the one in the poem above bearing that title, is impossible to say, the name was such a common one among the Northmen. The following translation of a song written in commemoration of this naval victory, appeared anonymously in the *Belfast Chronicle:*—

  Now sheathed is the sword, and the battle is o'er,
  The shouts of the victors have ceased on the shore;
  With blood, O Dundalgin, thy billows are dyed,
  O'er the mighty of Lochlin thy deep waters glide.

  O fierce was the conflict our warriors maintain'd,
  But bright is the triumph their valour has gain'd;
  Long Erin her tears and her praises shall give,
  For life they resign'd that her glory might live.

  Though no cairns do the bones of the valiant enclose,
  On the sands of the ocean though deep they repose,
  The patriot shall turn from the high-trophied grave,
  And seek, O Dundalgin, thy sanctified wave.

  There, in grateful remembrance, their fame shall recall,
  Exult in their glory, and envy their fall,
  Who each in his death-grasp encircled a foe,
  And plunged with his prize in the billows below.

OISIN.

Dost thou insult me to my face?
   Does thy presumption dare
With the bright glories of my race
   Thy wretched psalms compare?

  *   *   *   *   *   *

PATRICK.

Pardon, great chief!—I meant no ill;
   Sweet is to me thy song,
And high the themes and lofty skill
   Its noble strains prolong.

Sing, then, sweet bard, thy purpos'd tale,
   While gladly I attend,
And let me on thy grace prevail
   Its lovely sounds to lend.

OISIN'S TALE.

Once, while we chas'd the dark-brown deer
   Along the sea-girt plain,
We saw a distant fleet appear,
   Advancing on the main.

Quick ceas'd the hunt—to east, to west
   Our rapid mandate hied;
With instant march the Fenii prest
   To join their leader's side.

  *   *   *   *   *

Then Finn, the soul of Erin's might,
   With fame and conquest crown'd,
To deeds of glory to incite,
   Address'd the heroes round.

"Which of my chiefs the first will go
    To yon insulted shore,
And bravely meet the daring foe,
    Their purpose to explore?"
   *   *   *   *   *

Bright in the glittering blades of war
    The youthful Fergus goes;
Loud sounds his martial voice afar,
    And greets the distant foes.

FERGUS—"Whence are those hosts?—come they the force
    Of Finian arms to brave?
Or wherefore do they steer their course
    O'er Erin's guarded wave?"

HERALD—"Mac Mehee, of the crimson shields,
    Fierce Magnus heads our bands,
Who Lochlin's* mighty sceptre wields,
    And mighty hosts commands."—

FERGUS—"Why does he thus our coasts explore,
    And hither lead his power?
If peace conducts him to our shore,
    He comes in happy hour."—

The furious Magnus swift replied,
    With fierce and haughty boast
(The king whose navy's speckled pride
    Defied our martial host):

MAGNUS—"I come" (he cried) "from Comhal's son,
    A hostage to obtain,
And as the meed of conquest won,
    His spouse and dog to gain;

* "Lochlin is the Gaelic name for Scandinavia in general."

"His Bran, whose fleetness mocks the wind,
  His spouse of gentle love:
Let them be now to me resign'd,
  My mightier arm to prove."—

FERGUS—"Fierce will the valiant Fenii fight,
  And thin will be their host,
Before our Bran shall in their sight
  Perform thy haughty boast;

And Finn will swell green Erin's wave
  With Lochlin's blood of pride,
Before his spouse shall be thy slave,
  And leave his faithful side."—

MAGNUS—"Now, by that generous hand of thine,
  O Fergus, hear me swear,
Though bright your Finian glories shine,
  And fierce you learn to dare;

"Or Bran shall soon the dark-brown deer
  O'er Lochlin's hills pursue;
Or soon this arm shall teach you fear,
  And your vain pride subdue."

FERGUS—"Though strong that valiant arm you deem,
  Whose might so loud you boast,
And high those martial troops esteem,
  Whose numbers hide our coast,

"Yet never with thy haughty will
  Shall Erin's chief comply,
Nor ever deer o'er Lochlin's hill
  Before our Bran shall fly."

Mild Fergus then, his errand done,
    Return'd with wonted grace,
His mind, like the unchanging sun,*
    Still beaming in his face.

Before bright honour's generous chief,
    His noble sire, he goes,
And thus unfolds in accents brief
    The message of his foes.

"Why should I from the valiant ear
    The words of death withhold,
Since to the heart that knows no fear
    All tidings may be told?

"Fierce Magnus bids thee instant yield,
    And take the granted hour,
Or soon the dire contested field
    Shall make thee feel his pow'r;

"Fleet-bounding Bran his deer to chase,
    And prove his mightier arm;
And thy soft love his halls to grace,
    And his fierce soul to charm:

"These are his proud, his stern demands,
    Or soon from shore to shore
His spear shall desolate thy lands,
    And float thy fields with gore."—

---

* "How exquisitely is the character of Fergus supported! He greets the enemy with courtesy: he is answered with insolence: yet still he retains the same equal temper for which he is everywhere distinguished. We see his spirit rise, but it is with something more noble than resentment; for his reply to Magnus breathes all the calmness of philosophy, as well as the energy of the patriot and the dignity of the hero."

FINN—"From me shall my soft love be torn,
    A stranger's halls to grace?
Or my fleet Bran away be borne,
    A stranger's deer to chase?

"Oh, first shall cease this vital breath,
    And useless be this blade;
And low in earth, and cold in death,
    This arm be powerless laid!

"O Gaul! shall these redoubted bands
    Stand cold and silent by,
And hear such insolent demands,
    And not to vengeance fly?

"Shall we not chase yon vaunting host
    With rout and death away,
And make them rue their haughty boast,
    And rue this fatal day?"—

GAUL—"Yes, by that arm of deathful might,
    Oh, Comhal's noble son:
Soon shall our swords pursue their flight,
    And soon the field be won.

"Yon king, whose ships of many waves
    Extend along our coast,
Who thus thy power insulting braves,
    And dares our gallant host—

"Soon shall this arm his fate decide,
    And, by this vengeful blade,
Shall that fierce head of gloomy pride
    In humble dust be laid!"—

* * * * *

Finn—"Blest be your souls, ye arms of war!
    (The blooming Finn exclaim'd)—
May victory bear your triumphs far,
    To distant nations fam'd!

"But, my brave troops, your chief alone
    Shall chief in danger be;
And Magnus shall be all my own,
    Whate'er the fates decree.

"Strong though his arm the war to wage,
    I mean that arm to try;
Nor from his might nor from his rage
    Shall Erin's chieftain fly."

Then, girding on each warlike blade,
    And glorying in their might,
Our martial host advanc'd, array'd
    And ardent for the fight.

    *   *   *   *

Each chief with ardent valour glows,
    To prove the faith he swore,
And forth we march to meet the foes
    Encamp'd upon the shore.

    *   *   *   *

Before us on the crowded shore
    Their gloomy standard rose,
And many a chief their navy bore,
    And many princely foes.

And many a proud and bossy shield,
    And coat of martial mail,
And warlike arms of proof they wield,
    To guard or to assail.

And many a sword with studs engrav'd
  In golden pomp was there,
And many a silken standard wav'd
  Its splendid pride in air.

*   *   *   *

And many a chief of martial fame,
  And prince of mighty sway,
All rang'd beneath our banners came
  That memorable day.

*   *   *   *

At length we moved ; then was the shock—
  Then was the battle's roar !
Re-echoing shouts from rock to rock,
  Resounding, shook the shore !

With ten-fold might each nerve was strung,
  Each bosom glow'd with flame ;
Each chief exulting forward sprung,
  And rush'd to promised fame !

The foe recoil'd—fierce on we prest
  For freedom or for death ;
Each arm to vengeance was addrest,
  And victory gasp'd for breath.

Almost the bloody field was won,
  When through the ranks of fight
Dark Lochlin's king and Cumhal's son
  Rush'd forth, like flame, to sight.

Round on their falling hosts their eyes
  With rage and grief they threw ;
Then, swift as bolts from angry skies,
  They fierce to vengeance flew !

Each chief with the collected rage
    Of his whole host was fir'd,
And dire was the suspense, O sage,
    That dreadful fight inspir'd.

As when two sinewy sons of flame
    At the dark anvil meet,
With thundering sound, and ceaseless aim,
    Their mighty hammers beat.

Such are the fierce contending kings!
    Such strokes their fury sends;
Such thunder from their weapons rings,
    And sparkling flame ascends.

Dire was the rending rage of fight,
    And arms that stream'd with gore,
Until dark Lochlin's ebbing might
    Proclaim'd the combat o'er.

Beneath the mighty Finn he lay,
    Bound on the blood-stain'd field,
No more to boast his martial sway,
    Or hostile arms to wield.

    *   *   *   *

MAGNUS—"Not for thy favour e'er to call
    My soul shall I abase;
Beneath a hero's arm I fall,
    Beneath a hero's grace."

FINN—"Since then to me the glory fell
    Thy valour to subdue,
My arm shall now thy foes repel,
    Nor injure those who sue.

"For thou thyself an hero art,
 Though fortune on thee frown;
Rise, therefore, free, and free depart,
 With unimpair'd renown.

"Or choose, strong arm of powerful might,
 Choose, Magnus, now thy course:
With generous foes in peace unite,
 Or dare again their force.

"Better our friendship to engage,
 And be in peace allied,
Than thus eternal warfare wage,
 Defying and defy'd."

MAGNUS—"O never more my arm, through life,
 Against thee, Finn, shall rise—
O never such ungrateful strife
 Shall Mehee's son devise.

"And oh, that on their hills of snow
 My youths had still remain'd,
Nor thus against a generous foe
 Unprosperous war maintain'd.

"Exulting in their conscious might,
 And glorying in their fame,
And gay with spoils of many a fight,
 And flush'd with hope they came.

"O sad reverse! O fatal hour!
 In mangled heap to die;
Too mighty Erin, to thy power
 Pale victims here they lie."

Thus was the mighty battle won
 On Erin's sounding shore,
And thus, O Clerk, great Comhal's son
 The palm of valour bore.

Alas! far sweeter to my eyes
    The triumphs of that day,
Than all the psalming songs I hear
    Where holy zealots pray.

Clerk, thou hast heard me now recite
    The tale of Lochlin's shame,
From whose fierce deeds and vanquish'd might
    The battle took its name.

And by that hand, O blameless sage,
    Hadst thou been on the shore,
To see the war our chiefs could wage,
    The sway their prowess bore—

From Laogare's sweetly flowing stream,
    Hadst thou the combat view'd,
The Fenii then thy thoughts would deem
    With matchless force endued.

Thou hast my tale—though memory bleeds,
    And sorrow wastes my frame,
Still will I tell of former deeds,
    And live on former fame.

Now old—the streams of life congeal'd,
    Bereft of all my joys,
No sword this wither'd hand can wield,
    No spear my arm employs.*

Among thy clerks my last sad hour
    Its weary scene prolongs,
And psalms must now supply the pow'r
    Of victory's lofty songs.

---

* "How beautifully pathetic is the close of this poem! Surely every reader of sensibility must sympathize with a situation so melancholy, and so very feelingly described."

That these productions, which had found their way orally to the Scottish Highlands, were the sole ground-work of the epics of Macpherson, is evident beyond a doubt. They had long existed in MS., whilst it is admitted that there were no writings in the Highland dialect, and they are devoted to the celebration of the very same heroes as the "modern antiques" of Macpherson. However disguised and altered, the plots and allusions are so essentially the same as clearly show them to have had a common origin. In the MSS., allusions to the scenery of Ireland, and to many of its well-known localities, are interwoven through the poems. In the publication of Macpherson, these are carefully expunged or, in some cases, ingeniously altered. St. Patrick is addressed in the opening of most of the Fenian poems as the "son of Calfruin," and is converted by Macpherson into Mac Alpin, a Culdee, "with whom," he tells us in his introductory dissertation, "Ossian is said to have disputed, in his extreme old age, concerning the Christian religion." Yet it is an historical fact that the Culdees—first introduced into Scotland by Columba, an Irish missionary in the sixth century—did not exist until three centuries after the time of Ossian, nor did Christianity itself exist in any part of Scotland in his time. Almhuin (Alwin), the seat of Fion, in Leinster, which is frequently noticed, is also converted into Albin or Alba, the ancient name of Scotland.*

---

* Dr. Drake, one of the dupes of the Ossianic imposture, both English and Gaelic, has made it an argument in favour of Macpherson, that the Irish literati do not give to the ancient poems of their country an antiquity which they do not really possess—as if assumption and impudent pretension were not a very easy matter. He adds that, "as the productions ascribed to the

Many of the Fenian poems, as already stated, are devoted to descriptions of natural scenery, and prove the old Celtic poets to have been exquisitely susceptible to impressions of the beauties and charms of the outward creation. For such observations, indeed, their manner of life gave them peculiar facilities—living, as they did, amid the old patriarchal habits of their people, with all their wild, picturesque accompaniments—now watching the flocks up among the pleasant hills, now chasing the brown deer over the plains. They seem even to have entered into a sort of companionship with nature. Thus, in this Lay of Bin Bolbin, the poet personifies the hill, and apostrophizes it on its unwontedly serious aspect. They left no appearance of nature unnoticed, no sound unsung. Nothing was too high or too low for their notice, from the majestic mountain, the stately river rolling its volume of waters to the main, or the stunning cataract, down to

---

Caledonian Ossian *claim* not only a higher antiquity, but are entirely free from all modern allusions and gross anachronisms, which vitiate the pretensions of the Hibernian poet, it follows, as a result of the highest probability, that the minstrelsy of the Irish Oisin and his followers was founded on the prior inspiration of the bard of Morven." (*Mornings in Spring*, vol. ii., p. 38.) That is, according to this writer, it is highly probable that productions which had existed for ages in the Irish University and elsewhere in MS. were derived from pretended oral productions assuming to have descended by memory for fifteen hundred years! With regard to anachronisms, it is evident that the writer was entirely ignorant of the subject, or he would not have asserted that the productions of Macpherson were freer from them than the Irish poems, except such as would strike a superficial reader. An intimate acquaintance with Irish literary history could scarcely be looked for in an English author; but Dr. Drake might have

the song of the blackbird, the note of the cuckoo, or the cresses on the brook. There is in this simplicity something very delightful, amid the insipid conventionalities by which we are surrounded, that comes over the spirit with a sense of unspeakable freshness and purity, like issuing from the pent-up atmosphere of a close apartment to bathe in the pure air and sunshine of heaven.

The following is one of numerous sweet fragments of this description, which have celebrated in no unworthy spirit many a hill and glen in every quarter of this ancient

---

been aware of Gibbon's detection of the anachronism respecting Caracalla (*Decline and Fall*, vol. i., ch. vi.), against whom Fingal is represented as commanding the Caledonians, in the year 208, and, after the lapse of more than a century, we find this same "King of Woody Morven" engaged in single combat with Cathmor. But Dr. Drake has actually quoted, in the article referred to, a passage from Sir John Sinclair's dissertation, professing to be taken from a Danish historian, named Suhm, which involves an anachronism as gross as any of those which appear on the face of the Fenian poems; and if the passage be a *bonâ fide* translation, the writer must have made it subsequent to the publication of Macpherson, and have taken it from that source. Here it is:—
"Swaran was the son of Starus; he had carried on many wars in Ireland, where he vanquished most of the heroes that opposed him *except Cuchullin, who, assisted by the Gaelic or Caledonian king, Fingal,* not only defeated him," &c. We should like to see the original of this passage, with an authorized translation. It appeared very satisfactory and convincing to Sir John Sinclair, and Dr. Drake retails it on trust, little aware that Cuchullin preceded Fion (or Fingal), even allowing him to have been a Caledonian king, by about 250 years. The Fenian poems never in a single instance make them contemporaries. Indeed, almost the sole anachronism in them, which is consistently carried out, and adopted for an evident purpose, is the introduction of St. Patrick in company with Ossian.

land.* The locality here apostrophized is a hill in County Sligo, and the person addressed as "son of Calfruin" is St. Patrick.

---

* Dr. Petrie, to whose pencil and pen Ireland is so deeply indebted for his masterly delineation of her scenery and his antiquarian lore, with the true instinct of genius, seemed to delight in dwelling on the scenes so illustrated. Speaking of some of the objects and scenes of interest in the vicinity of the metropolis, he remarks: "We shall only say a few words on one more—the glorious Glanasmole, or Valley of the Thrush, in which the Dodder has its source. Reader, have you ever seen this noble valley? Most probably you have not, for we know of few that have even heard of it; and yet this glen, situated within six or seven miles of Dublin, presents mountain scenery as romantic, wild, and almost as magnificent, as any to be found in Ireland. In this majestic solitude, with the lovely Dodder sparkling at our feet, and the gloomy Kippure mountain, with his head shrouded in the clouds, two thousand four hundred feet above us, we have a realization of the scenery of the Ossianic poetry. It is, indeed, the very locality in which the scenes of some of these legends are laid, as in the well-known Ossianic romance called 'The Hunt of Glanasmole;' and monuments commemorative of Fin and his heroes—'tall grey stones'—are still to be seen in the glen, and on its surrounding mountains. We could conduct our readers to the Well of Ossian, and the tomb of Fin's celebrated dog Bran, in which, perhaps, the naturalist might find and determine his species by his remains. The monument of Fin himself is on a mountain in the neighbourhood, and that of his wife, Finane, according to the legends of the place, gives name to the mountain over the glen, called Sce-Finane. But there are objects of even greater interest to the antiquary and naturalist than those, to be seen in Glanasmole, namely, the three things for which, according to some of these old bardic poems, the glen was anciently remarkable, and which were peculiar to it: these were the large breed of thrushes, from which the valley derived its name, the great size of the ivy-leaves found in its rocks, and the large berries of the rowan or mountain ash, which formerly

THE LAY OF BHIN BOLBIN.*

VERSIFIED BY THE REV DR. DRUMMOND, M.R.I.A.

Bhin Bolbin, thou art sad to-day;
Thou that wast erst of aspect gay
   And lovely to be seen;
O son of Calfruin! then 'twas sweet
To find a soft and mossy seat
   On its lofty summit green.

---

adorned its sides. The ash woods, indeed, no longer exist, having been destroyed to make charcoal above eighty years since; but shoots bearing the large berries are still to be seen; while the thrush continues in his original haunt, in the little dell at the source of the river on the side of Kippure, undisturbed and undiminished in size, and the giant ivy clings to the rocks as large as ever; we have seen leaves of it from seven to ten inches in diameter. We should also state that to the geologist Glanasmole is as interesting as to the painter, antiquary, or naturalist, as our friend Dr. Schouler will show our readers."

* The original is preserved by Mr. Hardiman (*Irish Minstrelsy*, vol. ii., p. 386).

The reader may not be displeased with the following literal translation, from the *Dublin Penny Journal*, vol. iii., p. 128:—

"Thou art sad to-day, O Bin Bolbin! gentle height of the beauteous aspect! It was pleasant, O son of Calfruin! in other days to be upon its summit; many were the dogs and the youths; oft arose the sounds of the chase. There a tower arose: there dwelt a mighty hero. O lofty hill of contests! many were the herons in the season of night, and the birds of the heath on the mountains, mingling their sounds with the music of the little birds. 'Twas sweet to listen to the cry of the valleys, and the wonderful son of the rock [echo]. Each of our heroes would be present, with his beautiful dog in the slip. Many were the lovely maids of our race that collected in the wood. There grew the berries of fragrant blossom; the strawberries and the blackberries; there grew the soft, blushing flower of the mountain,

Thou hill of battles, stained with gore,
   How oft from thy fortress strong around,
Where dwelt a hero bold of yore,
   Rose music sweet of horn and hound;
The bittern round thee boom'd at night,
The grouse, loud-whirring in her flight,
Peopled thy heath, and every tree
Rang with the small birds' melody.

Yes, 'twas delight to hear the cry
   Of hounds along the valley sweep;
To hear the rock's wild son* reply,
   From every cliff and steep;
To see the chiefs of the Fenian band;
To slip, the grey-hounds ready stand;
And grouping maidens, young and fair,
That pluck'd, as they went, the flow'rets rare;
With berries of every form and hue,
Of crimson blush, or of glossy blue,
From bramble and bush; or cresses young,
That by the crystal streamlet sprung:
And passing sweet was the voice of their song,
As the fair-hair'd damsels roved along.

Sweet, too, by the source of the lonely stream
   To see, aloof, the eagle sail;
   To hear her solitary scream

---

and the tender cresses. There wandered the slender, fair-haired daughters of our race; sweet was the sound of their song. It was a source of delight to behold the eagle, and listen to her lonely scream, to hear the growl of the otters, and the snarling of the foxes; and the black-bird singing sweet on the tip of the thorn. I assure thee, O Patrick, that it was a pleasant place. We dwell on the top of this hill, the seven bards of the Fenians. But few are my friends to-night; is not my tale mournful?"

   * Echo—literally, son of the rock.

Burst startling o'er the vale;
To hear the otter's whining note;
  Or, 'mid the hollow mountain-rocks,
  The barking of the wary fox,
Or mellow song of the blackbird float
From bower and grove, o'er wood and lawn,
To evening hour from early dawn.
With joy it thrill'd my heart, I vow,
To sit upon the mountain's brow,
  And all the glorious landscape view,
The seven brave Fenian bands around,
In war, in peace, still faithful found—
  But now my friends are few!
Then, merry and gay, in the summer ray,
  They frolick'd and they shone;
With autumn's blast away they pass'd,
  And I am left alone.
My fate with tears may dim your eye,
And wake your tender sympathy.

    The following is another of the same description, all of which, if collected, would form an interesting illustration of the scenery of Ireland. It consists of a short, wild story of a blackbird, which, the poet says, was brought by Fion from Scandinavia, in an expedition which, it appears, he made to that country, if the author be not drawing upon his imagination. The translator says of the original of this piece, which he has preserved: "Here the alliterations, unions, correspondences, auricular harmonies, and other particulars requisite to the accuracy and elegance of Irish poetry, are most scrupulously and chastely preserved."*

---

   * *Trans. of Dub. Gaelic Soc.* The writer afterwards explains the nature and constituent elements of the ancient Irish poetry: "In Irish poetry there are several principal circumstances to be observed. The first is, that it must consist of stanzas of four lines (or quartans), including a determinate sense; each line, or

THE BLACKBIRD OF THE GROVE OF CARNA.

VERSIFIED BY WM. LEAHY.

Hail, tuneful bird of sable wing,
  Thou warbler sweet of Carna's grove !*
Not lays more charming will I hear,
  Tho' round the expansive earth I rove.

No melody's more soft than thine,
  While perch'd thy mossy nest beneath :
How sad to miss thy soothing song !
  When harmony divine you breathe.

O son of Calfron, cease thy bells,
  Cease thy hollow-sounding strain :
To Carna's grove thine ear incline—
  Thou wilt o'ertake thy psalms again.

    *   *   *   *

Found was the bird on Lochlin's† plains
  (Where purling flows the azure stream)
By Comhal's son, for goblets famed,
  Which bright with golden splendour beam.

---

quartan, must consist of seven syllables, and no irregular ellipsis is admitted; that is, no *poetic licence*, as it is so abusively called, is admissible. . . There must be alliteration between the different parts of speech, nouns, pronouns, and verbs, which the Irish poets name *concord;* there must be an agreement of words and syllables, which they call *correspondence;* there must be *union*, or *auricular harmony*, which is to have the vowels and diphthongs correspond in sound and rhythmical termination, not at all depending on unity, like English rhyme, but similarity of letters. These are the prominent features of Irish poetry, to all of which annexes many a critical adjunct."

  * "Derry-carn, in the Co. of Meath."

  † Lochlin, the general name for Scandinavia, signifying "the country of the lakes."

Yon lofty wood in Carna's grove,
    Which bends to west its awful shade,
Where, pleased with nature's wild display,
    The Fians—noble race—delay'd.

In that retired and dusky wood
    The bird of sable wing was laid:
Where the majestic oak extends
    His stately boughs in leafy shade.

The sable bird's harmonious note,
    The lowing hind of Cora's steep,
Were wont, at morning's early dawn,
    To lull the mighty Finn asleep.

The noise which haunts the weedy pond,
    That into triple straight divides:
Where, cooling in the crystal wave,
    The bird of silver plumage glides.

The twitt'ring hens on Croan's heath,
    And from yon water-girded hill,
The deepening voice of gloomy woe,
    Sad, pensive, melancholy, shrill.

The eagle's scream from Foat's vale,
    From the tall pine the cuckoo's song,
The music of the hounds, that fly
    The coral-pebbled strand along.

When lived brave Finn, and all his chiefs,
    The heath did more the heroes please—
Than church or bell they'd dearer deem
    The sable bird's melodious lays.

With one other specimen we take leave of this particular class of the Fenian poems. It is descriptive of the well-known and celebrated scene—once a favourite seat of the Fians—north of the highly picturesque bay of Dublin, under its ancient name of Ben Edir, and is not unworthy of the scene it describes.

ODE TO THE HILL OF HOWTH.

VERSIFIED BY THE REV. DR. DRUMMOND.

How sweet, from proud Ben Edir's height,
To see the ocean roll in light ;
And fleets, swift bounding on the gale,
With warriors clothed in shining mail.

Fair hill, on thee great Finn of old
Was wont his counsels sage to hold ;
On thee rich bowls the Fenians crown'd,
And pass'd the foaming beverage round.

'Twas thine, within a sea-wash'd cave,
To hide and shelter Duivne brave ;
When snared by Grace's charms divine,
He bore her o'er the raging brine.*

Fair hill, thy slopes are ever seen
Bedeck'd with flowers, or robed in green ;
Thy nut-groves rustle o'er the deep,
And forests crown thy cliff-girt steep.

---

* "The circumstance," says Mr. Hardiman, "alluded to in this stanza forms the subject of one of the finest-wrought romantic tales in the Irish language."—*Irish Minstrelsy*, vol. ii., p. 389.

High from thy raisèd peaks 'tis sweet
To see th' embattled war-ships meet;
To hear the crash—the shout—the roar
Of cannon, through the cavern'd shore.

Most beauteous hill, around whose head
Ten thousand sea-birds' pinions spread;
May joy thy lord's true bosom thrill,
Chief of the Fenians' happy hill.

The following will afford a specimen of the heroic class of the Fenian ballads, though it does not approach many others of its class in merit or interest, but is given to avoid drawing too largely from any one collection:—

TALC, THE SON OF TRONE.*

METRICAL VERSION BY W. LEAHY.

Behold yon hill of slaughter rise
  (For ever will it hold the name),
That bends the dreadful brow to west:
  Dire is the cause, but great the fame.

One day brave Finn and all his train,
  No strangers to the toil of fight,
With all their great and mighty hosts,
  Assembled on its airy height.

---

* "Signifies 'the firm, son of the mighty.'"—*Trans. Dub. Gaelic Soc.*

O'er steed-renown'd Ierne's plain,
    As paced a maid with mournful air—
The chiefs beheld, and saw the dame,
    Than sun's refulgent beam more fair.

She came, in purple robe array'd,
    And first great Cumhal's son address'd,
Whose graceful and majestic mien
    Transcendant shone above the rest.

" O speak again ! " exclaim'd the chief,
" And all reserve, fair maid, resign,
For more harmonious is thy voice
    Than sweetest melody divine !

" O speak ! and who thou art declare."
    She answer'd : " Nivra* is my name."†

    *   *   *   *

" Why hast thou fled thy father's halls ?
    To me the uncertain cause unfold :
My arm shall ever be thy guard—
    Then be thy sorrow's secret told."

" Hear, then, great chief, my woeful tale,
    And in my faithful word confide :
The monarch pledged his sacred oath
    That I should be the royal bride

" Of Tale, the dreadful son of Trone ;
    A monster of such horrid mien,
As fills my trembling soul with fear,
    And chills the blood within my vein !

---

* " Signifies 'splendid, youthful form.'"—*Trans. Dub. Gaelic Soc.*
† The next lines are omitted as out of keeping with the uniform Scandinavian origin of these legends.

"Between his brawny shoulders wide,
  A cat's terrific form he rears,*
With winding tail, uplifted paws,
  And fiery eyes, and frightful ears.

"Thrice round the earth I sought the aid
  Of every king, but sought in vain.
None dared to vindicate my cause.
  I now implore the Finian train."

"Sweet maid, I'll be thy sure defence,"
  Cumhal's conquering son replied :
"Nor shalt thou go before the strength
  Of all the Finian host be tried.

"Full seven legions in thy cause,
  Expert the brazen spear to wield,
Shall conquer—or expire, and leave
  Their breathless bodies on the field."

"Ah! by thy valorous hand, O Finn!
  I tremble, lest thy might be vain.
Beneath his stroke from whom I fly
  An hundred hosts would press the plain."

---

* "The warriors in ancient times were accustomed to wear on their armour the skins of the wild beasts they had slain; thus the celebrated casque of Ulysses, as he and Diomed prepare to go as spies to the Trojan camp, is described by Homer as covered with the skin of a wild boar—

————'without, in order spread,
A boar's white teeth grinn'd horrid o'er his head.'
                                                POPE.

The skin of the lion-cat in Persia, described by Dr. Goldsmith as larger and more fierce than even the wild one, may have covered the helm of this eastern warrior."

"Resplendent maid, of heav'nly mien,
　　Whose yellow tresses curling fold
And play around thy lily neck,
　　More beaming bright than purest gold,

"No region of the expansive earth
　　Could e'er a mighty champion boast,
Whose conqueror would not be found
　　Amid the Finians' fearless host."

Then distant, landing on the shore,
　　Appear'd a chief of stately mien,
Upon whose dire and hideous crest
　　A cat's fierce front was dreadful seen.

To where the assembled legions stood
　　He sternly turn'd with conscious might,
And proudly frowning on their chief,
　　Demanded or the maid or fight.

Three hundred leaders brave, who rush'd
　　Where'er the fire of battle burn'd,
Advanced to meet the stranger's rage,
　　But from his steel, ah! ne'er return'd.

O Patrick, of the creed severe,
　　Full ten hundred heroes slain
We lost that day in dreadful fight,
　　Which sad depress'd our weaken'd train.

When Osgar view'd the slaughter'd pile,
　　Fierce fury fir'd his rolling eye,
Finn's leave he ask'd—while I, intent,
　　Reluctant heard the chief's reply:

"Go, noble youth, I give thee leave,
    Though much thy gloomy fate I dread—
Forget not now thy deeds of fame;
    May glory beam around thy head."

For five long days and tedious nights
    Both heroes contest dire maintain'd—
Their weary limbs not eas'd by rest,
    Or fainting frames by food sustain'd.

Great Talc at length sinks pale to earth—
    In death his swimming eye-balls roll;
Yielding to Osgar's force supreme,
    He gasping breathes his mighty soul.

Three shouts resound aloud in air,
    And dreadful echo o'er the plain—
One to deplore our slaughter'd host,
    And two of joy that Talc was slain.

But Nivra fair, appall'd to see
    Such direful carnage all around—
Her crimson cheek grew silver pale—
    She, lifeless, sunk upon the ground!

And when the royal maid expired,
    Whose wrongs so bravely were redress'd,
More than the host of heroes slain,
    It fill'd with sorrow ev'ry breast.

O Patrick of the crosier fair,
    This dreadful tale will e'er be told;
Yon mount's the hill of slaughter dire
    Which now thy wond'ring eyes behold.

The tradition of Oisin having survived till the arrival of St. Patrick, to whom he is said to have narrated the Fenian exploits, which found its way into the *Book of Howth*, has evidently arisen from these supposititious ballads.

Though the power of the Norsemen had been effectually crushed for the time by King Brian, yet their restless energies had a salient power that only sunk under defeat to rebound again with elastic spring and redoubled force. Hydra-like, no sooner was one head cut off, than its place was supplied by many others. The same remarkable characteristic was also observable in their aggressions on the sister countries. The secret of this was, that they had settlements in the Orkneys, the Isle of Man, &c., which were in constant communication with each other. From the time of the Norman conquest of England, the Norsemen who still remained in the seaports of Ireland, and had never relinquished their ambitious designs upon the kingdom, entered into correspondence with that warlike people, with whom they were connected by the ties of ancient affinity, urging them to follow up what they had begun, by bringing this island also under their sway. And well had it been for the country if they had acted upon that advice, and had done their work as effectually as in the sister island, and not in that spirit of private enterprise and aggrandizement which afterwards characterized the undertaking, and was the fruitful source of all the subsequent miseries of the nation—a half-subjugation, an incomplete conquest. The invasion of this country was, therefore, a scheme which had long been contemplated, and if it had not taken place at the time and in the manner it did, would most probably have been undertaken, at the instigation of the resident citizens of Danish descent, by some other branch of the Norman race.

The distracted condition of the kingdom during the long period of the Danish incursions was perpetuated by the Anglo-Norman invasion, which occurred in the latter part of the twelfth century.*

A.D. 1169-70. This event was almost anomalous in its circumstances and results. In England, little more than a century previously, the Normans had effected a complete

---

* It is with regret that the writer observes in a publication so respectable and useful as Chambers's *Information for the People* (No. 9, p. 131) a series of the grossest errors and misstatements on this subject in the course of a few sentences. "The people of Ireland," it is there stated, "*being quite uncivilized*, were perpetually quarrelling among themselves; and this, *with their heathen religion*, furnished a flimsy pretext for invading them from England. Dermod Mac Morrough, King of Leinster, *having been dethroned by his subjects*, introduced an English warrior, &c. .... A body of 50 knights, 90 esquires, and 460 archers, *in all six hundred men, was enabled*, by its superior discipline, *to overthrow the whole warlike force that could be brought against them*." So it appears that our countrymen in the twelfth century were not only literally heathens, and quite uncivilized, but overcome by 600 Norman warriors. This beats even Cambrensis hollow. Perhaps a greater tissue of ignorance and misstatement was never put together in the same compass by any writer on the subject of which he professes to treat. Did this writer ever see the golden ornaments of curious workmanship of the people he stigmatises as *quite uncivilized*—specimens of which are preserved in the Museum of the Royal Irish Academy in Dublin—or the beautiful cross of Cong, manufactured by the goldsmith of O'Conor, brother of the King of Ireland, at the very period of the invasion? Or had he ever heard of such a person as St. Patrick, who, seven centuries previously, had converted these heathens to Christianity? If he had consulted Mosheim's Church History, Bede, and other authorities, instead of copying the slanders of Hume, with gratuitous additions, he would have found that these

and decisive conquest, that resulted in the recognised supremacy of a new dynasty, which, by the exercise of a vigorous power, of forbearance, and by the interchange of good offices with the conquered inhabitants, established a common language and interest in the kingdom. The English national character thus derived a positive advantage from this amalgamation with a polished and chivalrous race, superior in

---

people, professing, according to him, a "heathen religion," had, four or five centuries previously, even sent out a succession of the most eminent missionaries as well to England and Scotland as to the Continent, and that students flocked from all parts of the civilized world to study in Ireland. Neither was Mac Morrough dethroned *by his subjects*, but by a confederacy of the other powers of the island against him. Nor does the assumption that the 600 Anglo-Normans, even admitting their superior discipline—as Cambrensis tells us they were the *picked men* of Wales, and the power of the Norman cross-bows of their fathers had decided the fate of England in the single battle of Hastings—were enabled to overthrow the whole warlike force of the kingdom, rest on any better foundation. *Had the King of Leinster no men of his own* to aid his allies? Maurice O'Regan, who was Secretary to Mac Morrough, has left a fragment of the history of the transaction, which was translated from the Latin by Sir Geo. Carew, himself a descendant of Fitzstephen's, and President of Munster in the time of Elizabeth. From that most curious and interesting document we learn that, on the arrival of the Norman auxiliaries, "Dermond assemblid, with grete expedition, all his forces, *to the number of thre thousande*, besides thre hundreth Englishe, and marched towards Ossory," &c. (p. 15). But still further; when the additional supplies, under Raymond le Gros and Earl Strongbow, arrived, and they marched to Dublin, O'Regan informs us:—"Miles de Cogan was ordained to march in the vanguard with a regiment of 700 (Englishe) strong, and with Donnel Kevannagh, with his Irish, next unto him. Raymond le Gros led the battle, with his regiment of *eight hundreth English*, and with him the King of Leinster, with a thousand of his followers; the rear, with *thre*

civilization to their Saxon predecessors. In Ireland, however, the Anglo-Norman invasion was comparatively private. The settlement was confined to a few counties adjoining the metropolis, called the Pale ; The native chiefs of the other districts still ruled their clans in undisputed sovereignty, merely paying their stipulated tribute to the English crown,

---

thousand *English*, was commanded by the Earle (Strongbow), and in the rear of him a regiment of Irishmen " (p. 25).

So much for the statement of 600 Englishmen in all. It is really too bad that persons professing to write history should be guilty of such gross and invidious misstatements, to be disseminated among the masses. It is to be hoped that the Messrs. Chambers will in a future edition have the discreditable statements of this writer corrected, if not already done.

With regard to the general question of the facility with which the invaders succeeded in making good their footing in the country, it must never be forgotten that the king of one great province (Leinster) was their ally, while there was no central controlling power of sufficient authority over the provincial kings to counteract the designs of so formidable an enemy. But why should Ireland be made the subject of such illiberal and invidious remark, under the specious pretence of censuring the "flimsy pretext" of her invaders? She may at least boast that she did not, like the English at Hastings, with the forefathers of these very Norman invaders, relinquish her liberty after a single contest. In 1174, 1192, and 1195, the invaders met with three great defeats ; and Strongbow was obliged to remain in concealment till he effected his escape to Dublin.

But though truth and justice require thus much, it must be confessed no apology can be offered for the early, abject, voluntary submission of the southern chiefs, O'Brien, Mac Carthy, and others, to the English Crown, for they had not even the excuse of Mac Morrough. With the exception of the brilliant exploits of Cathal the Red-handed O'Conor, the northern chiefs alone— O'Neill, O'Donnell, and O'Kane—maintained for any length of time the dignity of their country, even after the cause of her independence had become hopeless.

and the great body of the nation continued to speak their own language, observe their own customs, and to be governed by their own laws. The spirit of aggression and retaliation, however, which such a state of things could not fail to engender, was fatal to the progress of civilization or the cultivation of refined pursuits. The liberal arts will not long dwell among a people who are ever engaged in warding off anticipated injuries or avenging inflicted wrongs. The poetic spirit naturally languished under such adverse influences. In the early part of the twelfth century, a few names of note are indeed found. Among these may be mentioned O'MULCONRY, whose poem on the aboriginal tribes of Ireland is preserved by the annalists; O'CASSIDY, a learned historical poet, one of the best of whose pieces is given in Dr. O'Connor's truly splendid work, the *Rerum Hibernicarum Scriptores;* and O'DUN, bard to the prince of Leinster, whose historical poems are also preserved by the annalists. The latter died about 1160.* These bards flourished immediately preceding the Anglo-Norman invasion. Subsequent to that event, scarcely another name occurs for a long period.

Though the poetical art languished, it appears from the glowing account of Giraldus Cambrensis, that its twin sister, music, was still cultivated and brought to exquisite perfection, the secret of which seems to have been altogether lost in subsequent times. Gerald Barry, commonly known as Giraldus Cambrensis, was a Welshman who came over to Ireland in the capacity of chaplain to King John, in 1185, and gained great notoriety by the calumnies which he published against the country; so his testimony with regard to

---

* *Irish Minstrelsy,* vol. i., p. 15.

its music cannot be attributed to any national prepossession. In music, Giraldus considered the skill of the Irish "incomparably superior to that of any other nation. For their modulations are not slow and morose, as in the instruments of Britain, to which we are habituated; but the sounds are rapid and precipitate, yet sweet and pleasing. It is wonderful that the musical proportion is preserved amidst such precipitate velocity of the fingers, and that the melody is rendered full and perfect by an undeviating art, amidst such trembling modulations, such organic tones, so infinitely intricate—possessed of such agreeable swiftness, such unequal parity, such discordant concord. Whether the chords of the diatesseron or diapente be struck together, they begin and terminate in dulce, that all may be perfectly completed in charming, sonorous melody. They commence and close their modulations with so much subtility, and the tinklings of the slender strings sport so freely with the deep tones of the bass chords, so delicately pleasing, so softly soothing, that it is manifest the perfection of their art lies in concealing art," &c. The Welshman little thought that it was not possible for a people cultivating, in such unrivalled perfection, one of the most civilized and civilizing of arts, to have been the barbarians he represents them. Many other testimonies to the high reputation of the early Irish minstrelsy might be adduced. Ranulph Higden, in the thirteenth century, styles the Irish "musica peritissimi;" and Fuller says that at the "Holy War" all the concert of Christendom would have made but imperfect music if the Irish harp had been absent. In the opinion of the great Bacon, "no harp hath the sound so melting and prolonged as the Irish harp;" and the famous John Evelyn considered it "far superior to the lute itself, or whatever speaks with strings."

The peculiar genius of the nation, however, could not be wholly suppressed, but would occasionally burst out under the most adverse circumstances. Accordingly, in the course of the thirteenth and fourteenth centuries, we find several bards of note. Among the first of these, both in point of time and ability, was Donogh More O'Daly, Abbot of Boyle, in Co. Roscommon, a man of great learning, whose sweetly flowing numbers gained for him the appellation of "the Ovid of Ireland." His poems were chiefly on divine subjects, and many of them are still retained among the peasantry. Conway, bard to the O'Donnells of Tyrone, who flourished about the same period, distinguished himself by some spirited productions in celebration of the great line of chiefs to whose house he was attached. Carol O'Daly, brother to the distinguished poet of that name, above mentioned, was the author of the celebrated song of "Eileen a Roon," which has been pronounced by competent judges to contain more music in fewer notes than almost any other lyric in existence. Handel and Geminiani, the great composers, united in eulogy of it. The former is stated to have declared that he would rather be the author of that simple air than of the most elaborate composition he had ever published. Like many other of our ancient songs, it has been plagiarized in Scotland, under the title of "Robin Adair." In the correspondence between the poet Burns and Thompson, the publisher of a collection of the melodies of Scotland, the former seems quite aware of the fact that many of the finest airs which were current in his country did not of right belong to it, and speaks of the Irish harpers, who in former times resorted thither, as the persons who introduced them. Our subject, however, is poetry, not music. The circumstances attending the production of this exquisite composition have in substance been thus stated :—

Carol O'Daly, who appears to have been one of the most accomplished men of his day, paid his addresses to Ellen, the daughter of a Leinster chieftain of the name of Kavanagh, a young lady of great beauty and merit. The attachment, however, though mutual, was no exception to the general "course of true love." The lady's friends, from whatever cause, were opposed to the match, and O'Daly being obliged to leave home for a considerable time, they took every means of representing him as false, and as having gone to wed another. In this belief the lady was persuaded to accept the addresses of a rival suitor. The day for the marriage was fixed, and O'Daly only returned the previous evening to hear of his blighted hopes. It was under the intense feelings which such a situation would naturally inspire, that he composed the song. Disguised as a harper, he presented himself on the eve of the wedding, and being called upon by Ellen herself to play, he drew forth tones of such exquisite tenderness from the strings as seemed to echo the feelings of his soul. The effect was irresistible, and the young lady, discovering her lover under his disguise, rewarded his fidelity and disappointed the treachery of her friends, by bestowing her hand upon the man of her choice.* The original words are exceedingly simple, and only remarkable as containing, and probably originating, the well-known expression of Irish hospitality, "Cead Mille Failte." The following version is by the spirited and lamented translator of Carolan :—

---

* *Irish Minstrelsy*, vol. i., p. 356.

EILEEN A ROON.*

TRANSLATED BY THOMAS FURLONG.

I'll love thee evermore,
    Eileen a Roon!
I'll bless thee o'er and o'er,
    Eileen a Roon!
Oh, for thy sake I'll tread
Where the plains of Mayo spread,
By hope still fondly led,
    Eileen a Roon!

Oh, how may I gain thee,
    Eileen a Roon?
Shall feasting entertain thee,
    Eileen a Roon?
I would range the world wide,
With love alone to guide,
To win thee for my bride,
    Eileen a Roon!

Then wilt thou come away,
    Eileen a Roon?
Oh, wilt thou come or stay,
    Eileen a Roon?
Oh! yes, oh yes, with thee
I will wander far and free,
And thy only love shall be,
    Eileen a Roon!

---

* *Eileen a Roon* signifies "Ellen, the secret treasure of my heart."

A hundred thousand welcomes,
                Eileen a Roon !
A hundred thousand welcomes,
                Eileen a Roon !
Oh, welcome evermore,
With welcomes yet in store,
Till love and life are o'er,
                Eileen a Roon.*

---

* Another version of this famed song is here given :—

EILEEN A ROON.*

METRICAL VERSION BY J. C. MANGAN.

For ever, for ever, you have my heart,
                O Eileen a-Roon!
'Tis rueful, 'tis woeful, when lovers part,
                O Eileen a-Roon!
Mayo would I travel from morn to night,
For one sweet smile of your face of light,
For one soft kiss from your red lips bright,
                My Eileen a-Roon!

O! how shall I woo you—how make you mine—
                Fair Eileen a-Roon?
Can warm words win you? can gold? can wine?
                Sweet Eileen a-Roon?
I would walk the wide world from east to west,
Inspired by love, if I could but rest
One heavenly hour on your beauteous breast,
                O Eileen a-Roon!

Come with me, come with me, then, darling one!
                Come, Eileen a-Roon!
The moments are precious—Oh, let us be gone,
                My Eileen a-Roon!

---

* *Dublin University Mag.*, vol. xxxii., p. 543.

The gift of poetry appears to have been hereditary in the family of O'Daly, there having been at least sixteen poets of that name.

The following very curious and interesting ballad on the fortification of Ross Mac-Bruin, since called New Ross, in Wexford, which was formerly a place of considerable importance, affords one of the earliest examples, on Irish ground, of the display of that corporate or municipal spirit to which we owe the birth of European liberty. The cause of the spirited resolution taken by the people of Ross to fortify their town was the lawless disposition of their neighbours, who would sometimes ride openly into their marts, and pillage their merchants with impunity, but chiefly the dread inspired by the deadly feud of two of the most powerful and turbulent barons in the kingdom—Maurice Fitzmaurice, chief of the Geraldine faction, whose descendants were afterwards Earls of Desmond, and the other probably Walter de Burgo, Earl of Ulster, in right of his wife, who was daughter of Hugh de Lacy. Mr. Croker, however, thinks it not improbable that

A.D. 1265.

> To the uttermost bounds of the world I'll go
> With you, my beloved, come weal or woe,
> You, you are my heaven on earth below,
>   O Eileen a-Roon!
>
> And all my glad kindred shall welcome you,
>   My Eileen a-Roon!
> With a hundred thousand welcomes true,
>   Sweet Eileen a-Roon!
> And love and rich plenty shall bless our home,
> As though 'twere a royallest palace dome;
> We both will be happy till death shall come,
>   O Eileen a-Roon!

this Sir Walter—for the Christian names only are given in
the poem—was rather one of the Le Poers, who is noticed
by Holinshed, in 1302, as having "wasted a great part of
Munster, burning many farmes and places in that countrie."
The original, which is in Norman-French, is preserved in
an ancient MS. volume, consisting of miscellaneous pieces
in prose and verse, sometimes called the Book of Ross or
Waterford, and now in the Harleian collection in the
British Museum. The author of the ballad was a friar
named Michael, of Kyldare, who was an eye-witness of the
transaction. The metrical translation was made by the
distinguished Mrs. Maclean, better known as Miss Landon
(L.E.L.), at the request of Mr. T. C. Croker, the ingenious
author of *Fairy Legends of the South of Ireland*, who
inserted it in the work which, by a singular misnomer, he
published under the title of *Popular Songs of Ireland*. In
that work the reader may find a very full and elaborate
account of the poem.

ON THE ENTRENCHMENT OF ROSS, A.D. 1265.*

METRICAL VERSION BY THE LATE MRS. MACLEAN (L.E.L.).

> I have a whim to speak in verse,
> If you will list what I rehearse,
> For an unheeded tale, I wisse,
> Not worth a clove of garlic is.

---

* We find an anonymous literal translation of this curious and
valuable poem in the *Dublin Penny Journal* (vol iii., p. 123), with
which the reader may feel gratified. The poem begins in the
following whimsical manner :—

" I have an inclination to write in romance, if it pleases you to
hear me ; for a story that is not listened to is of no more value

Please you, then, to understand
'Tis of a town in Ireland;
For its size the one most fair
That I know of anywhere.
But the town had cause of dread
In the feud two barons spread;
Sir Maurice and Sir Walter—see,
Here their names shall written be;
Also that fair city's name—
Ross they then did call the same.

---

than a berry. I pray you, therefore, to give attention, and you shall hear a fine adventure of a town in Ireland, the most beautiful of its size that I know of in any country. Its inhabitants were alarmed by the feud existing between two barons, whose names you see here written—Sir Maurice [Fitzmaurice] and Sir Walter [Sir Walter de Burgo]. The name of the town I shall now disclose to you: it is called Ros—it is the New Pont de Ros." The author then proceeds to relate how the principal men of the town, together with the commonalty, assembled to take measures for their safety; and they resolved to surround the town with mortar and stone. They commenced, accordingly, on the Feast of the Purification (Feb. 2, A.D. 1265), and marked out the fosse, or line of circumvallation. Workmen were speedily hired, and above an hundred each day came out to labour, under the direction of the burgesses. When this step was taken, they again assembled and determined to establish a by-law, such" (says the poet) "as was never heard of in England or France; which was publicly proclaimed next day to the people, and received with applause; this law was as follows: "That on the ensuing Monday, the vintners, the mercers, the merchants, and the drapers, should go and work at the fosse, from the hour of prime till noon." This was readily complied with, "and above one thousand men" (writes the poet) "went out to work every Monday, with brave banners, and great pomp, attended by flutes and tabors. So soon as the hour of noon had sounded, these fine fellows returned home, with their banners before them, and the young men singing loudly, and carolling through the town. The priests, also, who accompanied, fell to

'Tis the New Bridge town of Ross,
Which no walls did then enclose;
It therefore feared a stranger's blows.
Commons both and leading men
Gathered in the council then,
What for safety to devise,
In shortest time and lowest price:
'Twas that round the town be thrown
Walls of mortar and of stone.
For this war filled them with fear;
Much they dreaded broil so near.

---

work at the fosse, and laboured right well, more so than the others, being young and skilful, of tall stature, strong, and well-housed. The mariners, likewise, proceeded in good array to the fosse, to the number of six hundred, with a banner preceding them, on which was depicted a vessel; and if all the people in the ships and barges had been hired, they would have amounted to eleven hundred men. On Tuesday this party was succeeded by another, consisting of the tailors and cloth-workers, the tent-makers, pellers and celers [saddlers, from the French "selliers"], who went out in a similar manner as the former, but were not so numerous, amounting only to four hundred men. On the Wednesday a different set was employed, namely, the cordwainers, tanners, and butchers; many brave bachelors were among them, and their banners were painted as appertains to their craft. In number, I believe they were about three hundred, taken together, little and great; and they went forth carolling loudly, as the others did. On the Thursday, came the fishermen and hucksters. Their standards were of various sorts; but on one was painted a fish and a platter; these, five hundred in number, were associated with the wain-rights, who were thirty-two in number. On Friday went the . . . . [*illegible*] in number three hundred and fifty, with their banners borne before them unto the border of the fosse. On the Saturday succeeded the carpenters, black-smiths, and masons, in number about three hundred and fifty. Lastly, on the Sunday, assembled in procession the ladies of the town. Know,

Candlemas, it was the day,
They began to delve in clay,
Marking out a fosse, to shew
Where the future wall should go.
Soon 'twas traced, and then were hired
Workmen; all the task desired.
More than a hundred workmen ply
Daily 'neath the townsmen's eye;
Yet small advance these fellows made,
Though to labour they were paid.

---

verily, that they were excellent labourers, but their numbers I cannot certainly tell; but they all went forth to cast stones and carry them from the fosse. Whoever had been there to look at them, might have seen many a beautiful woman—many a mantle of scarlet, green, and russet—many a fair folded cloak, and many a gay-coloured garment. In all the countries I ever visited, never saw I so many fair ladies. He should have been born in a fortunate hour who might make his choice among them." The ladies also carried banners, in imitation of the other parties; and when they were tired of the duty assigned them, they walked round the fosse, singing sweetly to encourage the workmen. On their return to the town, the richer sort held a convivial meeting, and, as we are told, "made sport, drank whiskey, and sang, encouraging each other, and resolving to make a gate which should be called the Ladies' Gate, and there would fix a prison." According to the poet, "the fosse was made twenty feet in depth, and extended above a league. When it shall be completed," he adds, "they may sleep securely, and will not require a guard; for if forty thousand men were to attack the town, they never would be able to enter it, for they have sufficient means of defence; many a white hauberk and haubergeon—many a doublet and coat of mail, and many a savage Garçon—many a good cross-bowman have they, and many good archers. Never in any town beheld I so many good glaives, nor so many good cross-bows hanging on the wall, nor so many quarrels to shoot withal, and every house full of maces, good shields, and talevaces. They are well provided, I warrant you, to defend themselves from their enemies; for

So the council met again ;
Such a law as they pass'd then !
Such a law might not be found,
Nor on French, nor English ground.
Next day, a summons, read aloud,
Gathered speedily a crowd ;
When the law proclaimed they hear,
'Twas received with many a cheer.
Then a good man did advance,
And explained the ordinance ;
Vintners, drapers, merchants, all
Were to labour at the wall,
From the early morning time
Till the day was in its prime.

---

the cross-bowmen in reality amount to three hundred and sixty-three in number, as counted at their muster, and enrolled in the muster-roll. And of other archers have they one thousand two hundred, brave fellows, be assured ; and besides these, there are three thousand men, armed with lances or axes, in the town ; and knights on horseback one hundred and four, well armed for the combat."

The poet then assures us that the object of the inhabitants was by no means to court an assault, but simply their own protection; "for which," says he, "no one ought to blame them :" they, however, appear to have amply provided for their safety, for the writer continues : "When the wall shall be completely carried out and fortified, no one in Ireland will be so hardy as to attack them ; for, by the time they have twice sounded a horn, the people assemble and fly to arms, each anxious to be before his neighbour, so courageous and valiant are they to avenge themselves on an enemy. God grant they may obtain revenge, and preserve the town with honour ! And let all say Amen, for charite ! for it is the most hospitable town that exists in any nation, and every stranger is welcomed with joy, and may buy and sell at his will, without anything being demanded of him. I commend the town, and all who inhabit it, to God. Amen."

More than a thousand men, I say,
Went to the goodly work each day.
  Monday, they began their labours
Gay with banners, flutes, and tabours ;
Soon as the noon-hour was come,
These good people hastened home,
With their banners proudly borne.
Then the youths advanced in turn,
And the town they make it ring
With their merry carolling :
Singing loud and full of mirth,
Away they go to shovel earth.
And the priests, when mass was chanted,
In the fosse they dug and panted ;
Quicker, harder, worked each brother,
Harder far than any other ;
For both old and young did feel
Great and strong with holy zeal.
Mariners came next, and they
Pass'd along in fair array,
With their banners borne before,
Which a painted vessel bore.
Full six hundred were they then ;
But full eleven hundred men
Would have gathered by the wall,
If they had attended all.
  Tuesday, came coat-makers, tailors,
Fullers, cloth-dyers, and " selliers ;"*
Right good hands, these jolly blades,
Were they counted at their trades.
Away they worked like those before,
Though the others numbered more ;
Scarce four hundred did they stand,
But they were a worthy band.

---

  * The French for " saddlers."

Wednesday, following, down there came
Other bands who worked the same;
Butchers, cord-wainers, and tanners,
Bearing each their separate banners,
Painted as might appertain
To their craft, and, 'mid the train
Many a brave bachelor;
Small and great (when numbered o'er),
Singing, as they worked, their song,
Just three hundred were they strong.
  Thursday, came the fishermen
And the hucksters followed then,
Who sell corn and fish; they bear
Divers banners, for they were
Full four hundred; and the crowd
Carolled and sung aloud;
And the wain-rights they came too—
They were only thirty-two;
A single banner went before,
Which a fish and platter bore.
  But on Saturday the stir
Of black-smith, mason, carpenter,
Hundreds three, with fifty told,
Many were they, true and bold;
And they toiled with main and might,
Needful knew they 'twas and right.
  Then, on Sunday, there came down
All the dames of that brave town;
Know, good labourers were they,
But their numbers none may say.
On the ramparts there was thrown
By their fair hands many a stone;
Who had there a gazer been
Many a beauty might have seen;
Many a scarlet mantle, too,
Or of green or russet hue;

Many a fair cloak had they
And robes dight with colours gay.
In all lands where I have been,
Such fair dames working I've n't seen.
He who had to choose the power,
Had been born in lucky hour.
Many a banner was displayed,
While the work the ladies aid;
When their gentle hands had done
Piling up rude heaps of stone,
Then they walked the fosse along,
Singing sweet a cheerful song;
And, returning to the town,
All these rich dames there sat down;
Where, with mirth, and wine, and song,
Pass'd the pleasant hours along.
Then they said a gate they'd make,
Called the Ladies, for their sake,*
And their prison there should be;
Whoso entered, straightway he
Should forego his liberty.
Lucky doom, I ween, is his
Who a lady's prisoner is;

---

* "It appears from the quaint and pedantic Stanihurst that the ladies were well entitled to this compliment, the suggestion of the entrenchment having originated, according to that writer, with 'a famous Dido' of the town. 'The townsmen,' he says, 'put their heads together, consulting how to prevent either the sudden rushing, or the posthast flieng of anie such adventurous rake-hell hereafter.

"'In which consultation, a famous Dido, a chast widow, a politike dame, a bountiful gentlewoman, called Rose, who representing in sinceritie of life the sweetnesse of that hearbe [flower] whose name she bare, unfolded the devise how anie such future mischance should be prevented, and withall opened her coffers liberallie to have it furthered; two good properties in a councellor.'"

Light the fetters are to wear
Of a lady kind and fair;
But of them enough is said,
Turn we to the fosse instead.
Twenty feet that fosse is deep,
And a league in length doth creep.
When the noble work is done,
Watchmen then there needeth none;
All may sleep in peace and quiet,
Without fear of evil riot.
Fifty thousand might attack,
And yet turn them bootless back.
Warlike stores there are enough
Bold assailants to rebuff.
We have hauberks many a one,
Savage garçon, haubergeon;
Doublets, too, and coats of mail,
Yew-bows good, withouten fail.
In no city have I seen
So many good glaives, I ween.
Cross-bows hanging on the wall,
Arrows, too, to shoot withal;
Every house is full of maces,
And good shields and talevaces.*
Cross-bowmen, when numbered o'er,
Are three hundred and three score;
And three hundred archers shew
Ready with the gallant bow;
And three thousand men advance,
Armed with battle-axe and lance;
Above a hundred knights who wield
Arms aye ready for the field.
I warrant you the town's prepared
'Gainst all enemies to guard.

---

* Talevaces—large wooden shields.

Here I deem it meet to say,
No desire for war have they,
But to keep their city free,
Blamed of no man can they be.
When the wall is carried round,
None in Ireland will be found
Bold enough to dare to fight.
Let a foe-man come in sight,
If the city-horn twice sound,
Every burgess will be found
Eager, in the war-like labour,
Striving to out-do his neighbour;
God give them the victory!
Say Amen for charity.
In no other isle is known
Such a hospitable town;
Joyously the people greet
Every stranger in their street;
Free is he to sell and buy,
And sustain no tax thereby.
Town and people, once again,
I commend to God.   Amen.

This and the specimens of the Latin poetry of Columba and Columbanus do not come strictly within the scope of this volume, except as belonging to the early poetry of Ireland, though not of the Celtic poetry.

In the course of the fourteenth century almost the only poetical names which occur are those of O'Dugan and O'Daly. CARROLL O'DALY, the second, as he may be termed, to distinguish him from the former bard of the same name, was a native of Corcamroe, in Thomond, and flourished about the period last-mentioned (1372). From the specimens which have survived, he appears to have possessed an exquisite fancy, of which the following elegant conception would alone be sufficient evidence :—

CARROLL O'DALY AND ECHO.

TRANSLATED BY JOHN D'ALTON, M.R.I.A.

CARROLL.—Speak, playful echo, speak me well,
 For thou knowest all our care,
Thou sweet, responding sybil, tell,
 Who works this strange affair?
   Echo—A fair!

A fair—no, no, I've felt the pain
 That but from love can flow,
And never can my heart again
 That magic thraldom know.
   Echo—No!

Ah, then if envy's eye has ceased
 To mar my earthly bliss,
Speak consolation to my breast,
 If remedy there is.
   Echo—There is.

Gay, witty spirit of the air,
 If such relief be nigh,
At once the secret spell declare,
 To lull my wasted eye.
   Echo—To die.

To die!—and if it be my lot,
 It comes in hour of need;
Death wears no terror but in thought,
 'Tis innocent in deed.
   Echo (surprised)—Indeed!

Indeed, 'tis welcome to my woes,
  Thou airy voice of fate;
But ah! to none on earth disclose
  What you prognosticate.
          Echo (*playfully*)—To Kate.

To Kate—the devil's on your tongue,
  To scare me with such thoughts;
To her, oh, could I hazard wrong,
  Who never knew her faults.
          Echo—You're false.

If thy Narcissus could awake
  Such doubts, he were an ass
If he did not prefer the lake
  To humouring such a lass.
          Echo—Alas!

A thousand sighs and rites of woe
  Attend thee in the air;
What mighty grief can feed thee so,
  In weariless despair?
          Echo—Despair.

Despair not for Narcissus' lot,
  Who once was thy delight;
Another in his place you've got,
  If our report is right.
          Echo—'Tis right.

Dear little sorceress, farewell,
  I fear thou told'st me true;
But as thou'st many a tale to tell,
  I bid thee now adieu.
          Echo—Adieu.

One of the most, if not *the* most, voluminous of the poets of the fourteenth century was JOHN O'DUGAN, chief bard to O'Kelly of Hy Maine or Imania, an extensive district in Connaught. O'Dugan's works were principally historical and topographical. Among others were a metrical history of the ancient kings of Ireland down to Roderick O'Conor, the last native monarch; a poetical account of the principal tribes and districts of Meath, Ulster, and Connaught (which has been inserted piece-meal in the notes to O'Connellan's translation of the *Annals of the Four Masters*), and the chiefs who presided over them at the time of the Anglo-Norman invasion; an account of the actions of the illustrious monarch Cormac Mac Art; a poem on the principal festivals of the year; a poetical glossary of obsolete words; an account of the Kings of Leinster descended of Cathair Mor; and an account of the kings of the race of Eibhear (Heber), comprising a summary of the history of the kings of Cashel, from Corc, who flourished about A.D. 380, to his own time. This last poem, consisting of eighty-one stanzas, was translated by Michael Kearney in 1635,* "to preserve that ancient Rhyme," as he states, "from the overwhelming flouds of oblivion, which already devoured most part our Nationall Memoraryes." This translation is now of course very quaint, and in itself a literary curiosity. We here subjoin the first stanza, with some of the concluding ones, the body of it being taken up with hard names and dry historical details:—

A.D. 1350.

 Casshell the Citty was of noble Mogha's Sonnes,
  Its spetious hewe so flourished;
 From Corcke to Cormock Clurcaghe's Raignes,
  Their kinges that Pallace well nourished.

---

* Published and edited by the Irish scholar, Mr. John Daly.—Dublin, 1847.

* * * * *

Nineteen princes of a worthy race,
Warlike, comely, and vigorous,
Who never fail'd to maintain the Church,
Fell in the gory path of battle.

Seven,—being eminently just,—
Of those great kings, without a doubt,
Neither feared nor avoided death,
Received the blessed Viaticum, and died penitent.

And they, likewise, reigned kings supreme,
After Domhnall of the brown eye-brows,
Over Munster of the streams, of the rich rough crops,
And of the boughs drooping with loads of mellow fruit.

The most important part of pleasant Eire,
Is Munster of the mountain-studded plains,
On account of her nobility, her wealth,
Her store of precious stones, and the honour her people
 support.

I cannot conceal the good qualities of the men of
 Munster,
In whom no flaw was ever found ;
They were famed for love of freedom, comeliness of
 countenance,
And loftiness of spirit.

They were inured to war at all times,
They were hospitable and liberal ;
Their habits were calculated to win confidence,
Being in strict conformity with those of their ancestors.

Munster was also celebrated for the extent of her
    territory,
For the superiority of her women above those of the
    other provinces,
As well in the melody and cheerfulness of voice and
    charming features,
As in the excellent arrangement of their dress.

The two Munsters of the undulating plains,
Are the most delightful provinces of Eire;
A country of fertile glebe, of well-sheltered dales,—
'Tis a province befitting the monarch of Eire.

The death of the author, O'Dugan, is noted by the annalists in 1372.

A.D. 1380. The battle celebrated in the following poem was fought on the banks of the Roe, a river remarkable for the wild grandeur of its scenery, and in the vicinity of Dungiven in Derry, a locality which is also distinguished as the place of meeting of the famous assembly of Drumkeat in 590. This battle is erroneously ascribed by Walker* to the close of the twelfth instead of the fourteenth century. It is stated to have been the last of the many desperate conflicts between the English forces and those of O'Cahan, or O'Kane, prince of the territory comprising the present county of Derry and some of the northern portion of Antrim, and that it resulted in the complete extinction of the power of the Clan Saxon, as they were termed by the natives, in that locality. If this be so, it was probably fought after the time of his capture in 1376. O'Cahan, whose family was one of great dignity, being a branch of the

---

* *Memoir on the Dress, Armour, Weapons, &c., of the Ancient Irish*, 8vo edition.

O'Neills, acquired great renown by his military exploits, and was distinguished by the title of *Coo-ey na Gall*, or Terror of the Strangers, attached to his name. A fine monument to this distinguished chieftain still exists in a good state of preservation in the ancient abbey of Dungiven, one of the most beautiful and romantically situated pile of ruins in the kingdom, an interesting sketch of which has been furnished by the pen and pencil of our distinguished countryman, **Dr. Petrie**. " Dungiven," we are there informed, " was the burying-place of the sept of O'Cathan: . . . . the church and cemetery are filled with their graves. Their monuments, which are decorated usually with escutcheons, &c., in no mean style of sculpture, are, however, with the exception of one, of little interest. It is an altar tomb of much architectural beauty, situated in the south side of the chancel, and traditionally known as the monument of the chief of the O'Kanes, of great renown for his opposition to the inroads of the English, and hence called *Coo-ey na Gall*. This hero is represented in armour, in the usual recumbent position, with one hand resting on his sword. On the front of the tomb are figures of six warriors sculptured in relievo. The age of this extraordinary monument may be accurately ascertained. The style of its architecture points unequivocally to the close of the fourteenth century; and the name preserved by tradition as that of the distinguished chief for whom it was erected is conspicuous in our national annals of that period."*

In the *Annals of the Four Masters*, under the date 1376, is recorded the capture of O'Cahan by the English at Coleraine. He was conveyed to Carrickfergus Castle and there

---

* *Dublin Penny Journal*, vol. i., p. 404.

imprisoned. Neither the period nor the mode of his liberation is mentioned, but, nine years later, his death is noted among the obituaries, at the height of prosperity and fame. The last chieftain of note of this family, being implicated in the alleged treasonable practices with O'Neill and O'Donnel, early in the reign of James I., fled with them to the Continent in 1607, and his estates became forfeited to the Crown with theirs. A touching story is told of the venerable widow of the fallen chief. The Duchess of Buckingham, many years subsequently, having occasion to pass Limavady, was induced by curiosity to visit the ruins of the O'Cahans' demolished castle, where she discovered his unhappy widow in a condition characteristic of her fortunes, crouching beside the blaze of a few faggots in one of the ruined apartments of her once splendid residence, the broken casements of which were stuffed with straw.*

THE BATTLE OF THE ROE.

Loud the signal shield resounded,
   Shrill the horn of battle blew;
From the hill O'Cahan bounded,
   And along the valley flew.

He, the Saxon power despising,
   Then their marshall'd strength withstood;
Then, in all his vengeance rising,
   Dyed his rivers with their blood.

Towering in the front of danger,
   Ne'er by human power dismay'd;
Then the Terror of the Stranger
   Drew his slaughter-seeking blade.

---

* See Derry County Survey; *Dublin Penny Journal*, vol. iii., p. 89; and O'Connellan's *Four Masters*, p. 23.

Bright the brandished weapon gleaming,
    Lightened as the chieftain pass'd;
Loose his rustling banner streaming
    Gave the trophies to the blast.

All in vain, the ford defending,
    Firmly stood the Saxon band;
Vain their spears, on spears extending,
    Lined with death the shelving strand.

On his host, his red eye turning
    Ceased to flash upon his foes;
Breathing death, with vengeance burning,
    Thus O'Cahan's voice arose:—

"Warriors, Heaven and justice speed you
    To the meed your might has won:
Vengeance and O'Cahan lead you,
    Follow, warriors, and fall on."

First to tempt the threat'ning danger,
    First to dare the guarded flood,
Rush'd the Terror of the Stranger,
    Bathing deep his steel in blood.

Falling ranks the carnage swelling,
    Still their post the foe maintain'd;
Still his pressing strength repelling,
    Trench'd behind their fellows slain.

Till their chief, in blood extended,
    Pierced with wounds, resigned his breath;
Then the shout of conquest blended
    With the deep'ning groan of death.

Then triumphant o'er each danger,
    All his thirst of blood allayed,
Then the Terror of the Stranger
    Sheath'd his slaughter-seeking blade.

The fifteenth century was a period of greater intellectual darkness, at least so far as poetry was concerned, than any which had preceded it—a night illumined by scarcely a single star. "The art of poetry," says the venerable O'Conor, "declined as the nation itself declined; some eminent poets indeed appeared from time to time, but diverted in most instances from the ancient moral and political uses to the barren subjects of personal panegyric."*

One of the very few poetical productions of this period is supposed to have been written by the family bard of the Desmonds, on the incident which forms the subject of one of Moore's sweetest ballads—"By the Feal's wave benighted." The circumstance, which occurred about the commencement of the century under consideration, was briefly this. The youthful heir of Desmond having married Catherine, the beautiful daughter of one of his dependants named Mac Cormac, of whom he had become enamoured when resting in her father's house, after a hunting excursion at Abbeyfeale, in Co. Limerick, so outraged the feelings of his family and adherents by this inferior match, that, to escape the odium that it drew down upon him, he was forced into exile on the Continent.† The poet here cele-

---

* *Dissertations on History of Ireland*—Dissertation 6.
† The reader will remember the stanza of Moore's ballad—

"You who call it dishonour
  To bow to this flame,
If you've eyes, look but on her,
  And blush while you blame.
Hath the pearl less whiteness
  Because of its birth?
Hath the violet less brightness
  For growing near earth?"

brates the fair one under the name of Deirdre, the famed beauty of Irish romance, whose fatal charms were the occasion of the tragic fate of the celebrated heroes, the three sons of Usnoth.

BLOOMING DEIRDRE.

A.D. 1400.

TRANSLATED BY EDWARD LAWSON.

Sweet Deirdre 'bove all else I prize—
Such pearly teeth, such azure eyes!
O'er which, dispersed by zephyr's play,
Dark shining, twining tendrils stray,
In full luxuriant wreaths descending,
Those small, soft, heaving orbs defending,
Whose vestal snow no touch profane
Of man has ever dared to stain.

Like orient Venus, when she presses
The brine from her ambrosial tresses,
That down her sleek side glittering flows,
Like dew-star on the milk-white rose,
The dreary tenants of the tide,
With wondering gaze forget to glide;
Suspended in the liquid sky,
The plumy warblers cease to fly,
Choiring her praise to heaven above,
Where she'd depose the witching queen of love.

Her tutelary power I hail,
Though, like a cavern'd hermit pale,
Hopeless I pine, accusing death,
Whose barbarous shafts still spare my breath.

A martyr to protracted anguish,
Like joyless, sapless age I languish;
Nor read a line, nor time an air,
To all indifferent—whelm'd in deep despair.

The fascinating, white-arm'd maid
By some enchantment has betray'd
My hopeless bosom, which remains
Wrapt in inextricable chains;
In charity she ought to heal
The tortures that from her I feel.

A.D. 1468. A poem of this period, written by Donall O'Mulconry, chief bard to O'Brien of Thomond, though belonging to the class which it is the special object of this work to embody, is yet so prolix and discursive, and without any distinct and definite aim, that a small portion of it will perhaps satisfy the curiosity of the reader. It was an inauguration ode addressed to Turlogh O'Brien, who became chief of Thomond in 1468. Almost the whole poem, consisting of fifty-seven stanzas, is taken up with an encomium on the glories of Kincora, which, considering it was such an old story, and not the poet's immediate theme, might have sufficed with less—and, indeed, its praises would have been "more honoured in the breach than the observance," seeing that the O'Briens had been among the earliest and steadiest adherents of the English interest. The poet also introduces Finn Mac Cumhal as a prophet, which, with all his renown, is perhaps the only instance on record of his appearing in that character, which was indeed altogether out of his line. But he is made, notwithstanding, to foretell the future renown of Brian, and also of a long subsequent descendant of his house, which gives the poet an opportunity of indulging the hope that the present lord is to be the man; and this, at the forty-seventh stanza, is the first notice, excepting a very slight one at the fourteenth, of the immediate subject of his eulogy. This poem bears in its manner some resemblance to Ward's beautiful Ode to the Ruins of Donegal Castle, a metrical version of which will be subsequently given; but though not devoid of harmony and musical expression, in addition to the want of point, it is entirely deficient in the incomparable simplicity and pathos of that exquisite production. The last few verses are the best of the poem, and are certainly rather impressive.

ON THE INAUGURATION OF THE O'BRIEN.

A.D. 1469.

METRICAL VERSION BY J. C. MANGAN.*

Oh, great Kincora! 'tis my grief
  To gaze upon thy crumbling walls
    And chambers lone!
The O'Briens now forget their chief,
  And dwell, alas! in other halls,
    To him unknown.

Of yore, at royal Brian's call,
  The hundred kings of Banba's isle
    Would throng thy rooms;
But now how strangely changed is all!—
  Thy glories, O majestic pile,
    Are turned to gloom!

---

* *Dublin University Magazine,* vol. xxx., p. 66.

House of the drinking horns of old,
   Where chief and bard, with sword and lyre,
      So often met,
Wouldst thou thus mourn, all unconsoled,
   Were Morogh, or his regal sire,
      But reigning yet?

    *   *   *   *   *

But what avails it now to dwell
   Upon the glories, long since fled,
      Of those great men?
Nought! though their names are still a spell,
   And Erin ne'er shall see, I dread,
      Such hosts agen.

Still, royal Rath—wherein, long since,
   King Brian reigned, the conquering son
      Of Kennedy—
Another host, another prince,
   Shall win thee what may yet be won,
      Shall rescue thee!

Too long, Kincora, dost thou abide
   A sad sepulchral solitude
      Look cheerier now,
And cast thy weeds of woe aside;
   Thy glory shall shine out renewed,
      Thou loved one, thou!

New guards, new bards, new clansmen come;
   Comes hither Turlogh, son of Teague,
      To hold his court:
They make thy palace-halls their home,
   A brilliant band, a mighty league,
      Oh, once-proud Fort!

The Shannon, king of Erin's floods,
  For ever telleth, as a bell,
    Its love to thee;
While round thee bloom those walnut woods,
  So rich in copse and bowery dell,
    And flowery lea!

*   *   *   *   *

To Finn Mac Cool, the warrior sear,
  On these great heights was once revealed
    A wondrous tale—
Finn, who, through many a stormy year,
  Stood forward as the tower and shield
    Of Innisfail!

*   *   *   *   *

The darker hours drew on apace;
  So when the sun declined beneath
    The waves a-west,
Finn ceased a while the bootless chase,
  And stretched him on the mountain heath,
    And sank to rest.

Then, in the visions of the night,
  To him was Erin's fate foreshewn—
    He dreamed he saw
A palace on Kincora's height—
  A monarch, too, before whose throne
    All bent in awe.

He glanced around him. At a feast
  Sate silken dames and chiefs in steel;
    Rich music's mirth
Rang loud—when suddenly, all ceased.
  He felt the palace rock and reel,
    Then fall to earth!

Again he looked:—king, chiefs, dames, arms
   Were gone; crushed lay the golden throne;
      And, woe-the-while!
Strange hosts of steel-frocked knights, in swarms,
   Tore up the lowest fountain stones
      Of that proud pile!

Anon, a change came o'er his dream.
   Fierce battle stalked in iron might
      Throughout the land.
Thick lay the slain, till every stream
   Ran red with blood all day and night
      On either hand!

It was the glowing even-tide:—
   A light flashed from the west afar;
      And swiftly came,
Careering up the mountain side,
   A serried phalanx, like one star
      Of purple flame.

And heading this combined array,
   A chieftain rode, whose headlong course
      None could withstand.
With giant might he upheld the fray,
   And drove the invading foreign force
      From Erin's land!

Soon as the ruddy morning brake,
   Finn published this to all his bands,—
      The Fenian Lords;
And with prophetic power he spake—
   (Let him who reads and understands
      Weigh well his words!)

"The mystery of the dream," said he,
"I thus unveil:—in after time
A chief shall rise—
King Brian, son of Kennedy,—
A mighty prince, of soul sublime,
Great, brave, and wise.

"Long prosperously this king shall reign;
His golden throne shall stand in fair
Kincora's hall;—
But, woe-the-day, he shall be slain,
And, four-fold misery and despair,
His house shall fall!

"And ten-fold woe to Innisfail!
A people shall o'er-run her lands
Bad, fierce, and strong.
And fate shall overcome the Gael,
By crafty counsels, ruffian hands,
And fraudful wrong!

"And Tara and Kincora both
Shall lie through centuries desolate;
And force and guile
Shall tower to a gigantic growth,
And alien tyranny and hate
Shall rule the isle!"—

But Erin's life-blood yet is warm,—
Yes! in this world of joy and woe
God wills that bloom
Should chase decay, and sunshine storm;
And freedom's torch at length shall glow
Through Erin's gloom!

So, too, spake Finn: "A chief," he said,
  "Of Brian's line shall yet appear
    Whose mighty arm
Shall raise the land, as from the dead,
  And drive a-far, like hunted deer,
    The stranger swarm!

"Long after Brian's day and sway
  A nut shall grow, of dazzling gold,
    Upon his tree!"—
Thus far the seer. O Torlogh, say,
  Say, stalwart chief, do I behold
    That nut in thee?

   *   *   *   *   *

And should we not remember, we,
  Clontarf's great day? If men will dare—
    And *we are men!*—
They will be and they must be free!
  Can we not conquer *here* as *there*,
    And *now* as *then*?

   *   *   *   *   *

Warm winds waft fragrance round our shores;
  Gold fruit, from boughs o'er-laden, lies
    Among fair flowers;
Ships crowd our ports with choicest stores;
  The seas are calm; we have genial skies
    And gentle showers.

The grass teems under the bright scythe;
  The hills are ploughed even to their tops.
    Why should not we
Rejoice, then? Why not sing as blithe
  As the young throstle in the copse?
    We are not free!

> Thou, Torlogh, of a kingly race,
>   Mayest now retrieve, redeem, restore,
>   This fallen land!
> Up, then, and recognise thy place,
>   And bare the avenging sword once more,
>   And take thy stand!

Learning had now almost fled the island, or was only to be found within the secluded walls of the convent. The bards were no longer the favoured order, as in days of old; they were a proscribed race.* The kings and chiefs whose deeds it had once been their pride to sing, were fallen from their high estate, like the mighty oaks prostrated upon their hills by the strife of the elements; the halls that had once resounded to their minstrelsy were now silent and deserted; and we may well imagine that they struck their harps only in some congenial solitude, in plaintive strains, to mourn over the deep desolation of their country, or, like the Israelites of old, hung them in despair upon the willows.

The poetical spirit, however, was too deeply seated in the national mind to be wholly eradicated, even by the cruel persecutions to which the bards were exposed, and in the course of the sixteenth century it burst forth into a flame,

> "Like secret fire, which smouldering embers hide."

The legislative sages of those times, imagining, no doubt, that, like Samson, their strength lay in their hair, enacted

---

* By the Statute of Kilkenny, in the reign of Edward III., it was made penal to entertain any of the Irish bards, who had been in the habit, it appears, of making their profession subservient, like Alfred of England, to political purposes. These proscriptive measures were renewed in almost every succeeding reign.

that the "Coolin," or flowing ringlets, in which they took
so much pride, should be abolished, and would not even
allow them the poor privilege of a moustache, but ordered
that "the same be once at least shaven every fortnight."
Even the gentle poet, Spenser, in whom a more enlightened
and liberal mind might have been expected, recommended,
in his "View of the State of Ireland," published in the
year 1598, the utter extinction of the whole bardic order.
"They seldom choose unto themselves," he complains,
"the sayings and doings of good men for the argument of
their poems; but whomsoever they find most lawless in
life, most dangerous and desperate in all parts of his dis-
obedience, him they set up and glorifie, and make him an
example to the young men to follow. I have caused divers
of these poems," he adds, "to be translated unto me, . . .
*and surely they savoured of sweet wit and good invention, . . .
sprinkled with some pretty flowers of their natural device,*
which gave good grace and comeliness unto them, ... the
which with good usage would serve to adorn and beautify
virtue." This was surely praise enough from one of the
greatest masters of song in any age, and he a professed
enemy, and at a period when the bards had sunk so low.
But though stripped of their hereditary honours, and no
longer patronised in the mansions of the great, and though
the chiefs whose praises they had been wont to sing were
now prostrated, and not likely to relish in their present
humiliation the theme of their former glory, yet did these
sons of song still retain a powerful influence, and when occa-
sion offered, would effectually call on their countrymen to

"Burst the base foreign yoke, as their sires did of yore,
Or die like their sires, and endure it no more."
SCOTT.

Of this a striking instance occurred about this period. The Earl of Kildare, who had been called over to England to account for his administration, had appointed his son, the young Lord Thomas Fitzgerald, to act as lord deputy in his absence. It having been rumoured that the earl, on his arrival in London, had been committed to the Tower, and there beheaded, the young lord deputy, with the fire of the Geraldine race, indignant at the insults heaped upon his family and his country, resolved on taking the field in defence of both. Collecting his adherents, he entered the metropolis, proceeded to the council, and, rushing into the hall, cast down the sword of state, as he thus addressed them—" This sword of state is yours, not mine. I received it with an oath. I used it to your benefit. I should stain mine own honour if I turned it to your annoyance. I have now need of mine own sword, which I dare trust. As for this sword, it flattereth me with a painted scabbard; but it hath indeed a pestilent edge, bathed in the Geraldines' blood. I am now none of Henry's deputies—I am his foe. I have more mind to meet him in the field than to serve him in office." While the other lords remained mute and astonished at the chivalrous temerity of the young Geraldine, Cromer, who was both chancellor and primate, took him by the hand, and remonstrated with him, in the most soothing and affectionate terms, on the folly and madness of his rash attempt. The remonstrance might probably have had the desired effect; but, unfortunately, before reason had time to operate, a bard who was present broke forth into an extemporaneous rhapsody on the glory of the Geraldines, and the high destiny that awaited the present heir of the house; and the young lord, his passions thus roused, rushed from the hall to carry out his desperate enterprise.

The chief poetical names of the sixteenth century were: MAOLIN OGE MAC BRODIN, who was considered the first bard of his age; O'MULCONRY, the author of an admired piece, addressed to the chieftain O'Rourke, of Breiffny; TEIGE DALL O'HIGGIN, brother to the Archbishop of Tuam; and FEARFLATHA O'GNIVE, chief bard to the O'Neills of Claneboy (Antrim), who formed one of the train of the great Shane O'Neill, when he paid his famous visit to the court of Elizabeth, in 1562.* The following spirited lament for the fallen fortunes of the Gael, or ancient septs of Ireland, was the production of this bard :—

THE DOWNFALL OF THE GAEL.

TRANSLATED BY S. (LATER, SIR S.) FERGUSON, M.R.I.A.

> My heart is in woe,
>   And my soul is in trouble,
> For the mighty are low,
>   And abased are the noble.
>
> The sons of the Gael
>   Are in exile and mourning;
> Worn, weary, and pale,
>   As spent pilgrims returning;

---

* "O'Gnive (Agnew), bard of Claneboy in the reign of Elizabeth, to whose court he accompanied Shane (O'Neill) the Proud, in 1562. In Mr. Planche's lately published *Dissertation on British Costumes*, is a representation of the Irish as they appeared in London, taken from a valuable print in the possession of the late Mr. Douce, and curiously illustrative of Camden's account of their appearance."

Or men who, in flight
  From the field of disaster,
Beseech the black night
  On their flight to fall faster;

Or seamen aghast,
  When their planks gape asunder,
And the waves fierce and fast
  Tumble through in hoarse thunder;

Or men whom we see
  That have got their death omen:
Such wretches are we
  In the chains of our foemen!

Our courage is fear,
  Our nobility vileness;
Our hope is despair,
  And our comeliness foulness.

There is mist on our heads,
  And a cloud, chill and hoary,
Of deep sorrow, sheds
  An eclipse on our glory.

From Boyne to the Linn
  Has the mandate been given,
That the children of Finn
  From their country be driven;

That the sons of the king
  Oh, the treason and malice—
Shall no more ride the ring
  In their own native valleys;

No more shall repair
   Where the hill foxes tarry,
Nor forth in the air
   Fling the hawk at her quarry.

For the plain shall be broke
   By the share of the stranger,
And the stone-mason's stroke
   Tell the woods of their danger;

The green hills and shore
   Be with white keeps disfigured,
And the moat of Rathmore
   Be the Saxon churl's haggard;

The land of the lakes
   Shall no more know the prospect
Of valleys and brakes,
   So transformed is her aspect;

The Gael cannot tell,
   In the uprooted wildwood,
And red ridgy dell,
   The old nurse of his childhood;

The nurse of his youth
   Is in doubt as she views him,
If the pale wretch in truth
   Be a child of her bosom.

We starve by the board,
   And we thirst amid wassail;
For the guest is the lord,
   And the host is the vassal.

Through the woods let us roam,
  Through the wastes wild and barren;
We are strangers at home,
  We are exiles in Erin!

And Erin's a bark
  O'er the wild waters driven;
And the tempest howls dark,
  And her side planks are riven;

And in billows of might
  Swell the Saxon before her—
Unite—oh, unite.
  Or the billows burst o'er her!*

Incomparably the finest poetical production of this period, however, was by a non-professional poet. This was the noble maritime ode, written by a gentleman of the name of MAURICE M'DAVID FITZGERALD, on a voyage from Ireland to Spain. The translator remarks: "I should be accused of treason to the majesty of Horace (whose third ode was written on a similar occasion), did I say that he is surpassed by our Irish bard upon this subject;—I shall not, therefore, risk the censure; but my readers are at liberty to do it if they please."†

---

* "The remainder of the original, which becomes prolix, has been omitted." The above has been honoured with two versions besides the present—a literal translation in Charles O'Conor's *Dissertations on History of Ireland*, and the metrical one by J. J. Callinan, commencing—

  "How dimm'd is the glory that circled the Gael,
  And fall'n the high people of green Innisfail."

† *Reliques of Irish Poetry*, p. 179.

FITZGERALD'S MARITIME ODE.

TRANSLATED BY MISS BROOKE.

Bless my good ships, protecting pow'r of grace!
And o'er the winds, the waves, the destin'd coast,
Breathe, benign spirit!—let thy radiant host
    Spread their angelic shields!
Before us, the bright bulwark let them place,
And fly beside us, through their azure fields!

    O calm the voice of winter's storm!
    Rule the wrath of angry seas!
The fury of the rending blast appease,
Nor let its rage fair ocean's face deform!
    O check the biting wind of spring,
        And from before our course,
      Arrest the fury of its wing,
      And terrors of its force!
So may we safely pass the dang'rous cape,
And from the perils of the deep escape!

    I grieve to leave the splendid seats
      Of Teamor's ancient fame!
    Mansions of heroes, now farewell!
      Adieu, ye sweet retreats,
Where the fam'd hunters of your ancient vale,
    Who swell'd the high heroic tale,
      Were wont of old to dwell!
And you, bright tribes of sunny streams, adieu!
While my sad feet their mournful path pursue.
Ah, well their lingering steps my grieving soul proclaim!

Receive me now, my ship!—hoist now thy sails,
    To catch the favouring gales.
O Heaven! before thine awful throne I bend!
O let thy power thy servants now protect;
Increase of knowledge and of wisdom lend,
Our course through every peril to direct;
    To steer us safe through ocean's rage,
Where angry storms their dreadful strife maintain;
    O may thy power their wrath assuage!
May smiling suns and gentle breezes reign!

Stout is my well-built ship the storm to brave,
    Majestic in its might,
    Her bulk tremendous, on the wave
    Erects its stately height!
    From her strong bottom, tall in air,
    Her branching masts aspiring rise;
Aloft their cords and curling heads they bear,
And give their sheeted ensign to the skies;
While her proud bulk frowns awful on the main,
And seems the fortress of the liquid plain!

    Dreadful in the shock of fight,
She goes—she cleaves the storm!
Where ruin wears its most tremendous form
    She sails, exulting in her might;
On the fierce necks of foaming billows rides,
    And, through the roar
Of angry ocean, to the destined shore
    Her course triumphant guides;
As though, beneath her frown, the winds were dead,
And each blue valley was their silent bed!

    Through all the perils of the main
She knows her dauntless progress to maintain

Through quicksands, flats, and breaking waves,
Her dangerous path she dares explore;
Wrecks, storms, and calms, alike she braves,
And gains, with scarce a breeze, the wished-for shore!
    Or, in the hour of war,
  Fierce on she bounds, in conscious might,
    To meet the promis'd fight!
      While distant far,
  The fleets of wondering nations gaze,
And view her course with emulous amaze,
    As, like some championed son of fame,
    She rushes to the shock of arms,
And joys to mingle in the loud alarms,
Impell'd by rage, and fir'd with glory's flame.
Sailing with pomp upon the watery plain,
    Like some huge monster of the main,
    My ship her speckled bosom laves,
And, high in air, her curling ensign waves;
Her stately sides, with polish'd beauty gay,
And gunnel, bright with gold's effulgent ray.

  As the fierce griffin's dreadful flight,
    Her monstrous bulk appears,
    While, o'er the seas her towering height,
And her wide wings, tremendous shade! she rears.
Or, as a champion thirsting after fame,—
The strife of swords—the deathless name—
So does she seem, and such her rapid course,
    Such is the rending of her force;
When her sharp keel, where dreadful splendours play,
Cuts through the foaming main its liquid way—
Like the red bolt of heaven, she shoots along—
Dire as its flight, and as its fury strong!

    God of the winds! O hear my pray'r!
      Safe passage now bestow;
    Soft, o'er the slumbering deep, may fair
      And prosperous breezes blow!

O'er the rough rock and swelling wave,
  Do thou our progress guide!
Do thou from angry ocean save,
  And o'er its rage preside.

Speed my good ship along the rolling sea,
O Heaven! and smiling skies and favouring gales decree
Speed the high-masted ship of dauntless force,
Swift in her glittering flight and sounding course!
  Stately moving on the main,
  Forest of the azure plain!
  Faithful to confided trust,
  To her promis'd glory just;
  Deadly in the strife of war,
  Rich in every gift of peace,
    Swift from afar,
  In peril's fearful hour,
Mighty in force, and bounteous in her power,
  She comes; kind aid she lends,
  She frees her supplicating friends,
And fear before her flies, and dangers cease!

Hear, blest Heav'n, my ardent prayer!
My ship—my crew—O take us in thy care!
  O may no peril bar our way!
Fair blow the gales of each propitious day!
Soft swell the floods, and gently roll the tides,
While from Dunboy, along the smiling main,
We sail, until the destined coast we gain,
And safe in port our gallant vessel rides!

The seventeenth century produced a goodly array of poetical gems. Among the principal names of this period may be mentioned the erudite TEIGE MAC DARY, bard of the O'Briens of Thomond;* LUGAD, or LOUIS, O'CLERY, of Tyrconnell (Donegal); O'HUSSEY, of Orgiel, bard of the sept of Maguire, of Fermanagh; the WARDS, bards of the O'Neils and O'Donnells; O'CONNELLAN, O'RYAN, and many others too numerous to particularize. The two first were the rival leaders in the famous "Contention of the Northern and Southern Bards of Ireland," so spiritedly conducted about the year 1600, in which they respectively contended for the claim of the great northern and southern septs, particularly the O'Briens and O'Neills, to precedence. The various poems produced on this occasion were collected, under the title of the *Iomarba*, and are not less valuable in a historical than a poetical point of view.†

The following elegiac composition was written by MALMURRY WARD, son of the bard of Tyrconnell, on witnessing the ruins in which the celebrated Hugh Roe O'Donnell had left the castle of his ancestors, in 1601, in order to prevent it becoming a refuge for the enemy.

---

* That this philosophic bard had not forgotten the former importance of his profession, "when," in the words of the venerable O'Conor, "it answered, in ancient time, so many good purposes of religion and government," we are assured by a poem which he addressed to his patron, O'Brien of Thomond:—

"And though each loyal subject counsel bring,
And, to avoid misrule, instruct the king;
Yet 'tis alone the bard's peculiar claim,
As 'tis his only joy—his only aim—
To draw the attention of his monarch's ear;
The bard's advice he's always wont to hear."

THEO. O'FLANIGAN.

† *Irish Minstrelsy*, vol. ii., p. 345.

The life of Hugh Roe O'Donnell belongs to the romance of Irish history. His father, Hugh, was THE O'DONNELL, Prince of Tyrconnell, and his mother, daughter of M'Donnell, Lord of the Isles. At a very early age he evinced great capacity and energy of character, and great ambition. To these traits he united a generous disposition, and a personal appearance noble and engaging in the highest degree—a combination of qualities which made him equally dreaded by the government, and popular among his own people, who regarded him as destined to achieve some great exploit. The consequence was a most unworthy and, as it proved, impolitic plot, devised by Sir John Perrot, the Lord Deputy, to secure the person of the young O'Donnell. For this purpose, in the year 1587, he fitted out a vessel laden with Spanish wine, with orders to the commander to sail for some port in Donegal, and trade with the people in the assumed character of a Spanish merchant. Accordingly, directing his course to Lough Swilly, he cast anchor off the castle of the M'Swineys, near Rathmullen. The people of the castle and surrounding country were no way tardy in taking advantage of the unusually low price at which their favourite beverage was offered, and the report of the arrival soon spread to a distance. As was anticipated, the chief of the country, young O'Donnell, arrived at the castle to lay in a store, when a fresh order was sent for an additional supply for the chief and his train. The crafty commander sent back word that his stock for sale was nearly exhausted, but that if the young prince and a few of his friends would come on board, he would entertain them with some prime sack, and the best he had remaining. The bait took. O'Donnell, then only in his sixteenth year, embraced the proposal with boyish eagerness. He and a few of his friends immediately rowed off to the vessel, where they were received with the utmost cordiality by their *hospitable* entertainer. The mirth, revelry, and feasting soon commenced, and being well plied with potent drink, midnight found them in a state of profound oblivion. They were then deprived of any arms upon their persons. Having thus gained his object, the commander gave orders for the hatches to be closed, and the anchor to be weighed, and ere the morning's dawn his unconscious victims were on their way to the dungeons of Dublin Castle. In the latter part of 1591, however, after a confinement of better than three years in the castle tower, the prisoners effected their escape; but the unhappy O'Donnell was again basely betrayed by his friend, Phelim O'Toole, who had formerly been his fellow-prisoner, and under the shelter of whose roof he now sought protection. Seldom has an act of greater baseness been recorded. The unfortunate youth, his hope of freedom thus dashed by the hand of seeming friendship, was hurried back, heavily chained, and under stricter surveillance, to his cheerless dungeon, the gloom of which was no doubt aggravated by the bitter thought of the means of his renewed incarceration. A short time only elapsed, however, before he again effected his escape, by the aid of a faithful follower, and fled to the Wicklow hills. He was accompanied by his kinsmen and fellow-prisoners, two of the young O'Neills. It was in the depth of an unusually severe winter, and the tale of the sufferings they endured in their flight is touching in the extreme. Their progress was impeded by the thick drifting of the snow, which fell so heavily as to conceal almost every landmark, and thus they pursued their devious way through thicket and copse, briar and brake, a task to which, from the effects of their long confinement, their strength was unequal. At length they could proceed no further. One of the O'Neills was seized with a torpid drowsiness, and "slept the sleep that knows no waking." O'Donnell got into a spot that afforded a temporary shelter, and the attendants were despatched to the residence of O'Byrne, whither they had been proceeding, to obtain assistance. When they returned with warm clothes and refreshments, they found O'Neill dead, and O'Donnell, though still alive, terribly frost-bitten. By O'Byrne they were most cordially received, and hospitably entertained. With his assistance, O'Donnell, when sufficiently recovered, notwithstanding the scouts which were abroad to intercept him, succeeded in reaching his own territory in safety. His arrival was hailed by all the septs and chiefs of the north with the utmost enthusiasm; and he was unanimously chosen their leader, though he had not yet attained his twentieth year.

O'Donnell had suffered enough to rouse even one of a less ardent temperament; and for about ten years he proved the ablest and most dangerous foe that ever the arms of England had to contend with in this country. He showed himself more than a match for the most experienced of Elizabeth's generals, and carried his triumphant arms to the very extremities of Munster. An unfortunate misunderstanding with O'Neill, however, on one occasion, proved fatal to his cause. On that occasion—the only one—he was routed, and forced to seek refuge in Spain, where he died, in 1602.

TO THE RUINS OF DONEGAL CASTLE.

TRANSLATED BY JAMES CLARENCE MANGAN.

O mournful, O forsaken pile,
   What desolation dost thou dree!
How tarnished is the beauty that was thine erewhile,
   Thou mansion of chaste melody!

Demolished lie thy towers and halls;
   A dark, unsightly, earthen mound
Defaces the pure whiteness of thy shining walls,
   And solitude doth gird thee round.

Fair fort! thine hour has come at length,
   Thine older glory has gone by.
Lo! far beyond thy noble battlements of strength,
   Thy corner-stones all scattered lie!

Where now, O rival of the gold
   Emania, be thy wine-cups all?
Alas! for these thou now hast nothing but the cold,
   Cold stream that from the heavens doth fall!

Thy clay-choked gateways none can trace,
   Thou fortress of the once bright doors!
The limestones of thy summit now bestrew thy base,
   Bestrew the outside of thy floors.

Above thy shattered window-sills
   The music that to-day breaks forth
Is but the music of the wild winds from the hills,
   The wild winds of the stormy North!

What spell o'ercame thee, mighty fort,
    What fatal fit of slumber strange,
O palace of the wine!—O many-gated court!
    That thou shouldst undergo this change?

Thou wert, O bright-walled, beaming one,
    Thou cradle of high deeds and bold,
The Tara of Assemblies to the sons of Con,
    Clan-Connell's Council-hall of old!

Thou wert a new Emania, thou!
    A northern Cruachan in thy might—
A dome like that which stands by Boyne's broad water now,
    Thou Erin's Rome of all delight!

In thee were Ulster's tributes stored,
    And lavish'd like the flowers in May;
And into thee were Connaught's thousand treasures poured,
    Deserted though thou art to-day!

How often from thy turrets high,
    Thy purple turrets, have we seen
Long lines of glittering ships, when summer time drew nigh,
    With masts and sails of snow-white sheen!

How often seen, when gazing round
    From thy tall towers, the hunting-trains,
The blood-enlivening chase, the horseman and the hound,
    Thou fastness of a hundred plains!

How often to thy banquets bright
    We have seen the strong-armed Gaels repair,
And when the feast was over, once again unite
    For battle, in thy base-court fair!

TO THE RUINS OF DONEGAL CASTLE.

Alas, for thee, thou fort forlorn!
    Alas, for thy low, lost estate!
It is my woe of woes, this melancholy morn,
    To see thee left thus desolate!

O! there hath come of Connell's race
    A many and many a gallant chief,
Who, if he saw thee now, thou of the once glad face!
    Could not dissemble his deep grief.

Could Manus of the lofty soul
    Behold thee as this day thou art,
Thou of the regal towers! what bitter, bitter dole,
    What agony would rend his heart!

Could Hugh Mac Hugh's imaginings
    Pourtray for him thy rueful plight,
What anguish, O thou palace of the northern kings,
    Were his through many a sleepless night!

Could even the mighty Prince whose choice
    It was to o'erthrow thee—could Hugh Roe
But view thee now, methinks he would not much rejoice
    That he had laid thy turrets low;

Oh! who could dream that one like him,
    One sprung of such a line as his,
Thou of the embellished walls, would be the man to dim
    Thy glories by a deed like this!

From Hugh O'Donnell, thine own brave
    And far-famed sovereign, came the blow!
By him, thou lonesome castle o'er the Esky's wave,
    By him was wrought thine overthrow!

Yet not because he wished thee ill
  Left he thee thus bereaven and void;
The prince of the victorious tribe of Dalach still
  Loved thee, yea, thee whom he destroyed!

He brought upon thee all this woe,
  Thou of the fair-proportioned walls,
Lest thou shouldst ever yield a shelter to the foe,
  Shouldst house the black ferocious Galls!*

Shouldst yet become in saddest truth
  A *Dun-na-Gall*†—the stranger's own.
For this cause only, stronghold of the Gaelic youth,
  Lie thy majestic towers o'erthrown.

It is a drear, a dismal sight,
  This of thy ruin and decay,
Now that our kings, and bards, and men of mark and might,
  Are nameless exiles far away!

Yet, better thou shouldst fall, meseems,
  By thine own king of many thrones,
Than that the truculent Galls should rear around thy streams
  Dry mounds and circles of great stones.

As doth in many a desperate case
  The surgeon by the malady,
So hath, O shield and bulwark of great Coffey's race,
  Thy royal master done by thee!

The surgeon, if he be but wise,
  Examines till he learns and sees
Where lies the fountain of his patient's health, where lies
  The germ and root of his disease;

---

* "Foreigners." † "Fort of the foreigner."

Then cuts away the gangrened part,
    That so the sounder may be freed
Ere the disease hath power to reach the sufferer's heart,
    And so bring death without remead.

Now, thou hast held the patient's place,
    And thy disease hath been the foe;
So he, thy surgeon, O proud house of Dalach's race,
    Who should he be if not Hugh Roe?

But he, thus fated to destroy
    Thy shining walls, will yet restore
And raise thee up anew in beauty and in joy,
    So that thou shalt not sorrow more.

By God's help, he who wrought thy fall
    Will reinstate thee yet in pride;
Thy variegated halls shall be rebuilded all,
    Thy lofty courts, thy chambers wide.

Yes! thou shalt live again, and see
    Thine youth renewed! Thou shalt outshine
Thy former self by far, and Hugh shall reign in thee,
    The Tirconnellian's king and thine!

OWEN ROE WARD, bard to the O'Donnells, has left behind him an elegy on the melancholy death of Hugh O'Neill, the Earl of Tyrone, so celebrated by his successful opposition to the arms of Elizabeth, and Rory O'Donnell, Earl of Tyrconnell. These Ulster princes had fled from Ireland, in 1607, to escape a charge of conspiracy brought against them, on the authority of an anonymous letter dropped in the privy council, and both died shortly after, between 1608 and 1610, and were interred in one grave, on St. Peter's Hill, at Rome. On this charge, which was never proved on good evidence, and which subsequent writers have asserted to have been a conspiracy against these princes, six counties of Ulster were confiscated and forfeited to the crown.* The mourner addressed in this exquisite elegy was the female relative of one of the princes.

A LAMENT

FOR THE TIRONIAN AND TIRCONNELLIAN PRINCES BURIED AT ROME.†

METRICAL VERSION BY JAMES CLARENCE MANGAN.

Oh, woman of the piercing wail,
   Who mournest o'er yon mound of clay,
     With sigh and groan,
Would God thou wert among the Gael!
   Thou wouldst not then, from day to day,
     Weep thus alone.
'Twere long before, around a grave,
   In green Tirconnell, one could find
     This loneliness.

   *   *   *   *   *

---

* Dr. Anderson, an English writer, as quoted by Mr. Hardiman, states—"Artful Cecil employed one St. Lawrence to entrap the Earls of Tyrone and Tyrconnell, the Lord of Delvin, and other Irish chiefs, into a sham plot, which had no evidence but his. But those chiefs, being basely informed that witnesses were to be hired against them, foolishly fled from Dublin, and so, taking guilt upon them, they were declared rebels, and six entire counties were at once forfeited to the crown, which was what their enemies wanted."

† The present translation, including some verses here omitted, appeared in the *Irish Penny Journal*.

Beside the wave in Donegal,
  In Antrim's glens, or fair Dromore,
    Or Killilee,
Or where the sunny waters fall,
  At Assaroe, near Erna's shore,
    This could not be
On Derry's plains—in rich Drumcliaff—
  Throughout Armagh the great, renowned
    In olden years,
No day could pass but woman's grief
  Would rain upon the burial ground
    Fresh floods of tears!

Oh no! from Shannon, Boyne, and Suir,
  From high Dunluce's castle walls,
    From Lissadill,
Would flock alike both rich and poor,
  One wail would raise from Cruachan's halls
    To Tara's hill;
And some would come from Burron-side,
  And many a maid would leave her home
    On Leitrim's plains,
And by melodious Banna's tide,
  And by the Mourne and Erne, to come
    And swell thy strains!

    *   *   *   *

From glen and hill, from plain and town,
  One loud lament, one thrilling plaint
    Would echo wide.
There would not soon be found, I ween,
  One foot of ground among those bands
    For museful thought.
So many shriekers of the *keen**
  Would cry aloud, and clap their hands,
    All woe-distraught!

---

* *Caoine*, the funeral wail.

Two princes of the line of Conn
   Sleep in their cells of clay, beside
      O'Donnell Roe:
Three royal youths, alas! are gone,
   Who lived for Erin's weal, but died
      For Erin's woe!
Ah! could the men of Ireland read
   The names these noteless burial-stones
      Display to view,
Their wounded hearts afresh would bleed,
   Their tears gush forth again, their groans
      Resound anew!

*   *   *   *

Theirs were not souls wherein dull Time
   Could domicile decay, or house
      Decrepitude!
They passed from earth ere Manhood's prime—
   Ere years had power to dim their brows,
      Or chill their blood.

And who can marvel o'er thy grief,
   Or who can blame thy flowing tears,
      That knows their source?
O'Donnell, Dunnasava's chief,
   Cut off amid his vernal years,
      Lies here a corse,
Beside his brother Cathbar, whom
   Tirconnell of the Helmets mourns
      In deep despair,—
For valour, truth, and comely bloom,
   For all that greatens and adorns,
      A peerless pair.

Oh, had these twain, and he, the third,
  The Lord of Mourne, O Niall's son,
    Their mate in death—
A prince in look, in deed, and word—
  Had these three heroes yielded on
    The field their breath,
Oh, had they fallen on Criffan's plain,
  There would not be a town or clan
    From shore to sea,
But would with shrieks bewail the slain,
  Or chant aloud the exulting *rann**
    Of jubilee!

When high the shout of battle rose
  On fields where freedom's torch still burned
    Through Erin's gloom,
If one, if barely one of those
  Were slain, all Ulster would have mourned
    The hero's doom!
If at Athboy, where hosts of brave
  Ulidian horsemen sank beneath
    The shock of spears,
Young Hugh O'Neill had found a grave,
  Long must the North have wept his death
    With heart-wrung tears!

If on the day of Ballach-myre
  The Lord of Mourne had met, thus young,
    A warrior's fate,
In vain would such as thou desire
  To mourn, alone, the champion sprung
    From Niall the Great!

---

* Song.

No marvel this—for all the dead
   Heaped on the field, pile over pile,
     At Mullach-brack,
Were scarce an *eric** for his head,
   If Death staid his footsteps while
     On victory's track!

*   *   *   *   *

If on the day the Saxon host
   Were forced to fly—a day so great
     For Ashanee,†
The chief had been untimely lost,
   Our conquering host should moderate
     Their mirthful glee.
There would not lack on Lifford's day,
   From Galway, from the glens of Boyle,
     From Limerick's towers,
A marshalled file, a long array
   Of mourners, to bedew the soil
     With tears in showers!

If on the day a sterner fate
   Compelled his flight from Athenree,
     His blood had flowed,
What numbers all disconsolate
   Would come unmasked, and share with thee
     Affliction's load!
If Derry's crimson field had seen
   His life-blood offered up, though 'twere
     On victory's shrine,
A thousand cries would swell the *keen*—
   A thousand voices of despair
     Would echo thine!

---

* A compensation or fine.   † Ballyshannon.

Oh, had the fierce Dalcassian swarm
  That bloody night on Fergus' banks
    But slain our chief,
When rose his camp in wild alarm,
  How would the triumph of his ranks
    Be dashed with grief!
How would the troops of Murbach mourn,
  If on the Curlew mountains' day,
    Which England rued,
Some Saxon hand had left them lorn,
  By shedding there, amid the fray,
    Their prince's blood!

Red would have been our warriors' eyes,
  Had Roderick found on Sligo's field
    A gory grave,
No northern chief would soon arise
  So sage to guide, so strong to shield,
    So swift to save.
Long would Leith-Cuinn have wept, if Hugh
  Had met the death he oft had dealt
    Among the foe;
But had our Roderick fallen too,
  All Erin must, alas! have felt
    The deadly blow!

What do I say? Ah, woe is me!
  Already we bewail in vain
    Their fatal fall!
And Erin, once the great and free,
  Now vainly mourns her breakless chain,
    And iron thrall!
Then, daughter of O'Donnell, dry
  Thine overflowing eyes, and turn
    Thy heart aside,
For Adam's race is born to die,
  And sternly the sepulchral urn
    Mocks human pride!

Look not, nor sigh, for earthly throne,
   Nor place thy trust in arm of clay,
     But on thy knees
Uplift thy soul to God alone,
   For all things go their destined way
     As He decrees.
Embrace the faithful crucifix,
   And seek the path of pain and prayer
     Thy Saviour trod,
Nor let thy spirit intermix
   With earthly hope and worldly care
     Its groans to God!

And Thou, O mighty Lord! whose ways
   Are far above our feeble minds
     To understand,
Sustain us in these doleful days,
   And render light the chain that binds
     Our fallen land!
Look down upon our dreary state,
   And through the ages that may still
     Roll sadly on,
Watch thou o'er hapless Erin's fate,
   And shield at least from darker ill
     The blood of Conn!

The contrast is very striking between the conduct of Elizabeth (though a daughter of Henry VIII.) towards these princes, only requiring their submission, with the title of Earls, after ten years of successful opposition to her arms, until their final defeat, and that of the first of the Stuarts in confiscating their territory, without any overt act, merely on the authority of an anonymous letter. It forms a curious commentary on the fidelity of the Irish people to the Stuart race.

O'Hussey, the last hereditary bard of the great sept of Maguire, of Fermanagh, who flourished about 1630, possessed a fine genius. O'Hussey commenced his vocation when quite a youth, by a poem celebrating the escape of the famous Hugh Roe O'Donnell from Dublin Castle, in 1591, into which he had been treacherously betrayed, as already noticed. The noble ode which O'Hussey addressed to Hugh Maguire, when that chief had gone on a dangerous expedition, in the depth of an unusually severe winter, is as interesting an example of the devoted affection of the bard to his chief, and as vivid a picture of intense desolation, as could be well conceived. The present version, the only metrical one that has appeared, is one of those made expressly for the former edition of this work.

O'HUSSEY'S ODE TO THE MAGUIRE.*

TRANSLATED BY JAMES CLARENCE MANGAN.

Where is my Chief, my Master, this bleak night, *morrone?*
O, cold, cold, miserably cold is this bleak night for Hugh,
Its showery, arrowy, speary sleet pierceth one through and
    through,
Pierceth one to the very bone!

Rolls real thunder? Or, was that red livid light
Only a meteor? I scarce know; but, through the midnight dim
The pitiless ice-wind streams. Except the hate that persecutes *him,*
Nothing hath crueller venomy might.

---

* Mr. (later, Sir S.) Ferguson, in a fine piece of criticism on this poem, remarks: "There is a vivid vigour in these descriptions, and a savage power in the antithetical climax, which claim a character

An awful, a tremendous night is this, me-seems!
The floodgates of the rivers of heaven, I think, have been
 burst wide—
Down from the overcharged clouds, like unto headlong
 ocean's tide,
Descends grey rain in roaring streams.

Though he were even a wolf ranging the round green woods,
Though he were even a pleasant salmon in the unchainable
 sea,
Though he were a wild mountain eagle, he could scarce
 bear, he,
This sharp sore sleet, these howling floods.

Oh, mournful is my soul this night for Hugh Maguire!
Darkly, as in a dream, he strays! Before him and behind,
Triumphs the tyrannous anger of the wounding wind,
The wounding wind, that burns as fire!

It is my bitter grief—it cuts me to the heart—
That in the country of Clan Darry this should be his fate!
Oh, woe is me, where is he? Wandering, houseless, desolate,
Alone, without or guide or chart!

---

almost approaching to sublimity. Nothing can be more graphic, yet more diversified, than his images of unmitigated horror—nothing more grandly startling than his heroic conception of the glow of glory triumphant over frozen toil. We have never read this poem without recurring, and that by no unworthy association, to Napoleon in his Russian campaign. Yet, perhaps, O'Hussey has conjured up a picture of more inclement desolation, in his rude idea of northern horrors, than could be legitimately employed by a poet of the present day, when the romance of geographical obscurity no longer permits us to imagine the Phlegrean regions of endless storm, where the snows of Haemus fall mingled with the lightnings of Etna, amid Bistonian wilds or Hyrcanian forests."
—*Dublin University Magazine*, vol. iv.

Medreams I see just now his face, the strawberry-bright,
Uplifted to the blackened heavens, while the tempestuous
    winds
Blow fiercely over and round him, and the smiting sleet-
    shower blinds
The hero of Galang to-night!

Large, large affliction unto me and mine it is,
That one of his majestic bearing, his fair, stately form,
Should thus be tortured and o'erborne—that this unsparing
    storm
Should wreak its wrath on head like his!

That his great hand, so oft the avenger of the oppressed,
Should this chill, churlish night, perchance, be paralyzed
    by frost,
While through some icicle-hung thicket—as one lorn and
    lost—
He walks and wonders without rest.

The tempest-driven torrent deluges the mead,
It overflows the low banks of the rivulets and ponds—
The lawns and pasture-grounds lie locked in icy bonds,
So that the cattle cannot feed.

The pale bright margins of the streams are seen by none.
Rushes and sweeps along the untamable flood on every
    side—
It penetrates and fills the cottagers' dwellings far and wide—
Water and land are blent in one.

Through some dark woods, 'mid bones of monsters, Hugh
    now strays,
As he confronts the storm with anguished heart, but manly
    brow—
Oh! what a sword-wound to that tender heart of his were
    now
A backward glance at peaceful days!

But other thoughts are his—thoughts that can still inspire
With joy and an onward-bounding hope the bosom of Mac
    Nee—
Thoughts of his warriors charging like bright billows of the
    sea,
Borne on the wind's wings, flashing fire!

And though frost glaze to-night the clear dew of his eyes,
And white ice-gauntlets glove his noble fine fair fingers o'er,
A warm dress is to him that lightning-garb he ever wore,
The lightning of the soul, not skies.

AVRAN.*

Hugh marched forth to the fight—I grieved to see him so
    depart;
And lo! to-night he wanders frozen, rain-drenched, sad,
    betrayed—
*But the memory of the limewhite mansions his right hand hath
    laid
In ashes warms the hero's heart!*

    The great body of the poetical productions from this period are tinged with the political spirit of the times, which for better than half a century were marked by a succession of great and stirring events, in all of which Ireland took a conspicuous part, and always on the unsuccessful side; first, against the usurpation of Cromwell; next, in favour of the last of the Stuarts, at the Revolution; and again, in favour of the Pretender, in the several abortive attempts made for the restoration of his fated

---

    * A concluding stanza, generally intended as a recapitulation of the entire poem.

race. The chivalrous fidelity with which the people of this country adhered to the fallen fortunes of the Stuarts, considering how little they owed them, is, indeed, surprising. No doubt their leaning to the religious faith of the people was the chief ground of their attachment. But, in addition to this, there was superadded the tie of descent from the ancient princes of Ireland, which James I., previous to his accession to the British throne, had taken great pains to disseminate. Their claims, therefore, however slight they might be personally, appealed to the strong national, as well as the religious, feelings of the Irish people. Hence the numerous songs, termed Jacobite, are written in a spirit which the general reader might well be at a loss, at first, to comprehend; for while they breathe the utmost animosity against British rule, they are enthusiastic in aspirations for the return of the exiled family, recognising in them the descendants of their ancient kings.

It was formerly noticed that, in the time of Henry VIII., an order was issued, among many others, with reference to the persons and costume of the native inhabitants, prohibiting the custom of wearing the "Coolin," or flowing ringlets, in which they took so much pride. It was on this occasion that one of the bards composed the fine melody which goes by that name. Among the many verses to which this famous air has been wed at different times, the most popular are attributed to a bard named MAURICE O'DUGAN, who flourished about the middle of the century under review.

THE COOLIN.

TRANSLATED BY SAMUEL (LATER, SIR S.) FERGUSON, M.R.I.A.

Oh, had you seen the Coolin
   Walking down by the cuckoo's street,
With the dew of the meadow shining
   On her milk-white twinkling feet—
Oh, my love she is, and my colleen oge,
   And she dwells in Bal'nagar;
And she bears the palm of beauty bright
   From the fairest that in Erin are.

In Bal'nagar is the Coolin,
   Like the berry on the bough her cheek;
Brighty beauty dwells for ever
   On her fair neck and ringlets sleek:
Oh, sweeter is her mouth's soft music
   Than the lark or thrush at dawn,
Or the blackbird, in the greenwood singing
   Farewell to the setting sun.

Rise up, my boy, make ready
   My horse, for I forth would ride,
To follow the modest damsel,
   Where she walks on the green hill-side;
For ever since our youth were we plighted
   In faith, troth, and wedlock true—
Oh, she's sweeter to me, nine times over,
   Than organ or cuckoo!

Oh, ever since my childhood
   I loved the fair and darling child;
But our people came between us,
   And with lucre our pure love defiled:
Oh, my woe it is, and my bitter pain,
   And I weep it night and day,
That the colleen bawn of my early love
   Is torn from my heart away.

Sweetheart and faithful treasure,
    Be constant, still, and true;
Nor, for want of herds and houses,
    Leave one who would ne'er leave you:
I'd pledge you the blessed Bible,
    Without and eke within,
That the faithful God will provide for us,
    Without thanks to kith or kin!

    *   *   *   *

Another popular, though somewhat allegorical, lyric of this period, seems as if timed to the movements, and conveys the impressive solemnity, of a dead march. It was composed on a military leader, whose name it bears, who had distinguished himself in the southern counties, when, along with his followers, he took his departure for Spain, after the defeat of the royal adherents, and the sanguinary successes of the parliamentary forces in Ireland :—

JOHN O'DWYER OF THE GLEN.

TRANSLATED BY THOMAS FURLONG.

Blithe the bright dawn found me,
Rest with strength had crown'd me,
Sweet the birds sung round me,
        Sport was all their toil.

The horn its clang was keeping,
Forth the fox was creeping,
Round each dame stood weeping,
        O'er the prowler's spoil.

Hark, the foe is calling,
Fast the woods are falling,
Scenes and sights appalling
   Mark the wasted soil.

War and confiscation
Curse the fallen nation;
Gloom and desolation
   Shade the lost land o'er.

Chill the winds are blowing,
Death aloft is going,
Peace or hope seems growing
   For our race no more.

Hark, the foe is calling,
Fast the woods are falling,
Scenes and sights appalling
   Throng the blood-stained shore.

* * * * *

Nobles, once high-hearted,
From their homes have parted,
Scattered, scared, and started,
   By a base-born band.

* * * * *

Spots that once were cheering,
Girls beloved, endearing,
Friends from whom I'm steering,
   Take this parting tear.

Hark, the foe is calling,
Fast the woods are falling,
Scenes and sights appalling
   Plague and haunt me here.

A production of the period, called "The Roman Vision," written about 1650, would be a really fine historical poem, were it not so deeply tinged with the virulent sectarian and party spirit, so similar in all ages and all parties, which infects with an odious taint whatever it touches. It is true the times were such as to produce strong feelings, and afford a palliation for an equally strong expression of them. The poet, OWEN ROE MAC AN BHAIRD (WARD), supposes this vision to occur at Rome, over the grave of the Earls of Tyrone and Tyrconnell, previously noticed. After deploring the condition of the kingdom, and taking a rapid glance at the successive reigns from that of Henry VIII. downwards, he proceeds to sketch, with great spirit and power, the progress of the civil war, dwelling particularly on the exploits of the famous Irish general, Owen Roe O'Neill. In order to the understanding of the poem, it may be mentioned that the author was a strenuous supporter of Rinuncini, the pope's Nuncio, whose arrival in the country was the means of causing a breach between the Celtic and Anglo-Irish Catholics—the latter of whom the poet denounces as the authors of the misfortunes of the nation, and the sanguinary successes of Cromwell:—

THE ROMAN VISION.

TRANSLATED BY HENRY GRATTAN CURRAN.

No idle fiction this! too sadly true
Upon my wasting eyes the vision grew;
Too well my ears drank in the heavy sound.
Give it, ye winds, swift proclamation round.

   Lonely I strayed on Cepha's golden hill,
And memory came, my heart and eyes to fill,
While o'er the stone that shrouds the Gael in dust,
Bending, I mourned their country's fallen trust.
*   *   *   *   *   *

*　　*　　*　　*　　There slept
Tyrone, proud scion of the O'Niall race,
There too, O'Donnell, was thy resting-place,
Thou of the glittering blade! I brushed away
The mournful tribute to a better day—
When, lo, a nymph, whose brow, whose bosom's sheen,
Might shame the grace of beauty's fabled queen,
Came o'er the hill; her towering forehead bore
The impress of high thought—like molten ore
Gushed the gold ringlets o'er its polished plane:
Her cheek of snow confest one rose's stain;
She spoke, and vain, in sooth, were minstrel skill
To bid the chord such liquid sweets distil.

*　　*　　*　　*　　*

Her hands uplift to heaven, her streaming eyes
Raised with her fervid accents to the skies;
In words half broken by the labouring groan,
She poured her sorrows to the eternal throne.

　Say, thou Supreme, in pity dost thou deign
To bend thine ear, while suppliant I complain?
Or darkeneth thy brow? since mortals still
Should hail, nor dare to scrutinize thy will.
But deep and darkling doubts beset my soul;
For if one primal taint pervade the whole
Of the first parents' blighted race, and all
Are fallen alike with the first woman's fall,
Dread ruler! why doth the tremendous meed
Crush, with unequal force, the doomed seed?
Why doth the sinless bosom tinge the dart
That should have quivered to the guilty heart?
Why groan the lowly poor, while wealth and pride
Triumphant o'er the waves of fortune ride?
Shall they whose hearts confess thee holy, weep
Outcast, proscribed, and shall thy vengeance sleep?

*　　*　　*　　*　　*　　*

Say why doth Erin weep? what crime incurs
Thine ear averted?

   * * * *

Wilt thou look down in mercy?—say, oh say!
Or is thine ear for ever turned away?
And while the trusting spirit bends to thee,
Shall ruthless tyrants bow the neck, the knee?

   * * * *

Can we forget Elizabeth? Oh, never—
In Heber's heart she'll rankling live for ever;
The land grew waste beneath her—sex or age
Yielded no shelter from her bigot rage,
Till—bloodiest consummation—Mary fell,
To close her long account, but not the spell
That claimed her ruthless ministry; her sway
Devolved on James, and Phelim's land can say
How well the tyrant's sceptre graced his hand—
The " measuring chain " he cast upon the land—
Her nobles plundered for an alien race,
And with unhallowed rites defiled thy holy place.
Lo, next—his father's every taint and crime
Expanded in his soul's congenial clime—
His son succeeded, to embalm his fame
By deeds which let Leith Moath, Leith Cuin proclaim.
Spoiled of the rights long held from sire to son,
Their arms, and every glorious meed they won;
Of rank, of wealth, and—damned, foul decree—
Spurned from the shrines where they had knelt to thee
The very tongue, thy gift, in which they poured
Their souls, while at thy altars they adored,
Condemned to rudest jargon to give place.
For every woe he wrought upon her race,
The bitterness of Erin's heart ran o'er
In curses on the despot; and he wore

No amulet against the bolt that sped,
Retributive, to his devoted head.
'Twas a divine behest! high justice spoke,
And the pale tyrant's wily minions broke
Their hollow fealty; and the block and blade
Brought the stern quittance of man's rights betray'd.

   Yet ere it fell, to blast his glazing eye,
Maguire had tossed his banner to the sky—
Freedom's high priest; and kindling Ulster saw
Mac Mahon soon assert her bounteous law;
Last of the Finians, in whose ample mind
The gifts of his long lineage shone combined;
Of gentlest nature both, yet, thus pursued,
Two lions chafing in their might they stood;
Nor lured by conquest, nor athirst for fame,
Their rallying-word was the Eternal name.

       *   *   *   *

Nor yet unmarked by glory, Phelim's name,
Proud soul, and fitly shrined in such a frame!

       *   *   *   *

But see, what steadier lustre wins her gaze
Where, from Hispania's coast, O'Neill displays
His standard wide, and eager to sustain
Pours his proud chivalry athwart the main.
" Eogan the Red!"*   to freedom's strife he flies,
To veil the lustre of his vast emprise
With deeds of higher prowess— Cormac's blood
Bounds in the hero's heart—a tameless flood;
And all his grandsire's soul of flame he bears—
Attest it many a trophy that he wears,

---

    * The celebrated general, Owen Roe O'Neill.

The harvest of his hand in many a strife,
Waged in the tender spring-time of his life;
And when the greenness of his age went by,
The deeds he did are registered on high;
Those rife with living proofs let Spain avow,
Almania, richest wreath on Cæsar's brow:
Let France, the weeping Netherlands attest;
And oh! beyond them all, the brightest, best,
Let the Milesian race his glories tell;
Let Erin's voice the volumed record swell.

*　　*　　*　　*

Scarce the proud capital his course arrests,
While her high wall the girding fire invests—
Meath mourns the slaughter of her changling race;
Portlester's thousands, where is now their place?

*　　*　　*　　*

The echoing hills proclaimed to Inis-Con
His spreading conquests; Waterford o'erthrown;
Duncannon's waters in his course were dyed;
Wexford's keen blade hung useless by her side;
Nor Ross M'Truin, Ben Edar, stayed his tread;
Kilkenny bowed to him—his myriads spread
By Shannon's ample tide their long array;
The Avonmore was chequered with the play
Of his broad banners—by the Nore they stood,
And by the sedgy Barrow's headlong flood—
The Suir ran purpled with the stream of life;
Lough Erne rolled back proud tidings of the strife:
From Meane's high dome triumphant strains arose,
And Erin's centre caught the exulting close;
Thence to Beerhaven rolled the whelming tide,
And well might Sligo's unsupported pride
Droop at the sound of James'town's shattered wall,
Whose circling echoes thundered to appal.

*　　*　　*　　*

Hail to the conqueror, by the Gael upborne
(Bound these high hearts from shackles lately worn).
Mark, the proud flame his martial deeds avow
Burns in his breast, irradiates his brow;
Nor only battle's sterner lights illume,
There mercy smiles away impending doom,
From vanquished valour—and the warrior's eye,
As fixed dominion calm, hath ne'er been dry
O'er others' woe; and wise, albeit not yet
On his young brow had thought her impress set,
He weighs mankind, and, learning to appraise,
Hath learned to feel for frailty while it strays.
Strong as its iron mail, that kindling breast
To meek-eyed Ruth affords a shrine of rest.

* * * *

In council sage; in battle's fiery glow
Like the launched thunder 'mid the astonished foe.
And oh! when peace her gentle plume hath spread,
Mild as the melting tear that mourns the dead;
Witness, high Heaven, if yet his eagle gaze
Glared out to blast— no raven brood would raise
A wing, the sky-built eyry to invade:
Nor thus had cold succumbency betrayed
The land to Cromwell's sanguinary sway.

* * * * *

* * * * O great heart!
Proud gem of nature, so matured by art,
Had genius, culture, all, thou costly prey,
But decked thee for the tomb? thou envious clay,
Oh, what a mind thy leaden sleep hath bound;
Pure as pervading   lucid as profound!

* * * * *

Great spirits, fare you well! with mute regret
I gaze upon you, but my cheek is wet—
My tears shall number you; almighty power!
We had not dreamed of this disastrous hour.
Berean, Senan, our ancient prophets, saw
The dread revealings of thy mystic law;
Thy truth the breast of pious Kieran warmed,
Sage Columb's* lips thy spirit, Lord, informed—

* * * *

Nurtured with heavenly food, all these foreknew
Thy dispensations—but they bade us not
To deprecate this dark impending lot!
They said not "burning tears shall overflow,
Dark days shall come upon thee; shame and woe;
The reeking phial of a tyrant's hate
Shall waste thee, and thou shalt be desolate;
No joy or hope shall visit thy cold breast,
Till reason reel, with the huge weight opprest;
And thy soul, seared beneath the chastening rod,
Shall almost curse the high behest of God"—
And yet the burning tear had steeped my cheek,
And every pang that tyranny could wreak;
Shame, anguish,—all, save madness and despair,
To freeze my accents, or to warp my prayer,
All have I known; lost all; Oh God! my trust!
Faith only lives to raise me from the dust.

* * * *

Father of mercies! Oh, forgive the thought
That dared impugn thy fiat—if our lot
Have been a dark one, if defeat have bowed,
And trouble girded us as with a shroud,

---

* According to tradition, Columbkille foretold the invasion of Ireland.

Not thine the cruelty, but ours the crime
That stirred thee, slow to vengeance; in their prime,
Though sunk our thousands, Lord, we kiss the hand
Stretched, not to desolate, but purge the land.
Weigh well the lesson, ye surviving few,
Your country's hope, its moral points to you;
Scan the monition well, for it imparts
How human fate is shaped by human hearts;

   * * * *

The deep, the damning stains of cold deceit,
With virtuous seeming cloked—the deep retreat
Of the shut soul, with foulest treason rife—

   * * * *

These stains were yours—say not the hand of God
Hath armed the despot with an iron rod.
 Degenerate spirits! while my glazing eye
Dwells on these phantoms—when I hear the cry,
The long, low cry, whose quivering accents come
Back on me now—when I remember some,
True to the land, which glory had caressed,
And learning dignified, and affluence blessed—
But for the mean, malignant souls that strove,
By petty jealousies, and mean self-love,
And rankest perfidy, to render nought
The teeming promise of the deeds they wrought:
Scarce can my lips the struggling curse repress
On those who marred it into wilderness.
Weep for the treason! weep for the high race,
Its lordly victims! * * *

   * * * *

 Oh, what a lambent glory kindles now,
Chasing the shadows from Ierne's brow.

   * * * *

A vigorous race her children stand around,
Free as the billows, mighty as their bound.
Lo! where the opening clouds reveal a form
Tranquil as sunshine—stately as the storm.

* * * *

Peace o'er the prospect waves her mantling wing,
And bards, in Erin's tongue, her triumphs sing.
God of my hope! thou seest my soul's distress—
My tears—my anguish—God of mercy! bless
This union of the Gael!

* * * *

These suppliant accents breathed, all wildly clung
The maiden's hands, in holy transport wrung;
Her upraised brow with heaven's effulgence shone,
Then sudden wrapt from earth, the nymph was gone—
And solitude was on me, and the thought
Darker than solitude; in vain I sought,
With straining eye, to catch the lustrous hue
Of her unearthly vesture, as she flew;
And I was left alone with my despair,
Weeping the mighty hearts that mouldered there.
  Adieu to her, who poured beside the tomb
That wondrous tale of mingling joy and gloom.
Dear maid! blest tale! on every tear you drew
Sweet hope looked down—my soul remembers you.

The confiscation of the territories of O'Neill and O'Donnell, and the settlement of Ulster (which has been considered a brilliant success), in the beginning of the seventeenth century, stood pretty much in the relation of cause and effect to what is called the Great Rebellion, near the middle of it, to which the poet refers.

One of the most eminent minstrels of this period was THOMAS O'CONELLAN, who united to the most unrivalled skill on the harp high excellence as a poet, though, unfortunately, we must take this opinion upon the authority of his contemporaries. Conellan, as we learn from the "Bardic Remains," was born in the county Sligo, in the early part of the seventeenth century, of which he lived to see the close. Few particulars are known of his history. Many of his melodies were introduced into Scotland by the bard's brother, Lawrence O'Conellan, and have since continued, under different titles, among the most popular airs of what has been termed Scotch music. Of these may be mentioned "The Battle of Killiecrankie," and "Farewell to Lochaber"—the original titles of which were "Planxty Davis," and "The Breach of Aughrim." An ode, written with great spirit and elegance, in eulogy of O'Conellan's minstrelsy, by one of his contemporaries, has been preserved, and is here introduced in the absence of any specimens of his own poetic powers:—

ODE TO THE MINSTREL, O'CONELLAN.*

TRANSLATED BY SAMUEL (LATER, SIR S.) FERGUSON, M.R.I.A.

Enchanter, who reignest
  Supreme o'er the north,
And hast wiled the sole spirit
  Of true music forth;
In vain Europe's minstrels
  To honour aspire,
When thy swift, slender fingers
  Go forth on the wire.

---

* The present is one of three versions of this ode.

There is no heart's desire
  Can be felt by a king
That thy hand cannot match, from
  The soul of the string,
By the sovereign virtue
  And might of its sway.
Enchanter, who steal from
  The fairies your lay!

Enchanter, I say,
  For your magical skill
Can soothe every sorrow,
  And heal every ill;
Who hear you, they praise you,
  They weep while they praise;
For, charmer, you steal from
  A fairy your lays!

EDMOND O'RYAN, or Ned of the Hills, as he was called, a very noted person in his day, and one of the unhappy victims of the Revolution, who lost their property by following the fortunes of the last of the Stuarts, has left some pieces of elegiac poetry of great beauty. The author, who, after his loss of property, was forced to become the chief of a band of the daring freebooters termed Rapparees, appears, from the following tender effusion, to have been forsaken by his mistress for a more fortunate lover :—

EDMOND O'RYAN'S LOVE ELEGY.

TRANSLATED BY MISS BROOKE.

Bright her locks of beauty grew,
  Curling fair, and sweetly flowing;
And her eyes of smiling blue,
  Oh! how soft, how heavenly glowing!

Ah! poor plunder'd heart of pain!
    When wilt thou have end of mourning?
This long, long year I look in vain
    To see my only hope returning.

Oh! would thy promise faithful prove,
    And to my fond, fond bosom give thee:
Lightly then my steps would move,
    Joyful should my arms receive thee.

Then, once more, at early dawn,
    Hand in hand we should be straying,
Where the dew-drop decks the thorn,
    With its pearls the woods arraying.

Cold and scornful as thou art,
    Love's fond vows and faith belying,
Shame for thee now rends my heart,
    My pale cheek with blushes dying.

Why art thou false to me and love?
    (While health and joy with thee are vanish'd)
Is it because forlorn I rove,
    Without a crime unjustly banish'd?

Safe thy charms with me should rest,
    Hither did thy pity send thee:
Pure the love that fills my breast,
    From itself it would defend thee.

'Tis thy Edmond calls thee, love,
    Come, O come, and heal his anguish!
Driv'n from his home, behold him rove,
    Condemn'd in exile here to languish!

Oh, thou dear cause of all my pains !
   With thy charms each heart subduing,
Come on Munster's lovely plains,
   Hear again fond passion suing.

Music, mirth, and sports are here,
   Cheerful friends the hours beguiling ;
O wouldst thou, my love, appear,
   To joy my bosom reconciling !

Sweet would seem the holly's shade,
   Bright the clustering berries glowing ;
And, in scented bloom array'd,
   Apple blossoms round us blowing.

Cresses waving in the stream,
   Flowers its gentle bank perfuming ;
Sweet the verdant path would seem,
   All in rich luxuriance blooming.

O bright in every grace of youth !
   Gentle charmer !—lovely wonder !
Break not fond vows and tender truth !
   O rend not ties so dear asunder !

For thee all dangers would I brave,
   Life with joy, with pride, exposing ;
Breast for thee the stormy wave,
   Winds and tides in vain opposing.

O might I call thee now my own !
   No added rapture joy could borrow :
'Twould be like heaven, when life is flown,
   To cheer the soul, and heal its sorrow.

See thy falsehood, cruel maid!
  See my cheek no longer glowing;
Strength departed, health decay'd;
  Life in tears of sorrow flowing!

Why do I thus my anguish tell?—
  Why pride in woe, and boast in ruin?—
O lost treasure!—fare thee well!—
  Lov'd to madness—to undoing.

Yet, O hear me fondly swear!
  Though thy heart to me is frozen,
Thou alone, of thousands fair,
  Thou alone shouldst be my chosen.

Every scene with thee would please!
  Every care and fear would fly me!
Wintry storms and raging seas
  Would lose their gloom, if thou wert nigh me!

Speak in time, while yet I live;
  Leave not faithful love to languish!
Oh, soft breath to pity give,
  Ere my heart quite break with anguish.

Pale, distracted, wild, I rove,
  No soothing voice my woes allaying;
Sad and devious through each grove
  My lone steps are weary straying.

O sickness, past all medicine's art!
  O sorrow, every grief exceeding!
O wound, that in my breaking heart,
  Cureless, deep, to death art bleeding!

Such, O love! thy cruel power,
   Fond excess, and fatal ruin!
Such, O beauty's fairest flower!
   Such thy charms, and my undoing!

How the swan adorns that neck!
   There her down and whiteness growing;
How its snow those tresses deck,
   Bright in fair luxuriance flowing.

Mine, of right, are all those charms!
   Cease with coldness, then, to grieve me!
Take—O take me to thy arms,
   Or those of death will soon receive me.

Ah! what woes are mine to bear,
   Life's fair morn with clouds o'ercasting!
Doom'd the victim of despair!
   Youth's gay bloom, pale sorrow blasting!

Sad the bird that sings alone,
   Flies to wilds, unseen to languish,
Pours unheard the ceaseless moan,
   And wastes on desert air its anguish!

Mine, O hapless bird! thy fate!
   The plunder'd nest,—the lonely sorrow!
The lost, lov'd, harmonious mate!—
   The wailing night,—the cheerless morrow!

O thou, dear hoard of treasur'd love!
   Though these fond arms should ne'er possess thee,
Still, still my heart its faith shall prove,
   And its last sigh shall breathe to bless thee!

The peculiar aptitude of the Irish language for lyric poetry has been dwelt upon by all acquainted with its resources, and pronounced superior, in this respect, to any European language, the Italian excepted. Miss Brooke, who has laid her country under a deep debt of gratitude, by the patriotic exertion of her hereditary genius, remarks that "the poetry of many of our songs is indeed already music without the aid of a tune. . . . . Nor is this to be wondered at, when we consider the advantage the Irish has in this particular, beyond every other language, of flowing off in vowels upon the ear."* How either a people capable of conceiving, or a language embodying, sentiments so exquisite as some of the lyric effusions of the bards could ever have been deemed *essentially* barbarous, is truly a marvel; for theirs is indeed—

"The passionate strain that, deeply going,
Refineth the bosom it trembleth through."

The following stanzas are among the many beautiful fragments of this description, of which, unfortunately, the dates and writers are alike unknown. The translation is by Miss Brooke:—

As the sweet blackberry's modest bloom,
  Fair flowering, greets the sight;
Or strawberries, in their rich perfume,
  Fragrance and bloom unite:
So this fair plant of tender youth
  In outward charms can vie,
And, from within, the soul of truth,
  Soft beaming, fills her eye.

---

* *Reliques of Irish Poetry*, quarto edition, p. 229.

Pulse of my heart, dear source of care,
  Stolen sighs, and love-breath'd vows !
Sweeter than when, through scented air,
  Gay bloom the apple boughs !
With thee no day can winter seem,
  Nor frost nor blast can chill ;
Thou the soft breeze, the cheering beam,
  That keeps it summer still.

One other specimen of the same class may suffice. It was the joint production of two brother bards, named Fergus and M'Nally, and addressed to a young lady of the County Mayo, considered one of the greatest beauties of her time.*

BRIDGET FERGUS.

TRANSLATED BY JOHN D'ALTON, M.R.I.A.

What chief of Erin's Isle with coldness could regard,
  When wandering o'er
  Our western shore,
The flower of Rahard !
  Her eyes so blue,
  Like glistening dew
On summer rosebuds seen ;
  Her smile so bright,
  Her heart so light,
Her majesty of mien !

What wonder Erin's sons should be spell-bound in her gaze,
  For when I chance
  To catch her glance,
I startle in amaze.
  A swan-like grace
  Her neck displays ;

---

* *Irish Minstrelsy*, vol. i., p. 324.

  Her eye what witchery tells!
   Her budding breast,
   But half confest,
  Like living marble swells.

Should sickness weigh your frame, or sorrow cloud your mirth,
   One look upon
   This lovely one,
  This paradise on earth;
   Her winning air,
   Her tender care,
  Will put e'en death to flight;
   For though her eyes
   Beam witcheries,
  Her angel soul's more bright.

Her lips more sweet than honey, a pouting freshness warms,
   While all must own
   That beauty's throne
  Is centred in her charms;
   Though thousands prove
   The force of love,
  Deep cherished in her sight,
   A morning star
   She shines afar,
  On all with equal light.

Since the birth-day of creation, this sacred earth ne'er bore
   A heavenly mind
   So fairly shrined,
  As her's whom I adore;
   Just like the rose,
   The blush that glows
  O'er all her kindling cheeks;
   The dewy thyme
   In all its prime
  Seems breathing where she speaks.

Oh, that my fair and I were in some lonely place,
    Whose woods and groves
    Might hide our loves,
And none our wanderings trace:
    That bliss untold
    Beyond the gold
Of nations would I prize;
    For ever there
    Her love to share,
And triumph in her eyes.

The last specimen of the native poetry of the seventeenth century that shall be given, was written towards its close by some bard whose name has not survived, and is of a very different kind from any that has preceded it. It describes, in a highly humorous style, but apparently with a lurking moral, the progress of that epidemic vice, intemperance, which about this period commenced its frightful ravages in the land, and which Mr. Hardiman, perhaps not unjustly, attributes to the political degradation of the people. Prior to this period, indeed, there does not appear even a single allusion to the existence of such a vice; but it is significant of the spirit and manners of the times, that much of the subsequent poetry, including a large portion of the fine songs of Carolan, is of a Bacchanalian cast. Eternal honour to the man through whose patriotic exertions the nation purged itself, even temporarily, from this degrading vice. He left an example worthy of all imitation. In a poetical point of view, many of the compositions of this class are admirable. Of the present one, the first two stanzas are omitted.

ODE TO DRUNKENNESS.

TRANSLATED BY THOMAS FURLONG.

* * * * *

Chang'd by thy touch, the poor quite rich become,
   The low get lofty, and the timid bold;
Cripples get legs, speech bursts upon the dumb,
   And youth and vigour bless the weak and old;
The smile of joy steals o'er the face of trouble,
And folks, with scarcely half an eye, see double.

By thee the miser's purse is opened wide;
   The dolt, the dunderhead, thou renderest witty;
'Tis thine to lend meek lowliness to pride,
   Or melt the stony, selfish heart with pity;
Even old hell-daring, weather-beaten sinners,
When moved by thee, in grace become beginners.

How oft have I, dear spouse, inspired by thee,
   Poured the full tide of eloquence along;
How oft have other wights been chang'd like me,
   Now up and down, defending right or wrong;
Subtle thou art, and valorous, and strong:
'Tis thine to loose the slave, or bind the free,
   To paralyze with age the limbs of youth;
Void of all guile, with thee dwells barefaced truth.

* * * * *

Little thou heedest where thy head is laid;
   To thee the bog is as the bed of down;
Little thou mindest how thy clothes are made,
   Small thought hast thou of cloak, or cap, or gown;
For points of form thou carest not a pin,
But at the chimney would as soon come in—

Aye, just as soon as at the opening door;
The pelting rain may drench thee o'er and o'er,
The storm, the snow, the hail around may fall,
But still, my fearless spouse, thou smilest at them all.

To many an ancient house art thou allied—
   Oh, many a lordly one thy claim must own;
The soul of valour, and the heart of pride,
   Must stoop all humbly where thy face is shown.
   Wide round the land thy relatives are known,
The chiefs of might, O'Donnell and O'Neill,
   M'Guire, O'Rorke, M'Mahon, and O'Conor,
   Kildare's old earl, that pink of worth and honour,
O'Hanlons from the mountain and the vale,
Fair Antrim's chiefs, M'Donnell and O'Keane.
And hundreds more, that must unnam'd remain.
All these, though haughty, and though high they be—
These, darling drunkenness, are allied to thee.

Nor these alone—each doctor in the land,
   Each strutting soldier, drest in red or blue,
Each minstrel and each poet takes thy hand,
   Lawyers and ladies, and the clergy too.
   Knockgraney's head—the sky so fair to view—
Than thee, at moments, seem not more sublime,
But low thou liest again in little time:
Fill up the cup, may victory be thine own,
Go where thou wilt—for thee I'll live alone.

After making due allowance for political causes, however, it remains true—

> "How small, of all that human hearts endure,
>   That part which laws or kings can cause or cure!"

And it requires some other explanation adequately to account for what was a social vice of the time, even later and elsewhere than in Ireland, and as a preventative of which in ancient times the Greeks exhibited their slaves drunk publicly, in order to create disgust and contempt.

In the early part of the eighteenth century appeared several bards of eminence—the last bright flickerings of the light of song, ere it died out for ever. The principal of these were O'Neachtan, MacDonnell, and Carolan. The first and last of these belong almost equally to the latter part of the previous century. O'Neachtan and M'Donnell were two of the principal Jacobite writers. The Jacobite poetry being that of a party, and deeply tinged with its prejudices, is not now very interesting. It is, moreover, chiefly written in a sort of allegorical style, which, though the allusions were obvious at the time, detracts very much from the interest, to readers of the present day; for poetry, like wit, which requires to be explained at every step, however excellent in itself, loses half its charm. So pervading, indeed, is this figurative style throughout the Jacobite poetry, that, taken literally, much of it might pass for the love songs of the troubadours. Ireland, celebrated under the greatest possible variety of titles, is frequently represented as a lovely and disconsolate fair one, sometimes seen in visions, mourning the loss of her lover, and anxiously looking forward to his return. From these circumstances, few specimens of the Jacobite relics may suffice.

John O'Neachtan, of Meath, the first of these writers, appears to have been a person of considerable erudition, and an extensive miscellaneous author, from the list of his works furnished by O'Reilly. The following stanzas are from an elegiac tribute which he paid to the memory of Mary D'Este, the queen of the ill-fated James, on her decease, in the year 1718.

LAMENT
FOR THE QUEEN OF KING JAMES II.

TRANSLATED BY HENRY GRATTAN CURRAN.

* * * *

The stone is laid o'er thee! the fair glossy braid,
  The high brow, the bright cheek, with its roseate glow;
The bright form, and the berry that dwelt, and could fade
  On those lips, thou sage giver! all, all are laid low.

* * * *

Whatever of purity, glory, hath ever
  Been linked with the name, lovely Mary, was thine;
Woe! woe, that the tomb, ruthless tyrant, should sever
  The ties which our spirits, half broken, resign.

* * * *

The mid-day is dark with unnatural gloom—
  And a spectral lament, wildly shrieked in the air,
Tells all hearts that our princess lies cold in the tomb—
  Bids the old and the young bend in agony there!

* * * *

The most popular production of O'Neachtan, however, belongs to the Bacchanalian class, of which it is one of the very best, and as such is here given. Maggy Lauder is one of the innumerable Jacobite titles of Ireland.

MAGGY LAUDER.

TRANSLATED BY THOMAS FURLONG.

Here's, first, the toast, the pride and boast,
  Our darling Maggy Lauder;
Let old and young, with ready tongue,
  And open heart, applaud her;

And next prepare—here's to the fair,
    Whose smiles with joy have crown'd us;
Then drain the bowl—for each gay soul
    That's drinking here around us.

Come, friends, don't fail to toast O'Neill,
    Whose race our rights defended;
Maguire the true—O'Donnell, too,
    From eastern sires descended;
Up, up, again—the tribe of Maine
    In danger never failed us;
With Leinster's spear, for ever near,
    When foemen have assailed us.

*   *   *   *   *

Come, mark the call—and drink to all
    Old Ireland's tribes so glorious,
Who still have stood, in fields of blood,
    Unbroken and victorious:
Long, as of old, may Connaught hold
    Her boast of peerless beauty;
And Leinster show to friend and foe
    Her sons all prompt for duty.

A curse for those who dare oppose
    Our country's claim for freedom;
May none appear the knaves to hear,
    Or none who hear 'em heed 'em:
May famine fall upon them all,
    May pests and plagues confound them,
And heart-felt care and black despair
    Till life's last hour surround them.

May lasting joys attend the boys
  Who love the land that bore us ;
Still may they share such friendly fare
  As this that spreads before us.
May social cheer, like what we 've here,
  For ever stand to greet them ;
And hearts as sound as those around
  Be ready still to meet them.

Come, raise the voice, rejoice, rejoice,
  Fast, fast, the dawn 's advancing ;
My eyes grow dim, but every limb
  Seems quite agog for dancing :
Sweet girls, begin, 'tis shame and sin
  To see the time we 're losing ;
Come, lads, be gay—trip, trip, away,
  While those who sit keep boozing.

Where 's Thady Oge ?—up, Dan, you rogue,
  Why stand you shilly-shally ;
There 's Mora near, and Una 's here,
  And yonder 's sporting Sally ;
Now frisk it round—aye, there 's the sound
  Our sires were fond of hearing ;
The harp rings clear—hear, gossip, hear !
  Oh, sure, such notes are cheering.

Your health, my friend ! till life shall end,
  May no bad chance betide us ;
Oh ! may we still, our grief to kill,
  Have drink like this beside us ;
A fig for care !—but who 's that there
  That 's of a quarrel thinking ?—
Put out the clown, or knock him down,
  We 're here for fun and drinking.

> Tie up his tongue—am I not sprung
>   From chiefs that all must honour ?—
> The princely Gael, the great O'Neill,
>   O'Kelly, and O'Connor ;
> O'Brien the Strong ; Maguire, whose song
>   Has won the praise of nations ;
> O'More the Tough, and Big Branduff—
>   These are my blood relations !

John Claragh Mac Donnell, born in 1691, in a locality near Charleville, in the county of Cork, called "Claragh," from which he acquired that distinguishing appellation, was one of the chief bards of this period. O'Halloran has highly eulogized his antiquarian attainments and general scholarship, and states that he proposed to some gentleman in the county of Clare the project of translating Homer into Irish, which, however, he did not live to accomplish. Mac Donnell, who lived till about the middle of the century, was one of the last who maintained the ancient practice of holding stated bardic conventions. His poetry—at least such of it as has received an English dress—is almost exclusively of the Jacobite class, and possesses the allegorical style which characterizes most of the poetry of that description. In the following, taken from a recently published work,* the poet represents Albany, or Scotland, under the character of a lady mourning for her exiled lover, the unfortunate Pretender. In the song of "Grana Weal," he adopts the same figurative style, anxiously looking forward to the coming of the Stuart to espouse Grana Weal, under which name he celebrates Ireland.

---

* Daly's *Relics of Irish Jacobite Poetry.*

THE LADY OF ALBANY'S LAMENT FOR PRINCE CHARLES.

TRANSLATED BY EDWARD WALSH.

I'll not reveal my true love's name;
Betimes 'twill swell the voice of fame:
But, oh, may Heaven, my grief to quell,
Restore the hero safe and well!
  My hero brave, *ma ghile, m'fhear*,[*]
  My kindred love, *ma ghile, m'fhear;*
  What wringing woes my bosom knows,
  Since crossed the seas *ma ghile, m'fhear!*

His glancing eyes I may compare
To diamond dews on rosebuds rare;
And love and valour brighten o'er
The features of my bosom's store!
  My hero brave, &c.

No cuckoo's note by fell or flood,
No hunter's cry through hazel wood,
No mist-wrapt valley yields me joy,
Since cross'd the seas my royal boy.
  My hero brave, &c.

Oppress'd with grief, I hourly cry,
With bursting heart and tearful eye,
Since we, fair youth, did thee resign,
For distant shores, what woes are mine!
  My hero brave, &c.

---

[*] "The English reader will pronounce the Irish here as if written *ma yilli, mar.*"

The sun his golden glory shrouds
In mantle sad, of sable clouds;
The threat'ning sky of grief portends,
Since through far realms our lion wends.
    My hero brave, &c.

That haughty, noble, youthful knight,
Of feature bland, of spirit light—
Strong-handed, swift, in war's wild throng,
To chase to death the brave and strong!
    My hero brave, &c.

His wreathed hair, in graceful flow
Of ringlets rare, falls full below
His manly waist in yellow fold,
Like silken threads of curling gold!
    My hero brave, &c.

Like Aongus Oge, he bears command,
Or Louis of the trenchant brand,
Or Dairy's son, the great Conroy—
Brave Irish chiefs, my royal boy!
    My hero brave, &c.

Or Conall, who strong ramparts won,
Or Fergus, regal Rogia's son,
Or Conor, Ullad's glorious king,
Whom harp-strings praise, and poets sing—
    My hero brave, &c.

Wake, wake the wild harp's wildest sound,
Send sparkling flagons flowing round—
Fill high the wine-cup's tide of joy,
This health to thee, my royal boy!
    My hero brave, *ma ghile, m'fhear,*
    My kindred love, *ma ghile, m'fhear;*
    What wringing woes my bosom knows
    Since cross'd the seas *ma ghile, m'fhear!*

But all these must yield their "pride of place" to the gifted individual commonly considered as ending the line of the old national bards of Ireland. TURLOGH O'CAROLAN was born about the year 1670, near Nobber, in the county of Meath, of humble parents, but who still resided on the lands of Carolanstown, of which their ancestors had been disinherited. The bard, however, though he possessed the pride of ancestry, often expressed himself with great good sense and feeling on the subject. Instead of representing himself as a victim and martyr, he always said that, "never having possessed the property himself, he did not feel the loss of it;" well knowing, amid the various vicissitudes of fortune, how uncertain the portion which, under any circumstances, might have fallen to his own individual lot. To the kindness of Mrs. Mac Dermott, of Alderford House—a kindness which followed him through life— oung Carolan was indebted for all the education which he received, which was confined almost exclusively to the Irish language, then generally taught, as well as spoken. The representative of the ancient family of O'Conor, of Ballinagar, also interested himself in directing and promoting the mental improvement of the youthful bard; and a member of that family, the venerable Charles O'Conor, after a lapse of more than half a century, penned an elegant eulogy in memory of his departed friend. Before, however, he had attained the years of manhood, an event occurred which for ever deprived him of the aid of books. In his eighteenth year, he lost his sight by an attack of the small-pox; and this calamity, as in many similar cases, seems not only to have strengthened his mental vision and concentrated his intellectual resources, but was the means of deciding his future destiny in life. His harp then became his constant companion and solace under his bereavement; and in his twenty-second year, having procured a horse and attendant, he commenced as a professional minstrel, by visiting the houses of the nobility and gentry. It is recorded, that after his loss of sight he was much given to musing, and—as is told of Byron and the great Italian dramatist, Alfieri—for hours together

"His listless length at noontide would he stretch"—

and bask in the sun in motionless abstraction. Sometimes he would start up suddenly from these reveries, as in a fit of inpiration, call for his harp, and sweep the strings with an air of wild enthusiasm, as he gave expression, for the first time, to the notes of some of his exquisite melodies. The spot which he generally chose on these occasions was one of the small raths commonly called fairy mounds. And hence, it became a prevalent idea among the simple peasantry of the neighbourhood that the bard was favoured with fairy inspiration. Carolan, like a true poet, had been disappointed in love. To Bridget Cruise, the object of his earliest attachment, he addressed some of the first-fruits of his muse:—

BRIDGET CRUISE.

TRANSLATED BY THOMAS FURLONG.

Oh! turn thee to me, my only love,
  Let not despair confound me;
Turn, and may blessings from above
  In life and death surround thee.
This fond heart throbs for thee alone —
  Oh! leave me not to languish,
Look on these eyes, whence sleep hath flown,
  Bethink thee of my anguish:
My hopes, my thoughts, my destiny—
  All dwell, all rest, sweet girl, on thee.

Young bud of beauty, for ever bright,
　The proudest must bow before thee ;
Source of my sorrow and my delight—
　Oh ! must I in vain adore thee ?
Where, where, through earth's extended round,
Where may such loveliness be found ?
　Talk not of fair ones known of yore ;
　Speak not of Deirdre the renowned*—
　　　She whose gay glance each minstrel hail'd ;
　Nor she whom the daring Dardan bore
From her fond husband's longing arms ;
Name not the dame whose fatal charms,
　When weighed against a world, prevail'd ;
To each some fleeting beauty might fall,
　Lovely, thrice lovely, might they be ;
But the gifts and graces of each and all
　Are mingled, sweet maid, in thee !

How the entranc'd ear all fondly lingers
　On the turns of thy thrilling song ;
How brightens each eye as thy fair white fingers
　O'er the chords fly lightly along ;
The noble, the learn'd, the ag'd, the vain,
Gaze on the songstress, and bless the strain.
How winning, dear girl, is thine air,
How glossy thy golden hair ;
Oh ! lov'd one, come back again,
　With thy train of adorers about thee—
Oh ! come, for in grief and in gloom we remain—
　Life is not life without thee.

---

* Deirdre, a female much celebrated by our poets. She was the heroine of the tragical fate of the sons of Usneach, an Irish tale of the days of Conor, King of Ulster, and the foundation of Mr. Macpherson's Darthula.

> My memory wanders—my thoughts have stray'd—
>   My gathering sorrows oppress me—
> Oh! look on thy victim, bright, peerless maid,
>   Say one kind word to bless me.
> Why, why on thy beauty must I dwell,
> When each tortur'd heart knows its power too well?
> Or why will I say that favour'd and bless'd
>   Must be the proud land that bore thee?
> Oh! dull is the eye, and cold the breast,
>   That remains unmov'd before thee.

The irresistible fascination produced by the performance of this beautiful ode by the bard himself, in presence of the fair subject of it, has been recorded by Mr. O'Conor. From the following anonymous translation of some tender and elegant stanzas written in reply, it appears not to have been from any want of attachment for the bard, but in consequence of family circumstances, that his suit was not favourably received:—

Oh! tempt not my feet from the straight path of duty,
  Love lights a meteor, but to betray!
And soon wouldst thou tire of the odourless beauty,
  If grew not esteem upon passion's decay:
Then cease thee—ah! cease thee to urge and to plain!
I may not, I cannot, thy suit is in vain;
For filial affections a daughter restrain,
  And worthless were she who had slighted their sway.

Oh, how couldst thou trust for connubial affection
  The bosom untrue to its earliest ties?
Or where were thy bliss, when on sad recollection
  I'd sink, self-condemned, self-abashed, from thine eyes?
Then cease thee—ah, cease thee! 'tis fated we part!
Yet, if sympathy soften the pang to thy heart,
I will own, to this bosom far dearer thou art
  Than all that earth's treasure, earth's pleasure supplies.

But where am I urged by impetuous feeling?
   Thy tears win the secret long hid in my breast.
Farewell! and may time fling the balsam of healing
   O'er wounds that have rankled, and robb'd thee of rest.
Yet lose not, ah, lose not, each lingering thought
Of her who in early affection you sought,
And whose bosom, to cheer thee, would sacrifice ought
   But love to a parent, the kindest and best.

Carolan always maintained the dignity of his profession, and was above receiving any pecuniary remuneration. He was an honoured guest at the houses of all the nobility and gentry, where his company was eagerly sought and highly prized; and the hospitality of his entertainers was generally repaid by the tribute of his muse, either to the head of the house, or some of the fair members of the family. To follow him in all his wanderings would be impossible. Among many particulars of the bard's life, previously unknown, for which the public are indebted to the patriotic and indefatigable researches of the learned editor of the "Minstrelsy," is the following anecdote:—Though he seldom extended his peregrinations to the North, he visited, on one occasion, the county of Louth, and was brought without his knowledge into company with an eminent minstrel, named Mac Cuairt, or Macartney, whose skill upon the harp was superior to his own. The performance of Carolan, indeed, though correct, was never masterly or sweet, and he used the instrument chiefly as an accompaniment, and to aid him in the composition of his melodies. Both bards were blind, and neither knew the other. After listening for some time to the music of his rival, Carolan exclaimed, "Your music is soft and sweet, but *untrue.*" "Even truth itself is sometimes harsh," was the pointed rejoinder of Macartney. When, however, the minstrel learned on whom it was he had passed this censure, he burst out into an enthusiastic "Welcome," including these stanzas:—

* * * *

The prize of harmony, sent from afar,
   My Turlogh, that prize is thine;
It comes from Apollo, the old world's star,
   The guide of the sacred nine:
And each bard that wanders o'er earth and sea,
Seems proud to learn new lays from thee.

Oh! yes, from thee, thou son of song,
   Full many a strain may they borrow;
'Tis thine in their mirth to entrance the throng,
   Or soothe the lone heart of sorrow.

* * * * *

The Viscounts Mayo and Dillon were among his warmest patrons and admirers. It was probably at the mansion of one of them that the circumstance narrated by Goldsmith occurred. It is recorded that the poet, when very young, was taken to see Carolan, whose venerable and seer-like aspect made a deep impression on his youthful mind. In an elegant essay which he wrote on the genius of Carolan, he remarks: "His songs, in general, may be compared to those of Pindar, as they have frequently the same flight of imagination. . . . . Being at the house of an Irish nobleman, where there was a musician present, who was eminent in his profession, Carolan challenged him to a trial of skill. To carry the jest forward, his lordship persuaded the musician to accept the challenge, and he accordingly played over on his fiddle the fifth Concerto of Vivaldi.* Carolan immediately, taking his harp, played over the whole piece after him, without missing a note, though he had never heard it before. This produced some surprise; but their astonishment increased when he assured them that he could make a Concerto in the same taste himself, which he instantly composed, and that with such spirit and elegance, that it may be compared (for we have it still) with the finest compositions of Italy."†

Carolan, perhaps from his very imperfect knowledge of English, seldom extended his excursions beyond the bounds of Connaught, scarcely an old respectable family of which province he has left uncelebrated. His compositions are stated to have amounted in all to, at least, two hundred. Like the poets of the East, his muse delighted to expatiate on the theme of female loveliness. Very many of his lyrics are of that description. Of these, the following are among the best. In the first occurs a pathetic allusion to his blindness, which must remind the reader of a similar passage in Milton.

MILD MABLE KELLY.‡

TRANSLATED BY SAMUEL (LATER, SIR S.) FERGUSON.

Whoever the youth who, by Heaven's decree,
  Has his happy right hand 'neath that bright head of thine,
    'Tis certain that he
    From all sorrow is free,
Till the day of his death, if a life so divine

---

* The Italian composers he preferred to all others. Vivaldi charmed him, and with Corelli he was much enraptured.—O'CONOR.

† *Goldsmith's Essays.*

‡ The present is one of three versions of this fine song. The other two are in the "Minstrelsy" and Miss Brooke's "Reliques." The fair subject was one of the family of Castle Kelly, in the county of Galway.

Should not raise him in bliss above mortal degree.
Mild Mable Ni Kelly, bright coolun of curls!
    All stately and pure as the swan on the lake,
Her mouth of white teeth is a palace of pearls,
    And the youth of the land are love-sick for her sake.

No strain of the sweetest e'er heard in the land
    That she knows not to sing in a voice so enchanting,
        That the cranes on the sand
        Fall asleep where they stand.
Oh, for her blooms the rose, and the lily ne'er wanting
To shed its mild lustre on bosom or hand.
The dewy blue blossom that hangs on the spray,
    More blue than her eyes human eye never saw;
Deceit never lurked in its beautiful ray—
    Dear lady, I drink to you, *slainte go bragh!*

To gaze on her beauty the young hunter lies
    'Mong the branches that shadow her path in the grove;
        But, alas! if her eyes
        The rash gazer surprise,
All eyesight departs from the victim of love,
And the blind youth steals home with his heart full of sighs.
Oh, pride of the Gael, of the lily-white palm,
    Oh, coolun of curls to the grass at your feet;
At the goal of delight and of honour I am,
    To boast such a theme for a song so unmeet.*

---

* "The third verse of the original being either a repetition of the first and second, or an anticipation of the fourth, has been omitted." The following is Miss Brooke's version of the portion omitted in the above:—

    "As when the simple birds at night
      Fly round the torch's fatal light,
      Wild, and with ecstacy elate,
      Unconscious of approaching fate:

O'MORE'S FAIR DAUGHTER; OR, THE HAWK OF BALLYSHANNON.

AN ODE.

TRANSLATED BY THOMAS FURLONG.

Flower of the young and fair,
  'Tis joy to gaze on thee;
Pride of the gay hills of Maile,
Bright daughter of the princely Gael,
    What words thy beauty can declare?
    What eye unmov'd thy loveliness can see?
Fond object of the wanderer's praise,
Source of the poet's love-fraught lays,
    Theme of the minstrel's song,
    Child of the old renown'd O'More,*
    What charms to thee belong!

Happy is he who wafts thee o'er
  To yon green isle, where berries grow—
Happy is he who, there retired,
  Can rest him by thy side,
Marking, with love's delicious frenzy fir'd,
  Thy young cheek's changing glow,
And all the melting meaning of thine eyes;

  " So, the soft splendours of thy face,
    And thy fair form's enchanting grace,
    Allure to death unwary love,
    And thousands the bright ruin prove!

  " Ev'n he whose hapless eyes no ray
    Admit from beauty's cheering day,
    Yet, though he cannot *see* the light,
    He feels it warm, and knows it bright."

* " This family holds a conspicuous place in the annals of Ireland."

While round and round him, far and wide,
On the shore, and o'er the tide,
   Soft strains of music rise,
Varying thro' each winning measure,
Soothing every sense to pleasure.

    *   *   *   *   *

He to whom such joy is given,
Hath while here his share of heaven.

  Happy is he who hath gained thy love—
    Happy is he who hath won thee;
  Thy princely sires look from above,
    And smile in their pride upon thee:
The race of Tarah, the men of name,
First in the gory fields of fame.
Oh, fair one! wherever thou art
There is light for the eyes and balm for the heart;
The desire of desires, the essence of all
That can torture, or soften, or soothe, or enthrall;
  Thy step is life and lightness,
And thy glance hath a thrilling brightness;
    Thy waist is straight and slender,
    And thy bosom, gently swelling,
  Outdoes the swan's in whiteness,
    When she starts from her tranquil dwelling,
  And breasts the broad lake in splendour.

Sweet girl, those locks so wildly curled,
  Have snares and spells for many;
Oh, far may we range thro' this weary world,
  And find thee unmatch'd by any.
    Art thou a thing of earth
    A maid of terrestrial birth?
Or a vision sent from on high,
  In peerless beauty beaming,
Like those shapes that pass o'er the poet's eye,
  When he lies all idly dreaming?

Rejoice, rejoice, with harp and voice,
    For the hawk of Erne is near us;
She comes with a smile our cares to beguile,
    She comes with a glance to cheer us:
Not lov'd and lovely alone is she,
But bounteous as high-born dames should be.
On she moves, while the eyes of all
Hail the ground where her footsteps fall;
Sweet are her tones as the treasur'd store
    Which the weary, weary bee
Culls from the flowers he lingers o'er,
    When he wanders far and free;
Sweeter far than the cuckoo's lay,
That rings on the ear of a summer's day:
    But come, let this the rest declare—
    In this bumper flowing o'er
    We pledge the fairest of the fair—
    The daughter of old O'More.

This exquisite ode is one of the finest productions of Carolan. The English version is, no doubt, to a considerable extent, like many of the others, paraphrastical. But may not the same be said of the finest poetical versions of the classics we possess? Who imagines that the great Grecian bard possessed the polish in the original which he has received at the hands of his English interpreter, the poet of Twickenham, though he has thereby been shorn of much of his majesty? And perhaps, after all—literal translations apart—paraphrases are not the least satisfactory, for the great felicity is to translate the *spirit* as well as the letter of poetry. This is a task, doubtless, which requires great ability and great judgment—to preserve the essential spirit of the original, and yet to adapt it to the genius of the language into which it is transfused, and to the style of thought and feeling of the people, and the times for which it is intended. This is only to be attained by hitting the happy medium.

The lady to whom the following is addressed belonged to the family inheriting the possessions once the property of the bard's ancestors :—

GRACE NUGENT.*

TRANSLATED BY S. (LATER, SIR S.) FERGUSON, M.R.I.A.

Brightest blossom of the spring,
Grace, the sprightly girl, I sing :
Grace who bore the palm of mind
From all the rest of womankind :
Whomsoe'er the fates decree,
Happy fate for life to be,
Day and night my coolun near,
Ache or pain need never fear.

Her neck outdoes the stately swan,
Her radiant face the summer dawn :
Ah, happy thrice the youth for whom
The fates design that branch of bloom !
Pleasant are your words benign,
Rich those azure eyes of thine ;
Ye who see my queen, beware
Those twisted links of golden hair ! †

---

* "The fair subject of this song was sister to the late John Nugent, Esq., of Castle Nugent, Calumbre. She lived with her sister, Mrs. Conmee, near Balanagar, in county Roscommon, at the time she inspired our bard."—*Historical Memoirs of Irish Bards*, Appendix, p. 78.

† "Hair is a favourite object with all the Irish poets, and endless is the variety of their descriptions :—'Soft, misty curls'—'thick, branching tresses of bright redundance'—'locks of fair waving beauty'—tresses flowing on the wind, like the bright waving flame of an inverted torch.' They even affect to inspire it with expression, as 'locks of *gentle* lustre' 'tresses of *tender* beauty'—'the maid with the mildly flowing hair,' &c., &c."

This is what I fain would say
To the bird-voiced lady gay—
Never yet conceiv'd the heart
Joy that Grace cannot impart:
Fold of jewels, case of pearls!
Coolun of the circling curls!
More I say not, but no less
Drink your health and happiness.

In 1733 the bard was bereft of his wife. The beautiful elegy which he composed on this occasion has been much and deservedly admired. The following version by Miss Brooke appeared originally in Walker's Bards, where it was introduced with this just compliment:—" For the benefit of the English reader, I shall here give an elegant paraphrase of this monody, by a young lady whose name I am enjoined to conceal; with the modesty ever attendant on true merit, and with the sweet timidity natural to her sex, she shrinks from the public eye." There is also another version in the " Minstrelsy."

CAROLAN'S MONODY ON THE DEATH OF HIS WIFE.

TRANSLATED BY MISS BROOKE.

Were mine the choice of intellectual fame,
    Of spellful song, of eloquence divine,
Painting's sweet power, philosophy's pure flame,
    And Homer's lyre and Ossian's harp were mine,
The splendid arts of Erin, Greece, and Rome,
    In Mary lost would lose their wonted grace;
All would I give to snatch her from the grave,
    Again to fold her in my fond embrace.

Desponding, sick, exhausted with my grief,
   Awhile the founts of sorrow cease to flow ;
In vain—I rest not, sleep brings no relief—
   Cheerless, companionless, I wake to woe.
Nor birth nor beauty shall again allure,
   Nor fortune win me to another bride ;
Alone I'll wander, and alone endure,
   Till death restore me to my dear one's side.

Once, every thought and every scene was gay,
   Friends, mirth, and music all my hours employ'd ;
Now doom'd to mourn my last sad years away,
   My life a solitude—my heart a void !
Alas, the change ! to change again no more !
   For every comfort is with Mary fled ;
And ceaseless anguish shall her loss deplore,
   Till age and sorrow join me with the dead.

Adieu, each gift of nature and of art,
   That erst adorned me in life's early prime !
The cloudless temper, and the social heart,
   The soul ethereal, and the flight sublime ;
Thy loss, my Mary, chas'd them from my breast ;
   Thy sweetness cheers, thy judgment aids no more ;
The muse deserts a heart with grief opprest,
   And lost is every joy that charmed before.

   The bard only survived his partner about five years, having paid the debt of nature in the year 1738, at the moderate age of sixty-eight. To the last he showed "the ruling passion strong in death." Feeling that his hours were numbered, he called for his harp, and in the excitement of what he knew to be a final effort, produced his "Farewell to Music," to which he gave an expression so captivating and touching as to dissolve all present in tears. His remains, which were interred in the parish church of Kilronan, county of Roscommon, were accompanied to their last resting-place by the clergy of all denominations and the gentry from the neighbouring counties. Yet, though the spot is still well known, and pointed out to the pilgrims of his genius to this day, not even " some rude memorial " tells where his ashes moulder. Such has ever been, with few rare exceptions, the fate of Irish genius !

His memory, however, was not left unsung. His intimate friend and brother bard, M'Cabe, poured the tribute of verse over his grave. M'Cabe, who lived in a distant part of the country, unconscious of his decease, had gone to visit Carolan. As he passed the churchyard near his destination, he inquired after his friend of a peasant whom he met. The man pointed to his grave, and wept.* M'Cabe, cut to the soul, vented his grief in the following stanzas :—

ELEGY ON THE DEATH OF CAROLAN.
TRANSLATED BY MISS BROOKE.

I came, with friendship's face, to glad my heart,
But sad and sorrowful my steps depart !
In my friend's stead a spot of earth was shown,
And on his grave my woe-struck eyes were thrown !
No more to their distracted sight remain'd
But the cold clay, that all they lov'd contain'd,
And there his last and narrow bed was made,
And the drear tombstone for its covering laid !

Alas ! for this my aged heart is wrung !
Grief chokes my voice and trembles on my tongue.
Lonely and desolate, I mourn the dead,
The friend with whom my every comfort's fled !

---

* *Reliques of Irish Poetry*, p. 224.

There is no anguish can with this compare !
No pains, diseases, suffering, or despair,
Like that I feel, while such a loss I mourn,
My heart's companion from its fondness torn !
Oh, insupportable, distracting grief !
Woe that through life can never hope relief !
Sweet-singing harp !* thy melody is o'er !
Sweet friendship's voice ! I hear thy sound no more !
My bliss, my wealth of poetry,* is fled,
And every joy with him I lov'd is dead !
Alas ! what wonder (while my heart drops blood
Upon the woes that drain its vital flood)
If maddening grief no longer can be borne,
And frenzy fill the breast with anguish torn !

Though there were several writers in the native language subsequent to Carolan, yet he may justly be regarded as the last great representative of the ancient bards of Ireland. The language itself, indeed, after his time, began to fall into comparative disuse ; for, while the feelings and inclinations of the people led them to retain their ancient language, the irresistible circumstances and necessities of social life were fast compelling them to the adoption of another. To this transition state we must attribute the origin of those blunders, termed bulls, for which the people have acquired such an unenviable notoriety, which has been an endless source of dull facetiousness, and has been tacitly, though most unjustly, attributed to a defect of understanding.

Only one other specimen—a favourable one of the poetry subsequent to Carolan—shall be given. The author was JOHN O'CULLANE, or Collins, who was born in the county

---

* " Both of these expressions are exactly literal."

of Cork, about the middle of the last century, and educated with a view to orders, but devoted himself to the instruction of youth.* Collins, though not a professed bard like Carolan, has written several other pieces, which, from the merit of the present elegy, it would be desirable to see translated. He may be regarded as the last of the sons of song who have

"Entwined their name with their land's language."

That he was a true poet, this intensely and touchingly pathetic elegy would alone sufficiently evince :—

ELEGY
ON THE RUINS OF TIMOLEAGUE ABBEY.

TRANSLATED BY S. (LATER, SIR S.) FERGUSON, M.R.I.A.

 Lone and weary as I wandered
  By the bleak shore of the sea.
 Meditating and reflecting
  On the world's hard destiny;

 Forth the moon and stars 'gan glimmer
  In the quiet tide beneath,
 For, on slumbering spray and blossom,
  Breathed not out of heaven a breath.

 On I went, in sad dejection,
  Careless where my footsteps bore ;
 Till a ruined church before me
  Opened wide its ancient door ;

---

* *Hardiman's Irish Minstrelsy*, vol. ii., p. 410.

Till I stood before the portals,
    Where of old were wont to be,
For the blind, the halt, the leper,
    Alms and hospitality.

Still the ancient seat was standing,
    Built against the buttress grey,
Where the clergy used to welcome
    Weary travellers on their way.

There I sat me down in sadness,
    'Neath my cheek I placed my hand,
Till the tears fell hot and briny
    Down upon the grassy land.

There (I said in woeful sorrow,
    Weeping bitterly the while)
Was a time when joy and gladness
    Reigned within this ruined pile;

Was a time when bells were tinkling,
    Clergy preaching peace abroad,
Psalms a-singing, music ringing
    Praises to the mighty God.

Empty aisle, deserted chancel,
    Tower tottering to your fall,
Many a storm since then has beaten
    On the grey head of your wall!

Many a bitter storm and tempest
    Has your roof-tree turned away,
Since you first were formed a temple
    To the Lord of night and day.

ON THE RUINS OF TIMOLEAGUE ABBEY.

Holy house of ivied gables,
   That were once the country's boast,
Houseless now, in weary wandering,
   Are you scattered, saintly host.

Lone you are to-day and dismal,
   Joyful psalms no more are heard,
Where, within your choir, her vesper
   Screeches the cat-headed bird.

Ivy from your eaves is growing,
   Nettles round your green hearth-stone;
Foxes howl where, in your corners,
   Drooping waters make their moan.

Where the lark to early matins
   Used your clergy forth to call,
There, alas! no tongue is stirring,
   Save the daw's upon the wall.

Refectory cold and empty,
   Dormitory bleak and bare,
Where are now your pious uses,
   Simple bed, and frugal fare?

Gone your abbot, rule, and order,
   Broken down your altar-stones;
Nought see I beneath your shelter,
   Save a heap of clayey bones.

Oh, the hardship—oh, the hatred,
   Tyranny and cruel war,
Persecution and oppression,
   That have left you as you are!

I myself once also prospered,
  Mine is, too, an altered plight;
Trouble, care, and age have left me
  Good for nought but grief to-night.

Gone my motion and my vigour,
  Gone the use of eye and ear;
At my feet lie friends and children,
  Powerless and corrupting there.

Woe is written on my visage,
  In a nut my heart would lie;
Death's deliverance were welcome—
  Father, let the old man die!*

We are informed by Mr. Hardiman that "in the early part of the last century, periodical meetings or 'sessions' of the Munster bards were held at Charleville and Bruree, in the counties of Cork and Limerick, where the aspirants for poetic celebrity recited their productions before the assembly. They to whom prizes were adjudged . . . . were publicly crowned and distinguished by other marks of honour."† The same custom is still continued in Wales, and, apart from

---

* In the version by Furlong, in the "Minstrelsy," the concluding portion runs thus:—

"I too have chang'd—my days of joy are done—
  My limbs grow weak, and dimness shades mine eye;
Friends, kindred, children, dropping one by one
  Beneath these walls, now mouldering round me lie;
My look is sad, my heart has shrunk in grief—
Oh! death, when wilt thou come, and lend a wretch relief?"

† *Irish Minstrelsy*, Introduction, p. xxviii.

the production of any high order of poetry, it may at least claim to have been a custom which encouraged intellectual habits, for which the press may now be considered a substitute. In Wales at least it has the sanction of so distinguished a critic as Matthew Arnold.* But, whatever question there might be as to the feasibility or desirability of reviving these meetings, there could be no reason assigned why the national music should be a thing of the past, unless, indeed, as has been sometimes said, that it is a lost art. Instead of that morbid and injurious addiction to politics—injurious to the best material interests, public and private, as experience has sufficiently proved—it were to be desired that patriotism might take something of the form of that of Scotland and Wales, which cherishes with enthusiasm, without the aid of any professional agitators, its historic and literary memories, and without in any way detracting from their pride and loyalty as an integral part of a great empire—

"Above all Greek, above all Roman fame."

The cultivation of the ancient Celtic as a written language is a highly laudable pursuit, although unfortunately it has no material incentive; but there is at least a social one in the cultivation of our ancient music, which Mr. Bunting devoted himself with such pious labour to preserving. Under the influence of the wave of patriotism in the last century, induced by the enthusiasm of the Volunteer movement, a meeting of existing professors of the harp was held, but resulted in no permanent organization for its revival as a national instrument. Is it too late for such an effort by

---

* *Study of Celtic Literature*, Introduction, p. ix.

means of a society? Music is an element of social and individual happiness.

> "Verse aids the mind, however rude the strain:
> All at her work the village maiden sings,
> Nor, while she turns the busy wheel around,
> Revolves the sad vicissitudes of things."

Let us hope that some means may yet be found for the revival of this national instrument, or in time its existence, as such, may come to be considered a myth. It might at least become a valuable resource for those in some degree compensated for the deprivation of sight by a musical capacity.

In conclusion, there seems reason to hope that, with the new interest which has of late sprung up with regard to our ancient literature, and with the machinery of more than one society which has been put in operation, all the mutilated fragments which have hitherto been made public may be but the commencement of such a full and ample collection of our native poetry (for which there are, even yet, materials), as shall evince to the world that Ireland possesses literary monuments in its ancient, and still spoken, language, equal, at least, to those of any country of Northern or Western Europe. When such shall appear, it must place upon a valid and enduring foundation our national pretensions to an early and comparatively brilliant civilization—so long regarded as the offspring of national vanity—and fling back the oft-repeated calumny of our ancient barbarism and unlettered condition.

It is a matter of deep congratulation that many of the sources of discord and distraction which, through so many ages, made

> "Hearts fall off that ought to twine,"

and severed the bond of brotherhood among Irishmen, are no longer in existence; and now, when the mingled jealousy, distrust, and alienation, so long unhappily prevalent, promise soon to be numbered only with the things that were, we possess in our literature a common ground of deep sympathy and paramount interest, well calculated to cement the tie of returning confidence and mutual goodwill. In rescuing from oblivion the mouldering fragments which mutely testify of a comparative civilization, and early cultivation of letters, in our country, we have a labour of love, as well as of duty, which must commend itself to all men, whatever be their distinctions of sect or party, who would respect their country, or desire to see it respected of others; for it must be sufficiently obvious to every ordinarily enlightened mind, that in proportion to the elevated or depressed state of literature in a country, it rises or sinks in the scale of nations.

The remark by a distinguished politician, on the importance of a people's poetry, has been previously quoted; and when the full collection of our ancient lays shall have been given to the public in a worthy form, it cannot be that its streams, wafting with them the traditions and recollections of by-gone times, should enter into the popular mind without nationalizing its tone, and steeping it in patriotic feeling. Nor can it fail to produce a corresponding improvement, a reviving freshness, in our existing literature, similar to the marked change effected in that of England, by the illustrious labours of Percy and Ellis.

On this green spot of neutral ground—this charmed circle from the blighting influences of party—with this accumulation of fresh materials—with the new power of a united people, and the new hopes inspired by the incalculable resources of our country (only now beginning to receive their development), we may yet hope to rear up no unsightly temple of national literature, which shall be glorious as the spirit it fosters—beautiful as the land it adorns.

> "Long, long be my heart with such memories fill'd;
> Like a vase in which roses have once been distill'd,
> You may break, you may ruin the vase if you will,
> But the scent of the roses will hang round it still."
>
> MOORE.

MISCELLANEOUS ADDENDA.

THE DIRGE OF DARGO.*

TRANSLATED BY JOHN ANSTER, LL.D.

CHORUS.

Like the oak of the vale was thy strength and thy height,
Thy foot like the erne† of the mountain in flight;
Thy arm was the tempest of Loda's fierce breath!
Thy blade, like the blue mist of Lego, was death!

Alas! how soon the thin cold cloud
The hero's bloody limbs must shroud!
And who shall tell his sire the tale?
And who shall soothe his widow's wail?
—I see thy father, full of days—
For thy return behold him gaze.
The hand that rests upon the spear
Trembles in feebleness and fear;
He shudders, and his grey bald brow
Is shaking like the aspen-bough;
He gazes, till his dim eyes fail
With gazing on the fancied sail;—

---

* " The original is printed in Smith's Gaelic Poems."
† " Eagle."

Anxious he looks—what sudden streak
Flits like a sunbeam o'er his cheek !
—" Joy, joy, my child, it *is* the bark
That bounds on yonder billow dark !"—
His child looks forth with straining eye,
And sees the light cloud sailing by.
—His grey head shakes—how sad, how weak
That sigh !—how sorrowful that cheek !

His bride from her slumbers will waken and weep ;
But when shall the hero arouse him from sleep ?
The yell of the stag-hound—the clash of the spear,
May ring o'er his tomb—but the dead will not hear.
Once he wielded the sword—once he cheered to the hound—
But his pleasures are past, and his slumbers are sound.
—Await not his coming, ye sons of the chace—
Day dawns !—but it nerves not the dead for the race ;
—Await not his coming, ye sons of the spear—
The war-song ye sing—but the dead will not hear !

Oh, blessing be with him who sleeps in the grave,
The leader of Lochlin ! the young and the brave !—
On earth didst thou scatter the strength of our foes,
—Then blessing be thine in thy cloud of repose !

CHORUS.

Like the oak of the vale was thy strength and thy height ;
Thy foot like the erne of the mountain in flight ;
Thy arm was the tempest of Loda's fierce breath ;
Thy blade, like the blue mist of Lego, was death !

THE WOMAN OF THREE COWS.*

TRANSLATED BY J. C. MANGAN.

O Woman of Three Cows, agragh! don't let your tongue thus rattle!
Oh, don't be saucy, don't be stiff, because you may have cattle.
I have seen—and here's my hand to you, I only say what's true—
A many a one with twice your stock not half so proud as you.

Good luck to you, don't scorn the poor, and don't be their despiser,
For worldly wealth soon melts away, and cheats the very miser,
And death soon strips the proudest wreath from haughty human brows;
Then don't be stiff, and don't be proud, good Woman of Three Cows.

See where Mononia's heroes lie, proud Owen More's descendants—
'Tis they that won the glorious name, and had the grand attendants.

---

* "This specimen, which is of a homely cast, was intended as a rebuke to the saucy pride of a woman in humble life, who assumed airs of consequence, from being the possessor of three cows. Its author's name is unknown; but its age may be determined, from its language, as belonging to the early part of the seventeenth century; and that it was formerly very popular in Munster may be concluded from the fact that the phrase, 'Easy, O Woman of Three Cows,' has become a saying, in that province, to lower the pretensions of proud or boastful persons."—*Translator.*

If *they* were forced to bow to fate, as every mortal bows,
Can *you* be proud, can *you* be stiff, my Woman of Three Cows?

The brave sons of the Lord of Clare, they left the land to mourning,
Mavrone! for they were banished, with no hope of their returning;
Who knows to what abodes of want those youths were driven to house!
Yet *you* can give yourself these airs, O Woman of Three Cows.

Oh, think of O'Donnel of the Ships, the chief whom nothing daunted—
See how he fell in distant Spain, unchronicled, unchanted!
He sleeps, the great O'Sullivan, where thunder cannot rouse—
Then ask yourself should *you* be proud, good Woman of Three Cows.

O'Ruark, Maguire, those souls of fire, whose names are shrined in story—
Think how their high achievements once made Erin's greatest glory;
Yet now their bones lie mouldering under weeds and cypress boughs,
And so, for all your pride, will you, O Woman of Three Cows.

The O'Carrolls also, famed when fame was only for the boldest,
Rest in forgotten sepulchres, with Erin's best and oldest;
Yet who so great as they of yore in battle or carouse?
Just think of that, and hide your head, good Woman of Three Cows.

Your neighbours poor, and you, it seems, are big with vain
   ideas,
Because, *inagh,** you've got three cows, one more, I see
   than *she* has;
That tongue of yours wags more at times than charity
   allows—
But if you're strong, be merciful, great Woman of Three
   Cows.

THE SUMMING UP.

Now there you go, you still, of course, keep up your scorn-
   ful bearing,
And I'm too weak to hinder you—but, by the cloak I'm
   wearing,
If I had but *four* cows myself, even though you were my
   spouse,
I'd thrash you well, to cure your pride, my Woman of Three
   Cows.

TRANSLATIONS BY S. (SIR S.) FERGUSON, M.R.I.A.†

O'BYRNE'S BARD TO THE CLANS OF WICKLOW.

God be with the Irish host!
Never be their battle lost!
For, in battle, never yet
Have they basely earned defeat.

---

* "Forsooth."

† As all the remaining pieces are by this gentleman, the repe-
tition of the name at each is unnecessary.

Host of armour, red and bright,
May ye fight a valiant fight!
For the green spot of the earth,
For the land that gave you birth.

Who in Erin's cause would stand,
Brothers of the avenging band,
He must wed immortal quarrel,
Pain, and sweat, and bloody peril.

On the mountain, bare and steep,
Snatching short, but pleasant sleep,
Then, ere sunrise, from his eyrie,
Swooping on the Saxon quarry.

What although you've failed to keep
Liffey's plain or Tara's steep,
Cashel's pleasant streams to save,
Or the meads of Cruachan Maev.

Want of conduct lost the town,
Broke the white-walled castle down;
Moira lost, and old Taltin,
And let the conquering stranger in.

'Twas the want of right command,
Not the lack of heart or hand,
Left your hills and plains to-day
'Neath the strong Clan Saxon's sway.

Ah, had Heaven never sent
Discord for our punishment,
Triumphs few o'er Erin's host
Had Clan London now to boast.

Woe is me, 'tis God's decree
Strangers have the victory:
Irishmen may now be found
Outlaws upon Irish ground.

Like a wild beast in his den,
Lies the chief, by hill and glen,
While the strangers, proud and savage,
Creevan's richest valleys ravage.

Woe is me, the foul offence,
Treachery and violence,
Done against my people's rights—
Well may mine be restless nights!

When old Leinster's sons of fame,
Heads of many a warlike name,
Redden their victorious hilts
On the Gaul, my soul exults.

When the grim Gaul, who have come
Hither o'er the ocean's foam,
From the fight victorious go,
Then my heart sinks deadly low.

Bless the blades our warriors draw,
God be with Clan Ranelagh!
But my soul is weak for fear,
Thinking of their danger here.

Have them in thy holy keeping,
God be with them lying sleeping,
God be with them standing fighting,
Erin's foes in battle smiting!

MOLLY ASTORE.

Oh, Mary, dear—oh, Mary fair,
   Oh, branch of generous stem,
White blossom of the banks of Nair,
   Though lilies grow on them;
You've left me sick at heart for love,
   So faint I cannot see;
The candle swims the board above,
   I'm drunk for love of thee!
Oh, stately stem of maiden pride,
   My woe it is and pain,
That I, thus severed from thy side,
   The long night must remain.

Through all the towns of Innisfail
   I've wandered far and wide,
But, from Downpatrick to Kinsale,
   From Carlow to Kilbride,
Many lords and dames of high degree,
   Where'er my feet have gone,—
My Mary, one to equal thee
   I never looked upon:
I live in darkness and in doubt
   Whene'er my love's away—
But were the gracious sun put out,
   Her shadow would make day.

'Tis she, indeed, young bud of bliss,
   And gentle as she's fair—
Though lily-white her bosom is,
   And sunny bright her hair,
And dewy azure her blue eye,
   And rosy red her cheek,
Yet brighter she in modesty,
   More beautifully meek!

The world's wise men, from north to south,
  Can never ease my pain—
But one kiss from her honey mouth
  Would make me well again.

THE FAIR-HAIRED GIRL.

The sun has set, the stars are still,
The red moon hides behind the hill—
The tide has left the brown beach bare,
The birds have fled the upper air;
Upon her branch the lone cuckoo
Is chanting still her sad adieu,
And you, my fair-haired girl, must go
Across the salt sea under woe.

I, through love, have learned three things,
Sorrow, sin, and death it brings;
Yet, day by day, my heart within
Dares shame and sorrow, death and sin.
Maiden, you have aimed the dart
Rankling in my ruined heart;
Maiden, may the God above
Grant you grace to grant me love!

Sweeter than the viol's string,
And the note that blackbirds sing,
Brighter than the dew-drops rare
Is the maiden wondrous fair;
Like the silver swans at play
Is her neck, as bright as day.
Woe was me, that e'er my sight
Dwelt on charms so deadly bright!

CASHEL OF MUNSTER.

I'd wed you without herds, without money, or rich array,
And I'd wed you on a dewy morning, at day-dawn grey;
My bitter woe it is, love, that we are not far away
In Cashel town, though the bare deal boards were our
　marriage-bed this day!

Oh, fair maid, remember the green hill-side,
Remember how I hunted about the valleys wide;
Time now has worn me; my locks are turned to grey,
The year is scarce, and I am poor, but send me not, love,
　away!

Oh, deem not my blood is of base strain, my girl,
Oh, think not my birth was as the birth of the churl;
Marry me, and prove me, and say soon you will
That noble blood is written on my right side still!

My purse holds no red gold, no coin of the silver white,
No herds are mine to drive thro' the long twilight;
But the pretty girl that would take me, poor tho' I be and
　lone,
Oh, I'd take her with me kindly to the County Tyrone.

Oh, my girl, I can see 'tis in trouble you are,
And oh, my girl, I see 'tis your people's reproach you bear;
I am a girl in trouble, for his sake with whom I fly;
And oh, may no other maiden know such reproach as I.

NORA OF THE AMBER HAIR.

Oh, Nora, amber-coolun,
　It robs me of my rest,
That my head should be forbidden
　Its place upon thy breast!

It robs me of my rest, love,
　　And it breaks my heart and brain;
And oh, that I could bear my dear
　　Across the raging main!

Oh, valentine and sweetheart!
　　Be true to what you swore
When you promised me you 'd marry me
　　Without a farthing store:
Oh, we 'd walk the dew together,
　　And light our steps should be;
And Nora, amber-coolun,
　　I 'd kiss you daintily!

Hard by the holm
　　Lives this white love of mine;
Her thick hair 's like amber,
　　Which causes me to pine:
King of the Sabbath,
　　Oh, grant me soon to see
My own fat cattle grazing
　　Around sweet Ballybuy.

BOATMAN'S HYMN.

Bark that bear'st me through foam and squall,
You in the storm are my castle wall;
Though the sea should redden from bottom to top,
From tiller to mast she takes no drop.
　　On the tide top, the tide top,
　　　　Wherry aroon, my land and store!
　　On the tide top, the tide top,
　　　　She is the boat can sail *go leor*.

She dresses herself, and goes gliding on,
Like a dame in her robes of the Indian lawn;
For God has blessed her, gunnel and whale—
And oh! if you saw her stretch out to the gale,
　　On the tide top, the tide top, &c.

Whillan,* ahoy! old heart of stone,
Stooping so black o'er the beach alone,
Answer me well—on the bursting brine
Saw you ever a bark like mine?
    On the tide top, the tide top, &c.

Says Whillan—since first I was made of stone,
I have looked abroad o'er the beach alone—
But till to-day, on the bursting brine,
Saw I never a bark like thine,
    On the tide top, the tide top, &c.

God of the air! the seamen shout
When they see us tossing the brine about:
Give us the shelter of strand or rock,
Or through and through us she goes with a shock!
    On the tide top, the tide top, &c.

THE FAIR HILLS OF IRELAND.

A plenteous place is Ireland for hospitable cheer,
    Uileacan dubh O!
Where the wholesome fruit is bursting from the yellow barley ear;
    Uileacan dubh O!
There is honey in the trees where her misty vales expand,
And her forest paths, in summer, are by falling waters fanned;
There is dew at high noontide there, and springs i' the yellow sand
    On the fair hills of holy Ireland.

Curled he is, and ringleted, and plaited to the knee,
    Uileacan dubh O!
Each captain who comes sailing across the Irish sea,
    Uileacan dubh O!

---

* "Whillan, a rock on the shore near Blacksod harbour."

And I will make my journey, if life and health but stand,
Unto that pleasant country, that fresh and fragrant strand,
And leave your boasted braveries, your wealth and high
    command,
    For the fair hills of holy Ireland.

Large and profitable are the stacks upon the ground,
        Uileacan dubh O !
The butter and the cream do wondrously abound,
        Uileacan dubh O !
The cresses on the water, and the sorrels are at hand,
And the cuckoo's calling daily his note of music bland,
And the bold thrush sings so bravely his songs i' the forests
    grand,
    On the fair hills of holy Ireland.

INDEX.

	PAGE
ACADEMIES of Ireland, early fame of the	111
Addenda, Miscellaneous	291
Alba, Deirdre's Farewell to	19
Albany's, Lady of, Lament for Prince Charles—a Jacobite Relic	112
Aldfrid, Prince of Northumbria—his Itinerary of Ireland	112-14
Amergin, first Arch-bard of the Kingdom	11
Anster, J., LL.D., Version by—Dirge of Dargo	291
Anglo-Norman Invasion of Ireland	169
Aodh, Prince of Orgiall, Odes to	94-95
Ardan, one of the three sons of Usnoth	19
Argyleshire, Irish Colony in	65
Ath-cliath, ancient name of Dublin	114

BALLADS, Historic, Heroic, and Legendary, &c.	19, 33, 130, 140, 191
Bards, Historic Notices of the Origin and Progress of the	11
———— Reformation of the	41
————————— second	95
Bacchanalian Songs—Intemperance probably of recent origin	257
Bhin Bolbin, Lay of	155
Blackbird of Hill of Carna	158
Boatman's Hymn	302
Brehons, the judicial Bards	15
Bridget Cruise, Carolan's first love	268
Bridget Fergus	255
Brian Boroimhe (Boru)	118
Brooke, Miss Charlotte, Versions by—	
Carolan's Monody on the Death of his Wife	279
Conloch, a heroic Poem	33
Elegy on the Death of Carolan	281

W

INDEX.

	PAGE
Brooke, Miss Charlotte, Versions by—	
Fitzgerald's Maritime Ode	211
Lament of Cuchullin for his Son	45
Magnus the Great	140
Ode to Goll, the son of Morni	67
O'Ryan's Love Elegy	249
War Ode to Osgur, the son of Oisin	75
CAMBRENSIS', Giraldus, Eulogy of Irish Music in the twelfth century	170
Carbry Riada founds the Dalraidic Colony in Argyleshire	65
Carbre Liffecar, King, suppresses the Fenians at the Battle of Gabhra (Gaura)	74
Carolan (see O'Carolan)	267
Cashell, Kings of, O'Dugan	189
Cashel of Munster	300
Cathaeir, Mor, Testament of	45
Celtic Language	12, 254
—— War Songs	73
Chase, Poem of the	130
Christianity, Introduction and rapid spread of	88
Clontarf, Battle of	118
Columba, Saint, interferes on behalf of the Bards	100
—————— his Latin verse	101
—————— Notice of his Culdee Priory at Iona	105
Columbanus, Saint, Specimen of his Latin verse	106
Concluding Remarks	286
Conloch, Heroic Poem of	33
Conor Mac Nessa, King of Ulster	19
Coolin, The	236
Core, King of Munster, Lament for	83
Cormac Ulfada, King	55
—— his Lament	59
Cormacan Eigeas, Poem on Murkerta MacNeill	116
Cows, Woman of Three	293
Cruachan (or Croghan), the royal Palace of Connaught	113
—— Cemetery	36
Cuchullin, Knight of the Red Branch	33
—— Lament of, for his Son	40

INDEX. 307

	PAGE
Curran, H. Grattan, Versions by —	
Odes to Aodh, Prince of Orgiall	94-95
Lament for Dallan	97
The Roman Vision	239
Lament for the Queen of James II.	261
DALLAN FORGAIL, Notice of the Bard	93
——————— Odes of, to Aodh, Prince of Orgiall	94-95
——————— Seanchan's Lament for	97
Dargo, Dirge of	291
D'Alton, John, M.R.I.A., Versions by —	
Bridget Fergus	255
Carroll O'Daly and Echo	187
Torna's Lament for Core and Niall	83
Danes, Invasion of the	115
——— Checked by Brian (Boroimhe) Boru	118
Deirdre, Lament of, for the Sons of Usna	30
——— Blooming (Earl of Desmond's song)	196
Donat's, Bishop, Verses in Eulogy of Ireland	115
Donegal Castle, Elegy on the Ruins of	219
Dr. Drake on the Ossianic Poems (note)	151
Drummond, Rev. Dr., Versions by	119, 121, 155, 160
Dubtach (Duvach), the Arch-bard, becomes a Convert to Christianity	88
Dublin, Notice of ancient	114
Duffy, C. G. (now Sir C.), note respecting Brian Boru	118
Dundalgin, the seat of Cuchullin	40
——————— Sea-fight at	140
Dunkin's, Rev. Dr., Translation of Donat's Verses	115
EGEAS, Torna, the last Pagan Bard	81
Elegies 26, 40, 77, 83, 119, 219, 224, 249, 261, 279, 281, 283	
Elizabeth, Queen, contrast between her policy and that of James I. towards the disaffected chiefs.	230
FAIR-HAIRED GIRL, the	299
Fair Hills of Ireland	302
Fenian Militia	67
——— Poems	27, 29, 31, 72, 129, 151, 158

	Page
Fergus, the Fenian Bard and Brother of Oisin	65
——— His Ode to Gaul, the son of Morni	55-67
——— His War Ode to Osgur, the son of Oisin	75
Fergus, Bridget	255
Ferguson, S. (Sir S.), M.R.I.A., Versions by—	
Farewell to Alba	21
Deirdre's Lament for the sons of Usna	30
Torna's Lament for Core and Niall	83
Lament for the Downfall of the Gael	207
Ode to the Minstrel, O'Connellan	248
Mild Mable Kelly	273
Grace Nugent	278
Elegy on the Ruins of Timoleague Abbey	283
O'Byrne's Bard to the Clans of Wicklow	295
Molly Astore	298
The Fair-Haired Girl	299
Cashel of Munster	300
Nora of the Amber Hair	300
Boatman's Hymn	301
The Fair Hills of Ireland	302
Fiech's Hymn to St. Patrick	89
Finn Mac Cumhal, or M'Cool	88
Fitzgerald's Maritime Ode	211
Frogs supposed formerly unknown in Ireland	116
Furlong, Thomas, Versions by—	
Eileen a Roon	171
John O'Dwyer of the Glen	237
Ode to Drunkenness	258
Maggy Lauder	261
Bridget Cruise	268
O'More's Fair Daughter	275
Gabhra (Gaura), Battle of	75
Gael, Lament for the Downfall of the (O'Gnives)	207
Giraldus (see Cambrensis)	170
Goll, or Gaul, the Son of Morni, Eulogy on	53-67
Goldsmith, Anecdote of Carolan	272
Heroic Poems (see Ballads)	19

INDEX.

	PAGE
Hostages, Niall of the Nine	82
Howth, Hill of, Ode to	160
ITINERARY, Prince Aldfrid's, of Ireland	112
Irish Language—its aptitude for lyrical poetry	251
KINCORA, Palace of, M'Liag's Lament for its Desolation	119
King Ollamh Fodhla (Ollav Foala)	16
—— Cormac Ulfadha	55
—— Niall of the Nine Hostages	82
—— Conn of the Hundred Battles (note)	55
—— Conor Mac Nessa	19
LAMENT of Cuchullin for his Son	40
For Core and Niall	83
For the Bard Dallan	97
For Kincora and Brian	119
For the Gael	207
For Prince Charles	265
Lawson, Edward, Version by—	
Blooming Deirdre	196
Lament for Prince Charles	265
Leahy, Wm., Metrical Versions by	19, 22, 23, 25, 26, 158, 161
MAGGY LAUDER	261
Magnus the Great, a Heroic Poem	140
Mangan, James Clarence, Versions by—	
Testament of Cathaeir Mor	45
Lament for Dallan	58, 98
Prince Aldfrid's Itinerary of Ireland	112
Lament for the Palace of Kincora	119
Lament for the Tironian and Tirconnellian Princes	224
O'Hussey's Ode to the Maguire	231
On the Ruins of Donegal Castle	219
The Woman of Three Cows	293
Mary, Queen of James II., Lament for	261
M'Nally and Fergus	255
Molly Astore	298
Mac Brodin, Maolin Oge	207
Mac Cuairt's Meeting with Carolan	271

	Page
Mac Dary, Teige, Bard of Thomond	215
Mac Donnell, John Claragh	260
M‘Liag's Lament for Kincora	119
———— in Exile remembers Brian	121
M‘Nally	255
NIALL of the Nine Hostages	82
Nora of the Amber Hair	300
Norman, Anglo-, Invasion of Ireland	169
Norsemen, earliest Incursion of	115-117
———— checked by reign of Brian Boru	118, 166
O'BRIEN, Earl of Thomond, Mac Dary's Instructions to	215
O'Brien, Inauguration of the — Donald O'Mulconry	197
O'Cahan, one of the Northern chiefs	191
O'Carolan, Turlogh, Biographic Notice of	267
O'Cassidy, the Bard	170
O'Connellan, the Minstrel, Ode to	248
O'Daly, Donogh More, Abbot of Boyle	172
———— Carroll — his Eileen a Roon	174
———— Carroll (the Second) and Echo	187
Odes	53, 67, 75, 94, 95, 231, 248
O'Donnell, Hugh Roe, Prince of Tyrconnell, Notice	215, 219
———— Lament for Ruin of his Castle	219
O'Dugan, Bard of the O'Kelly, Maurice	235
O'Dugan, John	189
O'Dun, the Bard	170
O'Gnive, Fearflatha	207
O'Higgin, Teige Dall	207
O'Hussey, Bard of, to the Maguire of Fermanagh	270
O'Mulconry	170
O'Mulconry, Donald	197
O'Neachtan, John, Biographic Notice of	260
O'Ryan, or, Ned of the Hills	219
Ossianic Heroes	59
PATRICK, Saint	82, 89
Petrie, G., LL.D., on Valley of the Thrushes, &c.	154
———— on the O'Cahans	192

	PAGE
Prince Aldfrid's Poem on Ireland	112-114
——— of Orgiall, Aodh, Odes to	94-95
——— of Tyrconnell, Hugh Roe O'Donnell	215, 219
ROMAN Vision, the	231
Ross, Fortification of	177
Rhyme, Earliest European Examples of, among the Irish Bards	89
Roe, Battle of the	193
SCOTIA, Ireland the ancient	62
Seanachan Torpest	97
Sheil, or Sedulius, the Poet—his Latin metre	90
Stuart, the Royal Family of, of Irish Extraction	60
TORNA Egeas, last Pagan Bard	81
USNA, tragic fate of the three sons of	19
VERSES on the Royal Cemetery of Croghan	86
WALSH, Edward, Versions by—	
Blooming Deirdre	196
Lament for Prince Charles	265
Wards, the Bards of the O'Donnell	215, 223, 239
Wicklow, O'Byrne's Bard to the Clans of	295

THE END.

C. W. GIBBS, Printer, Dublin.

ERRATUM.

Page 51, line 5 from top, *for* "N'as," *read* "Naas."

SELECT LIST

OF

WORKS RELATING TO IRELAND

PUBLISHED OR SOLD BY

HODGES, FIGGIS, AND CO.

---

7 Vols., Medium 4to. £12 12s.

THE ANNALS OF IRELAND BY THE FOUR MASTERS.

TRANSLATED

By the late JOHN O'DONOVAN, LL.D.

Profusely Illustrated. Imperial 8vo. 28s.

THE ROUND TOWERS & ANCIENT ARCHITECTURE OF IRELAND.

By the late GEORGE PETRIE, LL.D.

With 186 Engravings. Small 4to. 15s., net.

THE TOWERS AND TEMPLES OF ANCIENT IRELAND.

By the late MARCUS KEANE, M.R.I.A.

WORKS RELATING TO IRELAND

Fcap. 8vo. 3s.

THE IRISH FLORA:

Comprising the Phœnogamous Plants and Ferns.

With Frontispiece Portrait of Carolan. Crown 8vo. 5s.

SPECIMENS OF THE EARLY NATIVE POETRY OF IRELAND.

In Metrical Translations, with Historical, Biographical, and Explanatory Notes.

By HENRY R. MONTGOMERY.

Crown 8vo, Cloth. 5s.

DR. POCOCKE'S TOUR IN IRELAND IN 1752.

Edited, with Introduction and Notes,

By GEORGE T. STOKES, D.D., M.R.I.A.

Fcap. 8vo, Cloth. 1s.

HENRY GRATTAN: A HISTORICAL STUDY.

By JOHN GEORGE MacCARTHY.

8vo, Cloth. 12s. 6d.

A HISTORY OF THE UNIVERSITY OF DUBLIN.

From its Foundation to end of XVIII. Century.

By REV. JOHN W. STUBBS, D.D., S.F.T.C.D.

SOLD BY HODGES, FIGGIS, & CO.

Fcap. 8vo, Cloth. 9s.

Archæologia Hibernica:
HANDBOOK OF IRISH ANTIQUITIES.
By Wm. F. WAKEMAN, M R.I.A.
Second Edition, with numerous Engravings.

8vo, Cloth. 7s. 6d.

THE REFORMED CHURCH IN IRELAND, 1537–1889.
By RT. HON. JOHN T. BALL, LL.D.

Crown 8vo. 9s.

IRELAND AND THE CELTIC CHURCH.
By GEORGE T. STOKES, D.D.

Crown 8vo. 9s.

IRELAND AND THE ANGLO-NORMAN CHURCH.
By GEORGE T. STOKES, D.D.

WORKS BY COLONEL W. G. WOOD-MARTIN.

SLIGO AND THE ENNISKILLENERS. *Second Edition. 5s.*
HISTORY OF SLIGO. *2 Vols., 8vo, each, 10s.*
THE LAKE DWELLINGS OF IRELAND. *Royal 8vo, Cloth. 25s.*
THE RUDE STONE MONUMENTS OF IRELAND. *Royal 8vo. 21s.*

WORKS RELATING TO IRELAND

Crown 8vo. 2s. 6d.

IRELAND BEFORE THE UNION.
By W. J. FITZPATRICK.

Fcap. 8vo, Cloth. 3s. 6d.

THE FLORA OF HOWTH.
With Map, and an Introduction on the Geology and other features of the Promontory.
By H. C. HART, B.A., F.L.S.

Crown 8vo. 3s. 6d.

A HANDY BOOK ON
THE RECLAMATION OF WASTE LANDS IN IRELAND.
By G. H. KINAHAN, M.R.I.A.

New and Revised Edition. Crown 8vo. 7s.

THE PHYSICAL GEOLOGY AND GEOGRAPHY OF IRELAND.
By EDWARD HULL, LL.D.

Imperial 8vo. 21s.

EARLY CHRISTIAN ARCHITECTURE IN IRELAND.
By MARGARET STOKES.

Also, by same Author,

EARLY CHRISTIAN ART IN IRELAND. 4s.

SOLD BY HODGES, FIGGIS, & CO.

---

2 Vols., Folio. £8 8s.

NOTES ON IRISH ARCHITECTURE.

By the late EARL OF DUNRAVEN.

Edited by MARGARET STOKES.

Fifth Edition. 2 Vols., Post 8vo. 10s.

ORIGIN AND HISTORY OF IRISH NAMES OF PLACES.

By P. W. JOYCE, LL.D.

Also, by same Author,

IRISH LOCAL NAMES EXPLAINED. *1s.*

Folio, Cloth. £1 11s. 6d.

THE ANCIENT MUSIC OF IRELAND.

Collected and Arranged by E. BUNTING.

Second Edition, with Plan. Sewed, 1s.

MELLIFONT ABBEY IN THE COUNTY LOUTH:

ITS RISE AND DOWNFALL.

By K. F. B.

8vo. 10s. 6d.

HISTORY OF THE CONNAUGHT CIRCUIT.

By OLIVER J. BURKE.

WORKS RELATING TO IRELAND

4to, Cloth. 18s.

THE O'CONORS OF CONNAUGHT:

AN HISTORICAL MEMOIR,

Compiled from a MS. of the late DR. JOHN O'DONOVAN, with Additions from the State Papers and Public Records,

BY

THE RT. HON. CHARLES OWEN O'CONOR DON.

With numerous Engravings by George Hanlon.

New Edition. Cloth, 6s.

HISTORICAL REVIEW OF THE LEGISLATIVE SYSTEMS IN IRELAND.

By RT. HON. JOHN T. BALL, LL.D.

Small 4to. 15s.

ECCLESIASTICAL ANTIQUITIES OF DOWN, CONNOR, AND DROMORE.

With copious Notes.

By RT. REV. WILLIAM REEVES, D.D., M.R.I.A.

Ninth Edition. Boards, 1s. 6d. net.

TWENTY YEARS' RECOLLECTIONS OF AN IRISH POLICE MAGISTRATE.

By THE LATE FRANK THORPE PORTER, A.M., J.P.

SOLD BY HODGES, FIGGIS, & CO.

8vo, Cloth.

A SHORT HISTORY OF THE IRISH PEOPLE

Down to the date of the Plantation of Ulster.

BY THE LATE A. G. RICHEY, Q.C., LL.D.

Edited, with Notes, by R. R. KANE, LL.D.

HANDY GUIDE BOOKS FOR DUBLIN.

DUBLIN: What's to be seen and how to see it. By W. F. WAKEMAN. 1s.

HISTORICAL HANDBOOK OF S. PATRICK'S CATHEDRAL.
By Rev. ALEXANDER LEEPER, D.D. *Third Edition.* 1s.

MONUMENTAL INSCRIPTIONS, &c., IN CHRIST CHURCH CATHEDRAL.
By the late Rev. JOHN FINLAYSON. *Cloth.* 2s. 6d.

THE CHURCH OF S. WERBURGH. By Rev. S. C. HUGHES, LL.D. *Cloth.* 1s. 6d.

THE CHURCH OF S. JOHN. By Rev. S. C. HUGHES, LL.D. *Cloth.* 1s. 6d.

A DAY AT HOWTH. By HUBAND SMITH. *Sewed.* 6d.

HODGES, FIGGIS, AND CO.,

Publishers to the University,

104, GRAFTON STREET,

DUBLIN.

www.ingramcontent.com/pod-product-compliance
Lightning Source LLC
Chambersburg PA
CBHW021202230426
43667CB00006B/524